Henry D. B. Bailey

Local Tales and Historical Sketches

Henry D. B. Bailey

Local Tales and Historical Sketches

ISBN/EAN: 9783337088507

Printed in Europe, USA, Canada, Australia, Japan

Cover: Foto ©ninafisch / pixelio.de

More available books at **www.hansebooks.com**

LOCAL TALES

—AND—

HISTORICAL SKETCHES,

BY

HENRY D. B. BAILEY.

FISHKILL LANDING:
JOHN W. SPAIGHT, PUBLISHER.
FISHKILL STANDARD OFFICE.
1874.

INDEX.

	Page.
PREFACE,	7

POETRY.

THE MONTHS OF THE YEAR,	12

TALES.

DOMINIE VAN NIST'S COURTSHIP,	17
THE SUBALTERN,	65
VAN HORN,	86
THE SQUATTER'S DAUGHTER,	103
THE HAUNTED TAVERN,	119
WITCHCRAFT IN NEW HACKENSACK,	132
THE BROKEN HEARTED,	137
THE HIGHLAND FARMER VS. THE WESTERN FARMER,	149
DEACON JONES, THE PIONEER,	161
THE FARMER'S DAUGHTER,	172
A TALE OF THE REVOLUTION,	183
FARMER JONES, THE DISCONTENTED MAN,	193
THE MECHANIC'S WIFE,	203
FARMERS THRIFTY AND UNTHRIFTY,	212
THE OLD FARM HOUSE,	222

	Page.
The Ungrateful Father,	232
The Tailor and the Bachelor,	242
A Tale of the Early Settlers,	250
The Mysterious Pack,	259
Ten Cents a Day,	266
A Tale of the Great Rebellion,	273

HISTORICAL SKETCHES.

Early History of Dutchess County,	283
The First Churches in Dutchess County,	297
Poughkeepsie,	307
Early History of the Town of Fishkill,	314
Historical Sketch of Fishkill Village,	355
Early Settlers near Fishkill Landing,	373
A Visit to Fort Hill,	380
The Brick Meeting House,	384
Pine Plains,	393
Isaac Van Amburgh,	399

ESSAYS.

Civilized and Savage Life Contrasted,	409
Books the Great Source of Information,	421
Sleep,	424
Adversity,	426
Fashion,	428
April Days,	430

ILLUSTRATIONS.

	Page.
PORTRAIT OF THE AUTHOR,	Frontispiece.
THE VAN KLEECK HOUSE,	24
THE WHARTON HOUSE,	42
A COUNTRY SCENE,	136
EPISCOPAL CHURCH, FISHKILL VILLAGE,	361
REFORMED DUTCH CHURCH, FISHKILL VILLAGE,	364
VERPLANCK HOUSE, FISHKILL LANDING,	374
THE AGENT OF CIVILIZATION,	420

ERRATA.

On pages 323 and 325, for General Abram Van Wyck, in three places, substitute James Van Wyck.

On page 324, for C. Delevan, substitute Isaac Gildersleeve.

PREFACE.

This volume of local tales and historical sketches is the result of many years, and not the product of a day. When the author began his literary labors, he had no idea that his writings would ever be voluminous enough to make a book, or of sufficient value to be collected in such permanent form. He was in the habit of writing a tale or a sketch, and contributing the same, either to THE FISHKILL STANDARD or the POUGHKEEPSIE TELEGRAPH, in which they were eagerly read by the subscribers to those papers. His first published tale was "The Tailor and the Bachelor," a simple story of life's vicissitudes. This was followed at irregular intervals by others, culminating in his latest and most pretentious effort, "Dominie Van Nist's Courtship." Having a deep love for the olden times, he took a great interest in historical matters, and has brought to light many facts bearing upon the early history of Dutchess County, and especially the towns of Fishkill and East Fishkill, which the future historian will find of great value. To obtain these facts has cost him considerable time and labor, but his love for the work incited him to go on without expectation of pecuniary reward. A great many historical facts are woven into Mr. Bailey's tales. In fact, these are written with such a degree of naturalness that the only fear is that those who are not well acquainted with the early history of the County, may take fiction for fact, and so be unconsciously led astray. The chapters devoted to sketches of history, however, may be relied upon as correct—at least so far as the author has been able to get information.

Mr. Bailey is a native of this County, having been born at Johnsville, in the town of East Fishkill, on the 27th of December, 1813. He has resided in the County nearly all his life, and is well known to thousands of people. He did not commence his literary labors until in his forty-second year, but since that time has been a valued contributor to the local press. This book, which has been the result of so many years labor, and written while in the prime of his manhood, contains so many facts of historic interest that it will be regarded as an authority in many respects, and will be looked to by future historians as a mine from which to gather facts relating to the early days of this section of the County.

Mr. Bailey did intend writing a history of Dutchess County, but his advancing years, and other difficulties of a physical nature, have deterred him from the work. He has expressed to us his regrets that he did not, ten years ago, make a systematic canvass of the County, with that end in view. Knowing his industry and capabilities, we can but join in the regrets which he has expressed.

The fact is, we are drifting along with scarcely an effort to preserve from fast approaching oblivion the thousands of interesting facts, recollections, and reminiscences of the past, relating to our county, which are attainable now, but which in a few years more will be utterly lost. How many have passed away within the decade just closed, whose memories could recall incidents of three and four score years past, which would have been of great value to the historian; but they are gone, and with them is buried the knowledge they possessed. Our county is rich in material, and under a master hand would yield a fund of authentic historical incidents that would make a book of surpassing interest and value. We hope the historical researches begun this year by a gentleman in one of our neighboring towns, will result in the publication of a full and reliable history of the county.

The photographic portrait of Mr. Bailey, which forms a frontispiece, is an admirable one, and will be so accepted by all who know him. The engravings are mostly from "Lossing's Field Book of the Revolution," published by the Harper Brothers, New York, to whose kindness we are indebted for the privilege of using the same. They add very much to the interest of the book.

J. W. S.

Fishkill Standard Office, October, 1874.

Poetry.

THE MONTHS OF THE YEAR.

JANUARY.

Lakes and rivers now are frozen,
  Icy fetters bind in chains;
Earth in winter's garb reposing,
  Winter now triumphant reigns.

FEBRUARY.

Storms are raging, blustering, blowing;
  Snow in whirling eddies fly,
But the days are longer growing—
  Seasons brief, they soon pass by.

MARCH.

Storm and sunshine intervening,
  Sullen Winter yields at last,
To his Arctic den retreating,
  Driven by the Southern blast.

APRIL.

Vernal season now approaching,
  Mildly do the zephyrs play,
Light upon the night encroaching,
  Lengthens out the beams of day.

MAY.

Cattle in the pastures grazing,
  Fields are looking fresh and green,
Man his great Creator praising
  For the balmy days of Spring.

JUNE.

Busy season now arriving,
 Weeds in great profusion grow,
Farmers in their cornfields driving,
 Strong they wield the spade and hoe.

JULY.

Laborers in the fields are toiling
 Through the long and listless day;
In the West dark clouds are lowering,
 Raindrops wet the new mown hay.

AUGUST.

Early morn the dew drops shining,
 Hanging on the bushes low,
Lovers in the shades reclining,
 Love does in their bosoms glow.

SEPTEMBER.

Orchards now their boughs are bending,
 Filled with fruitage rich and rare,
Choicest blessing thick descending,
 Fills all hearts with thankful prayer.

OCTOBER.

Leaves now from the trees are falling,
 Cool and frosty is the morn,
Farmers to their cribs are hauling
 Golden ears of Indian corn.

NOVEMBER.

Autumn hues the landscape blending,
 O'er the face of Nature spread—
Gloomy, dreary days portending—
 Birds to warmer climes have fled.

DECEMBER.

Ah! the closing year reminds us
 Of the changing scenes of life—
Friends whose ties were of the kindest,
 Have left this world of woe and strife.

Local Tales.

Historical Tales and Sketches.

DOMINIE VAN NIST'S COURTSHIP.

Poughkeepsie is the shire-town of the wealthy and flourishing county of Dutchess. It is situated on the east bank of the noble Hudson, equidistant between New York and Albany, and contains about twenty-two thousand inhabitants. The original name of Poughkeepsie was Apokeepsing, an Indian word signifying safe harbor. The first settlers were Dutch, who came from Long Island about 1700. Boltus Van Kleek built the first house within the present limits of the city, in 1702. Jacobus Vander Bogart, Peter Velie, Johannas Van Kleek, and other pioneers, soon erected dwellings where the present city is now located, and a highway was opened east through the great Nine Partners patent, purchased by Caleb Heathcote and others, May 27th, 1697. This patent extended from the Hudson river to the west line of Connecticut. In 1709 building lots were laid out in Poughkeepsie and the Dutch Reformed Missionaries had commenced their labors there and at Fishkill. The Rev. Peter Vas, of Kingston, Rev. Gualterus Du Bois, of New York ; Rev. Vincentius Antonides, of Kings county, Long Island, and the Rev. Mr. Van Deusen, of Albany, would in turn visit Poughkeepsie and Fishkill and preach to the then few inhabitants, in their houses, and administer the ordinances of Baptism and the Lord's Supper. In 1716 the Reformed Dutch Church was organized at Poughkeepsie and Fishkill by the Rev. Peter Vas. A lot for a church and parsonage at Poughkeepsie was given by Captain Jacobus Vander Bogart, in 1716. This deed is recorded in the County Clerk's office, where it may be seen at the present day. The church stood in what is now known as Market street; the burying ground extended south near to what is now Cannon street, and along Main street east for several rods, and west of the church to the lot owned by the Court house. West of the Court house was the parsonage lot, where the present First Reformed Church is now located. This lot then contained several acres of land, and was conjointly owned by the congregations of Poughkeepsie and Fishkill, and remained so until the separation of the two churches, which took place in 1772. Since the separation, great alterations have taken place on the parsonage lot. The old parsonage has long since been demolished and a new one erected. The first church, which was erected in 1718, was taken down in 1782 and a new one erected on the opposite side of the street, near the Poughkeepsie Hotel, where the old burying ground is still to be seen. In 1822 they abandoned that ground and built a church on the parsonage lot. This church was destroyed by fire in 1857, when the present noble structure was erected on the same site.

As we have said, the parsonage formerly contained several acres of land, but portions of it have been sold at different times, the last in 1848. A number of lots were then sold to Matthew Vassar, the money, which amounted to some $8000, was given to the Second Church, which had just been erected. We will now attempt to give the architecture of the first church, which, in 1718, stood in what is now known as Market street. The material of which the church was built was stone, the height of the walls was two stories, and it was covered with a gambrel roof. A tower went up in front of the church, rising above the apex of the roof a moderate distance, and there the bell was suspended, and over the same was a small tapering spire, and surmounting that was the rooster. There was but one entrance and that was in the tower, which fronted Main street. Passing through the entrance to the interior, two aisles led the way through the church, flanked with high backed pews on either side. The pulpit was reached by a high flight of stairs from one of the aisles, and it was shaped like a wineglass. Over it was the sounding board, fastened securely to the rear walls of the church. An arch spanned the building, and galleries extended all around the church, excepting the rear, which was supported by heavy columns. The window lights were very small, set in heavy sash frames. This was the first church erected in the county. It is about one hundred and fifty-six years since the corner stone was laid.

From 1716 until 1731 the congregations of Poughkeepsie and Fishkill had no settled minister; they were too feeble to maintain one, for the country was as yet a wilderness. Dark tangled forests lined the banks of the Hudson, extending east over the country. Here and there the pioneer and squatter had made an opening, and erected log huts for a shelter, and the traveler in passing through the country then for miles nothing would greet his eye but dreary wastes, and occasionally a wolf or bear would emerge from some thicket, alarmed at the unusual noise occasioned by the traveler's horse. Although the county had been purchased by the patentees from the Aborigines for some twenty-five years, yet Indian tribes roved through the country, living by the chase. Their villages yet existed in Fishkill Hook and along the Wappingers Creek. After 1720, settlements increased rapidly, but Missionaries from New York, Kingston (then called Esopus) and Albany supplied the church at Poughkeepsie and the station at Fishkill until 1731. That year the congregation at Fishkill had erected a substantial stone church and then an effort was made by the two congregations to raise money sufficient to support a minister. A committee, one from each congregation, was appointed. Captain Jacobus Vander Bogart, of Poughkeepsie, and Abram Brinckerhoff, of Fishkill, visited the families in their respective congregations, and after ascertaining what salary each member of the congregation would give, reported at the church in Poughkeepsie. The sum was found sufficient to warrant the maintenance of a clergyman. The two congregations had just completed their parsonage in Poughkeepsie, which stood in the rear of the present one, located on the brow of the hill, on the south side of Main street, descending to the river. It was an airy, comfortable structure, sided and roofed with red cedar, and inclosed with a substantial fence. Accordingly a call was made out and accepted by the Rev. Cornelius Van Schie, who had been educated in Holland. He was installed in office by the Rev. Gualterus Du Bois, of the city of New York, October 4th, 1731. Mr. Van Schie's salary was five hundred gilders a year and fire wood, which cost but little, except the labor of cutting and hauling, which was done by the congregation. Mr. Van Schie's pastorate continued five years, when he was released from his charge and removed to Albany. The second pastor was the Rev. Benjamin Meynema, who also was educated in Holland. His pastorate commenced in 1745 and continued until 1755, when he resigned his charge. During his ministry he lost his wife, who was buried in the church yard at Fishkill, and September 9th, 1761, he died, and at his request he was buried beside his wife, where their tombstones can be seen at the present day with epitaphs in the Low Dutch language. The third pastor was the Rev. Jacobus Vannist, who was educated in this country. He was only twenty-four years old when he accepted the call to become pastor of the congregations of Poughkeepsie and Fishkill; Mr. Vannist having just completed his studies, and with little or no experience in preaching the Holy Gospel and imparting spiritual consolation to his flock, which then extended all over the western portion of the county, then called Poughkeepsie and Fishkill precincts. When Mr. Vannist arrived at Poughkeepsie, in the summer of 1758, he was cordially received by his congregation, and his time was occupied in visiting his parishoners and preaching at Poughkeepsie and Fishkill on alternate Sabbaths. Mr. Vannist was unmarried, and having no use for the parsonage, he wanted to get a permanent place to board at some private house, not wishing to board at a Hotel, deeming it an unsuitable place for a minister.

The Van Kleek House was then the most conspicuous Hotel in the county. The Court House had just been erected, and Poughkeepsie being the county seat, business centered there. Judges, lawyers and learned men, merchants, artisans, &c., located at Poughkeepsie. One of the most prominent men that lived there was Paul Schank, who engaged in the mercantile business. His customers came from far and near, north to what was then known as the Little Nine Partners, east to the Connecticut line, and south as far as New Hackensack and Beekman, which then contained a few settlers. The sturdy pioneers could be seen riding on horseback, with their frows seated on a pillion behind, trudging through Main street to Paul's store, the Christian name which his neighbors always called him by. Others again in their wagons would be wending their way to Paul's store to purchase articles of merchandise which the pioneers really needed. Paul owned several acres of land on the south side of Main street, east of the Dutch Church, adjoining the burying ground, where he had built him a house and store and was doing a thriving business. Paul's lot covered a part of what is now known as Cannon street, and extended east along Main street, opposite to where the Morgan House is now located. His family consisted of his wife, two sons, and his daughter Rebekah, and a number of negro slaves, for then slavery existed throughout the country.

In those days traveling through the country was

slow and difficult. New York city could be reached from the river by sloops, which sometimes would consume a fortnight going to and from Poughkeepsie. Paul only went to New York to purchase goods once or twice a year, and then he would have to take his bed and provisions with him, for the Captains of sloops did not supply their passengers with berths and board in those days. Paul, as soon as he had purchased what goods he thought he needed, would have them all carted to the sloop, which then lay at Coenties slip, for the city then lay all on the east side of the Island, and contained only thirteen thousand inhabitants. When the hour arrived for the Captain to sail, Paul had his business all perfected, and if nothing unusual occurred, and with favorable wind and weather, they would arrive at Poughkeepsie the second or third day after leaving New York.

In 1758, when Dominie Vannist was pastor of the two congregations at Poughkeepsie and Fishkill, the now populous and beautiful city of Poughkeepsie made but a sorry appearance. On the south side of Main street, east of the Dutch Church and burying ground, was the residence of Paul Schank; his store stood adjacent the burying ground. East of his residence was the school-house, a small building painted red. West of the Dutch Church was the Court House, a stone structure which was destroyed by fire in the Revolution. The next building west of the Court House was the Dutch Parsonage, and along the sloping hillsides to the river there were some twenty houses. The Van Kleek house, a substantial stone structure, was the most prominent Hotel, and under the eaves the walls were pierced with loopholes for musketry. In 1777 this Hotel was used as a State house and the Legislature convened there. George Clinton was then governor of the State, and Pierre Van Cortlandt lieutenant governor. In 1797 the Poughkeepsie Hotel was built, and then the Van Kleek House was abandoned as a public house, and finally it got in possession of Matthew Vassar, who demolished the building in 1835. On the

VAN KLEEK HOUSE, POUGHKEEPSIE.

north side of Main street, east of where the Poughkeepsie Hotel is now located, there were a few houses and stores, and west of the Hotel were a few lawyers' offices, and you have all there was of Poughkeepsie in 1758. One of the most prominent lawyers then was Bartholomew Crannell, a gentleman of note as an able counsellor and eloquent advocate. John H. Livingston, one of the ablest dominies of the Reformed Dutch Church, who was born at Poughkeepsie in 1746, commenced reading law in his office in the Autumn of 1762, and at the close of 1764, his health being a good deal impaired, in consequence of close application to reading and writing, he left Mr. Crannell's office. After that he experienced a change of heart, and connected himself with the Dutch Church, and his health was in a measure recovered. He became impressed that he was called to preach the Gospel, and in May, 1766, he sailed for Europe, studied in the University of Utrecht, and returned in September, 1770, and became pastor of one of the Collegiate Churches in the city of New York.

Dominie Vannist had as yet no permanent place to board; he had lived among his parishioners, preaching at intervals in New Hackensack and Hopewell, which now had become Missionary stations. His labors were now very arduous, and it was necessary that he should have some place where he could spend more time in his study. Often times he had been subjected to great inconvenience in preparing his sermons, and Paul Schank politely invited him to come and board at his house, which offer the dominie gladly accepted. Paul's dwelling was a stone structure, with low walls and steep roof. The entrance from the front door was through a box entry, with a stairs, which led to the garret. This entry communicated with the parlor, through a large door, and adjoining this was the sitting room. Two bedrooms, which were separated by a partition from the sitting room, completed the first floor, excepting the kitchen, which projected from the east end of the main building, and was set apart for the negroes. A large fire place occupied one side of the kitchen, with jambs of sufficient height to admit a tall man. Adjacent one of the jambs was a huge oven embedded in the walls, where the bread for the family was baked. In those days they had no knowledge of stoves, and their chimneys were so wide that one could drive through them with a cart and horses, with fireplaces of such immense wings that the consumption of wood was enormous. Two iron bars were fastened in the fireplace near the mouth of the chimney; across these bars another one was laid, which held the trammels where the pots and kettles were suspended over the fire, in which the cooking was done.

But as yet the country was comparatively a wilderness, and the forests were in close proximity to every settler's cabin. The negro then was the only laborer, and he was owned by the Dutch pioneer, and a half a score or less were in every Dutch farm house. They helped clear the forests and enclose and cultivate their farms. When Dominie Vannist came to Paul's to board, he gave him the privilege to select which room he wished to occupy. He selected one of the bedrooms adjoining the sitting room, and found it very convenient. Mrs. Schank had ordered it thoroughly cleaned. Fillis and Juda were set to work scouring the floors and the huge beams over head, for there were no walls over head, nor carpets on the floors, in the Dutch houses in those days. Rebekah was busily engaged arranging the furniture her father had recently purchased for Mr. Vannist's room. When his room was ready, he took possession, and was highly pleased with his new quarters, for Rebekah and her mother had prevailed on her father to get some nice furniture for his room when he went to New York to buy goods. Paul was willing to comply with their request, for he thought a great deal of his dominie, and when in New York he purchased a book case, writing desk, and rocking chair, and they were luxuries in those days. The fireplace in Mr. Vannist's room was located in a corner, and occupied less room than usual, and he was furnished with tongs, shovel and bellows, and Paul had instructed Sanco to fetch no wood but hickory in his room. Mr. Vannist having now a place to study prepared his sermons with the greatest care. The Dutch language was then the only one used in the Dutch churches, in fact it was almost the only language used in the county, especially in the western portion. Mr. Vannist always preached in the Dutch language, and his congregation used none other, but he understood both the Dutch and English languages, and could speak them fluently, but he always wrote his sermons in Dutch. Mr. Vannist had now become a popular preacher, and on every alternate Sabbath when he preached at Poughkeepsie, the people would come north from beyond Hyde Park, east to the center of the county, and south from New Hackensack and Beekman. Pioneers, in their large lumber wagons, seated on chairs taken from their houses, and their negro slaves squatted on bundles of straw in the rear of the wagon; young men on horseback, with their sweethearts behind seated on a pillion, clinging to their lovers, could be seen coming through Main street to the Dutch church. Wagons and horses would line Main street on either side beyond the churchyard to where Paul's store was located, during the time of service. Although there was occasionally preaching in Poughkeepsie then by the Rev. Samuel Seebury, an Episcopalian minister, they had not as yet erected a house of worship. Once in a month, perhaps, he would preach in the Court House. The interior of the Dutch church at Poughkeepsie then, when Mr. Vannist held forth, presented an impressive scene. He was only twenty-four years of age, tall, his height was six feet two inches, his appearance in the pulpit was prepossessing in the extreme. For one so young, he was a fervent and eloquent speaker, and the pathetic appeals that fell from his lips when in the pulpit, and his winning manners among his people, all contributed to his popularity. Paul and Rebekah led the singing in Dutch, and the congregation joining, presented a striking contrast from the mode of worship at the present day. The sexton's labors in those days were not arduous, and as no fires were used in churches, there was but little to do. On Saturday preceeding the Sabbath that Mr. Vannist was to preach in Poughkeepsie, Paul would send Sanco to the church, who would open it and sweep the aisles and sand the floor, and then Paul would see if anything was wanting for the church. If a broom or sand was wanting, he furnished those items from his store.

Paul and his wife were two of the leading members of the church, having united during the ministry of the Rev. Benjamin Meynema, and they had the supervision of the church and parsonage. Rebekah was their only daughter, and when Dominie Vannist came there to board, she was twenty years of age, and she was the idol of her parents. Modest and unassuming in her manners, her sweetness of disposition, filial affection, and love of domestic life, won the admiration of all who knew her. Dominie Vannist's room was on the south side of Paul's house, which was entirely secluded. The city of Poughkeepsie had not extended outside of Main street; not a habitation could be seen from his window, and when he rested from his studies, nothing greeted his eye beyond Paul's little farm, but a monotonous view of forest scenery.

A century and a quarter ago, the time to which we refer, education was confined to a few. A large class of the inhabitants could not read nor write; schools and books were scarce. The board of Supervisors, which then sat in Poughkeepsie, some of them in signing documents had to make their marks. No newspapers were printed in the county until after the Revolution. The first was printed in Poughkeepsie in 1785. Nicholas Power was editor. The education of women was thought to be of little consequence, and but a few were instructed beyond reading and writing. Many could not write their names. Rebekah's opportunities were as good as the times would admit; she was perfectly versed in Dutch writing and reading, and often she would spend hours with the Dominie in his room, trying her skill with her pen and reading aloud to him from books taken from his library. Her mother often remonstrated with her for spending so much time in his room. "Why, Rebekah," she would say, "you will hinder him from studying; he will not be prepared on Sunday," and one day at dinner she mentioned to Mr. Vannist that she was afraid that Rebekah was trespassing on time which he wished to devote to study, and if that was the case, she would not allow her to visit his room so frequently. Mr. Vannist replied that Rebekah did not often interfere, and when he wished to be alone in his room, Rebekah immediately left. But Rebekah's visits continued, and sometimes were prolonged, and the Dominie in his leisure hours would instruct her in various branches—reading, writing, and arithmetic, and her improvement was rapid, and it pleased him to see her so apt a scholar. Often when Mr. Vannist had hours of recreation, he would ask Rebekah to take a walk through the village and call on some of his congregation. Sometimes they would stroll to the river and take a sail to the opposite side, and there sit on the river's bank, secluded and alone. Rebekah would assist in rowing the boat. Again they would take a walk to where the Morgan House is now, which then was an open field, and wend their way to the woods near by, gathering wild flowers; and then they would take a circuitous route home, crossing ravines; anon they would cross lots, until they arrived on Main street, and on their way home they would stop at her father's store, who was pleased to see his Dominie pay so much attention to his daughter, perhaps thinking that it would be the forerunner of a closer union that could only be severed by death.

The communion season was now approaching, and Mr. Vannist was making preparations for that solemn event. He had held his last commemorative service at his church in Fishkill, and now it was his turn to administer the sacraments at Poughkeepsie, and on the Sabbath preceeding the communion he invited those who wished to connect themselves with the church of Christ to meet him and the elders of the church at the house of Mr. Paul Schank, at two o'clock. The preparatory lecture was to commence at three o'clock, and he sincerely hoped that there would be some that would feel the necessity of a preparation for death, as life is so uncertain. Among the number that presented themselves to unite with the church, was Rebekah Schank. Oh, how it gladdened the hearts of her parents when their daughter made a public profession of religion, when she renounced the world and gave her heart to God, and the joy of her parents on that Sabbath noon, when they were all seated around that sacramental table to commemorate the Saviour's dying love, can better be imagined than described. Mr. Vannist was encouraged, for his labors at Poughkeepsie and Fishkill had been blest during the brief time he had been with this people. Besides preaching alternate Sabbaths at Poughkeepsie and Fishkill, he had stations at New Hackensack and Hopewell, and as the county was becoming more thickly populated, his congregations multiplied and their numbers increased. Mr. Vannist now confined himself more closely to his room, and with close application to study left little time for leisure. He often had to ride miles to visit the sick and the afflicted, and with no way of traveling but on horseback, for the country would not admit of wheel vehicles, for the by-roads were so rough and uneven that if the traveler had to deviate from the main road, fallen trees would often obstruct his passage, and on horseback this difficulty could be avoided by finding an opening through the woods of sufficient width for his horse to pass through. Mr. Vannist often met with this difficulty, and he always could find a way in which to avoid sunken holes and fallen trees. The pioneers, when they traveled in their lumber wagons, took their axes with them, and in traveling through the woods, if they met with any obstruction caused by trees falling across the road, which had blown down by violent storms of wind, they would fall to work with their axes and remove the obstruction, but this could be avoided by traveling on horseback; and Mr. Vannist always traveled over his parish on horseback, then extending over a circuit of some twenty miles.

A strong attachment now existed between Mr. Vannist and Rebekah, and it created a great deal of gossip in the village. The matrons would meet at each other's houses and talk the matter over, wondering if their Dominie would marry Rebekah Schank. The young ladies, too, would collect together and tell how they had seen them at different times walk out, engaged in close conversation. Such circumstances strengthened their belief that they would soon be married. "But then," said Mrs. L., "he is such a fine young minister, so dignified, so engaging in his manners, one cannot but help admire him." "Yes," said Miss V., "and Rebekah Schank is a lucky girl." Rebekah was spotless to a fault, and she now might be described as a model of beauty and loveliness. Her figure was tall and graceful, her hair a light auburn, soft and lustrous, which flowed in silken ringlets over her neck and shoulders: her ardent love for the church and her devotion to religious duties, particularly in the prayer meeting, all conspired to elevate her in the esteem of those who were the followers of the meek and lowly Saviour.

On the week preceeding the Sabbath that Mr. Vannist was to preach at Fishkill, he invited Rebekah to accompany him, which invitation she readily accepted. As provender was very cheap in those days, Paul volunteered to keep the Dominie's horse gratis. He supplied him with hay and meal, and whatever else he wished. Sanco was ordered to give the Dominie's horse a thorough brushing on the morning they were to set out for Fishkill, and Paul saddled his horse and fastened a pillion on behind, and then led him to the front of the house in Main street, and after the Dominie helping Rebekah on the pillion, he placed himself in the saddle, and then bidding her parents good-bye, they moved slowly out of the village on their way to Fishkill. Their course lay through New Hackensack. It was the latter part of June, and the country wore a beautiful aspect, for nature was decking herself in her most brilliant garments. The purple willows had on their full dress, and the wild ivy was clambering the forest trees, whose giant arms stretched across the highway and often interlocking each other, shutting out the sun's rays, presenting a scene wild and picturesque. Again the sunbeams would be streaming through every crevice, and pouring a flood of light through intervening forests; anon they would emerge into open fields, where the Dutch pioneers had erected substantial dwelling houses and barns, and many of them had their farms enclosed, and cattle and sheep were feeding in luxuriant pastures that lay on either side of the highway where they passed. Arriving at New Hackensack, they concluded to stop and refresh themselves and horse, and alighted at Mr. Van Benschoten's, who was a large landholder. He had just returned from the field with his negro slaves, where he had been superintending the work. He ordered Pompey to take the Dominie's horse and put him in the stable and give him a half skipple of wheat, (skipple is a Dutch measure containing three pecks.) Mr. Van Benschoten politely invited Mr. Vannist and Rebekah into the house, and after the customary salutations and inquiring the news at Poughkeepsie, Mrs. Van Benschoten set to work preparing dinner for their guests. Mr. Vannist had frequently stopped at Mr. Van Benschoten's when on his way to Fishkill to preach, and he knew the hospitality that he always received at his house, and when he lectured at New Hackensack, he often made his home there. A good substantial dinner was prepared, and the Dominie and Rebekah, with the family, were soon seated at the table, and after Mr. Vannist invoking the divine blessing, they partook of the bountiful supply that had been set before them.

After dinner, Mr. Vannist and Rebekah remained one hour at Mr. Van Benschoten's, who were members of his church. He gave a short exhortation before leaving, to his family, who had gathered in the room, including the negro slaves, and then Mr. Vannist said that he would be obliged to leave, as he wished to reach Col. John Brinckerhoff's before night. Pompey was ordered to saddle his horse and lead him to the house, and then taking leave of Mr. and Mrs. Van Benschoten, thanking them for their kindness, they left for Col. John Brinckerhoff's. The day was wearing away, and as they ascended the high rolling ridge now known as Mt. Hope, a half mile south of Myers' Corners, the scenery was of more than ordinary beauty. The sun was receding to the western horizon, and the song birds were warbling on the tree tops, making the air ring with their melody. The valleys on the east of the Hudson was the foreground of the picture; in the centre, like a beautiful panorama, lay the noble river; beyond, for some twenty miles, the valleys extended to the base of the Shawangunk mountains, whose blue tops reached the furtherest limits of the landscape. The checkered shadows of the declining sun reflected over the scene. Conversation had lagged for some time, and Rebekah, who was getting fatigued with her journey, lay half reclining on his shoulder. The day was moderately warm, and the balmy breezes were sifting her clustering curls, occasionally sweeping his face, who made no effort to push them aside. But they jogged slowly along, and before sunset they reached Col. John Brinckerhoff's, now the residence of Alfred White. The house is the same which Col. Brinckerhoff then occupied. The Colonel was expecting Dominie Vannist, as it was the Sabbath when he was to preach at Fishkill, and he often remained with him, particularly when night overtook him before reaching Fishkill Village. The Colonel told Cæsar to take his horse, and Mr. Vannist and Rebekah were ushered into the parlor, where Rebekah was introduced to Mrs. Brinckerhoff and family, who soon spread a bountiful table, knowing that Rebekah must be tired traveling on horseback, exposed to a warm sun through the day. Soon they were all seated at the table, and after Mr. Vannist asking the blessing, their wants were supplied and the kind attention that Rebekah received at

Col. Brinckerhoff's made her feel very much at home. They spent a very pleasant evening with the Colonel and family. After tea they all took a walk to the large creek, which was but a little way from the house, and spent an hour sailing down the stream which broke through the forests that lined its banks. The silvery moonbeams reflected over the water at the splash of the oars, which were handled dexterously by Mr. Vannist. Martha Jane Brinckerhoff and Rebekah, who accompanied Mr. Vannist in the boat, admired his skill in gliding it so swiftly over the water.

Returning home after such pleasant recreation, which was very much enjoyed by Rebekah and Martha Jane, the time for retiring soon arrived. Col. Brinckerhoff gathered his family and slaves together in the parlor, and then the Dominie opened the large Dutch Bible, which lay on the stand, and read the twenty-third Psalm, and after making a few remarks on the Psalmist, his faith in God, and that He would sustain him when passing through the dark valley of the shadow of death, fearing no evil, for his rod and staff they comforted him, so all who put trust in the Saviour could feel as David did when he penned this Psalm, and death would present to us no terrors, if we placed our firm reliance in Him who died to save such sinners as we are. He then closed with prayer; and all retired for the night. Mr. Vannist, after retiring to his room, seated himself in his chair for some time in deep meditation. He at length opened his satchel, which he always carried with him, and taking his manuscript out, commenced examining his sermon, which he had to deliver to his congregation at Fishkill on the morrow. In looking over it he thought if he had the time he could improve it. He had spent hours with Rebekah, which he thought he ought to have devoted to his studies, and he felt that he had neglected his duty to his God and to his people. He was an embassador of Christ, and his mission was to labor for the salvation of his guilty fellow men, but, thought he, have I not been instrumental in bringing many to the Saviour; has not my ministry been successful, and through the instrumentality of my preaching have not souls been converted? Such thoughts seemed to thrill the very fibres of his soul, and he felt encouraged to work with more zeal than ever. Hastily looking over his manuscript and making some alterations, he laid it aside, and after closet devotions, he sought to refresh himself with sleep, but this was denied him. He was fatigued with his day's journey, yet he had no disposition to sleep. His God, his labors on the Sabbath, and the object of his affections, came rushing through his mind. He had not as yet offered her his hand and heart, but the love that he cherished for her penetrated his inmost soul, and no finite love could compare with that for his beloved Rebekah.

The nights in the months of June are the shortest of the year, and Mr. Vannist had scarce got asleep ere the east was again streaked with the broad crimson of the dawn, and over the blazing hills the morning sun was again pouring his rays upon a regenerated world, and it was not seven o'clock when he was awakened by a loud rap at his door, and a voice from without saying that breakfast would be ready in a quarter of an hour. Mr. Vannist hastily commenced dressing himself, and in less time than specified his toilet was all adjusted, and he then made his appearance in the parlor, where the Colonel and his family were sitting. The Colonel then invited his guests to breakfast, and Rebekah was ushered into the room by Martha Jane, who seated her at the table by the side of Mr. Vannist. After giving thanks to the giver of all good for his protecting care through the night and refreshing sleep, the Dominie gave each one a verse in Scripture to repeat in turn, while they were at breakfast, commencing with himself. His was Psalms, forty-second chapter, fifth verse, "Why art thou cast down, O my soul, and why art thou disquieted in me; hope thou in God, for I shall yet praise him for the help of his countenance." Col. Brinckerhoff's turn came next, and the Dominie asked him if he could think of a passage of Scripture, who said yes: "If any man serve me, let him follow me, and where I am there shall also my servant be. If any man serve me, him will my Father honor." Mrs. Brinckerhoff was asked next if she could think of a passage of Scripture, who replied in the affirmative, and hers was very appropriate; and then he asked Martha Jane if she could repeat a verse, who said, "Be kindly affectioned one to another, with brotherly love; in honor preferring one another." And last of all he asked Rebekah if she knew a passage, who replied, "And said, For this cause shall a man leave father and mother, and shall cleave to his wife, and they twain shall be one flesh. What, therefore, God hath joined together, let not man put asunder." What Mr. Vannist's thoughts were after hearing this passage of Scripture from Rebekah, was known only to himself. Breakfast being over, the Colonel called in his domestics, and then Mr. Vannist read a chapter from the Gospel of St. Matthew, and closed with prayer. He then informed the Colonel that he would like to have his horse saddled, for it was time for him to leave for Fishkill. His request was complied with, and he then set out for Fishkill Village, leaving Rebekah at Col. Brinckerhoff's, who was to follow immediately with his family, with Rebekah in his wagon.

Mr. Vannist soon arrived at Fishkill, and stopped at Stephen Purdy's, who then lived on the opposite side of the street from where the National Bank is now located. The house was demolished in 1836, by Nelson Burrough, who then owned the premises, and built the present mansion, now (1874) owned by O. H. Barnes. Mr. Purdy took charge of the Dominie's horse, and in a little while the sound of the bell was reverberating through the valleys, calling the people to the house of God, and when Mr. Vannist arrived at the church he found a large congregation assembled, who had come from New Hackensack, Hopewell, Fishkill Plains, Fishkill Landing, and the Highlands, filling the main body of the church. Rebekah was seated in Col. Brinckerhoff's pew with Martha Jane. Mr. Vannist took his text in St. Matthew's Gospel, twenty-fifth chapter, last verse, "And these shall go away into everlasting punishment, but the righteous into life eternal." After his introductory remarks, he proceeded to review the condition of the two classes, the righteous and the wicked, in the world to come, that punishment hereafter was eternal, and he exhorted all the impenitent to make their peace with God, and if they put off the time until a more convenient season, that season may never come, but the righteous would attain everlasting felicity, and all at last would be numbered among his Saints in glory everlasting. The speaker produced a profound impression on his hearers, and the vivid pictures that he drew of the two classes at the close of his sermon seemed to penetrate every heart. After the services were concluded, Mr. Vannist stated to his congregation that he would preach at either New Hackensack or Hopewell before he returned to Poughkeepsie, if any member of the church had a convenient place for him to hold service, and as he saw a goodly number of his congregation from there present, he would appoint preaching if any one would say where the service might be held. Peter Monfort, from Fishkill Plains, arose and said that he could preach in his barn. It was the warm season of the year, and he had not yet commenced haying; his barn being empty, there would be ample room to accommodate all that would be present. This offer was accepted, and then Mr. Vannist said that he would preach in Mr. Monfort's barn on Tuesday of that week, services to commence at 10 o'clock a. m. He then remarked that if any wished or was willing to hold a prayer meeting at their house that evening, they could signify by rising. Johannas Swart arose and said that he could appoint a prayer meeting at his house. The Dominie then said that a meeting for prayers would be held at the house of Johannas Swart that evening, and then dismissed the congregation.

In those days there was preaching only once on the Sabbath; the country was too sparsely settled to collect a congregation more than once, and the village of Fishkill then contained so few inhabitants that only a small number lived in convenient distance even to attend prayer meeting. Mr. Vannist and Rebekah spent the remainder of the Sabbath with Stephen Purdy, and in the evening, with Mr. Purdy and family, they attended the prayer meeting at Mr. Swart's. The house is now the residence of John P. Green, and has been rebuilt several times. A little band of Christians had assembled to spend an hour in prayer. Mr. Vannist opened the Bible, which had been laid on a stand for the occasion, and then read a chapter in Revelations and offered a brief prayer, and then said that the meeting was open for prayer and remarks. An hour was spent profitably in singing and praying, and then Mr. Vannist closed the meeting, and he and Rebekah remained over night with Mr. Swart. On Monday they spent the day calling on his people in the village, and dining at Robert R. Brett's, now the residence of Mrs. John C. Van Wyck. The house, which was then a stone structure, was demolished in 1819 by Obadiah Bowne, who then owned the premises, and built the present beautiful edifice. The close of the day Mr. Vannist and Rebekah arrived at Cornelius Van Wyck's, now the residence of Sidney E. Van Wyck, of Revolutionary fame, known in Cooper's novels as the Wharton House. The architecture of this house is the same as it was originally, covered with scollop shingles, which were taken off about 1805 by the grandfather of the present owner. They remained over night with Mr. Van Wyck, whose family spared no pains to make it pleasant for them. Rebekah was entertained by Mrs.

Van Wyck and daughters, who accompanied her through their yards and garden. It was her first visit there and she admired the mountain scenery, the majestic highlands, whose tops were then gilded with the rays of the setting sun, painting with purple and gold a cloud that rested on Beacon, presenting a scene to her of indescribable beauty. After family worship, Mr. Vannist retired for the night, and spent an hour preparatory to rest in meditation, as he had an appointment on the morrow at Mr. Monfort's. A good night's

WHARTON HOUSE, FISHKILL VILLAGE.

rest refreshed him very much, and he awoke just as he heard the summons at his door that breakfast was waiting; when he hastily arose and made all haste to get ready, and when he entered the parlor he apologized for his not rising earlier, but Mrs. Van Wyck said that he was in time for breakfast, and then all were soon seated around the table, and Mr. Vannist returned thanks for past mercies, and His protecting care through the night. He then informed Mr. Van Wyck that they would be obliged to leave as soon as breakfast was over, as his appointment at Mr. Monfort's was at 10 o'clock. After breakfast, Mr. Vannist read a chapter from the Psalms, and offered a prayer, in which Mr. Van Wyck and family were remembered at the throne of grace. Pompey was told to saddle the Dominie's horse and lead him to the front yard. Mr. Vannist, after thanking Mr. Van Wyck for the kind treatment that he had received from himself and family, and the many pleasant hours spent at his house during his stay at Fishkill, helped Rebekah on the pillion, who invited the Miss Van Wycks to return her visit, hoping they might enjoy a visit at Poughkeepsie as hers had been at Fishkill. They set out for Peter Monfort's. It was a lovely June morning, and the country just emerging from a wilderness, presented a wild and romantic scene. Primitive forests, dark and dense, yet covered the country, untouched by the woodman's axe, and as they journeyed over the solitary road, they passed the time in conversation. Occasionally a squirrel would arrest their attention, leaping through the tree tops, and a grouse or rabbit would flee from their seclusion at the noise of their approach, and disappear in the depths of the woods. Their progress being so slow, and time passed away so unheeded, that they did not arrive at Mr. Monfort's until half an hour past the time appointed. But a goodly number of his congregation from New Hackensack and Hopewell had collected in the barn, which was well arranged for the occasion. The ancient Dutch barns were built with a double frame work. The outer frame arose but a little way, when the roof commenced. A second frame work, twelve feet from the first one, went up, which supported the roof, and between the two frame works were the linters, where the hay and grain were stored. These linters being empty at this season of the year, and the weather warm, Mr. Vannist would once a month hold meetings in barns in New Hackensack, Hopewell or vicinity, before he returned to Poughkeepsie, after preaching on the Sabbath at Fishkill, as no church had yet been erected at either place. The congregation seated themselves in the linters, and an open space in the center of the barn was allotted for Mr. Vannist, who commenced the services by addressing the throne of grace. He opened the Bible and read the one hundred and thirty-fifth Psalm, and then the singing was led by Rebekah in Dutch. After which a practical discourse was delivered from the first verse of the Psalm just read: "They that trust in the Lord shall be as Mount Zion, which cannot be removed, but abideth forever." The congregation listened with interest while he delivered his sermon, and after the services were over, they all gathered around their Dominie, shaking him by the hand and inviting him to go home and take dinner with them. After thanking them all for their kindness, they dispersed for their homes, and the Dominie and Rebekah took dinner with Mr. Monfort, who entertained them very pleasantly. After an hour's rest after dinner, spent in pleasant conversation with Mr. and Mrs. Monfort, they set out for Poughkeepsie.

The heat now was oppressive, and Mr. Vannist and Rebekah were exposed to its scorching rays, and after having traveled a few miles they concluded to take shelter under a large oak tree that stood near the highway and remain there an hour or more until the sun's rays should be less penetrating, and oh, what a precious hour that was to Mr. Vannist. They sat for some time in silence and nothing broke the stillness but the occasional chattering of the squirrel and the singing of birds. He at length became tearfully agitated, so much so that Rebekah perceived it, and she gazed at some object to hide the secret throbbings of her heart, and at last the stillness was broken by Mr. Vannist, who then offered her his hand and his heart. Rebekah was so overwhelmed with emotion, that she had not the power to express herself, but placing her hand in his, nodded assent. A gleam of joy irradiated the Dominie's face, and as the heat was subsiding, they commenced their journey, he urging his horse, for the day was getting towards its close, and they were yet several miles from Poughkeepsie. A sudden shower obliged them again to stop and seek shelter under a tree, as no house was near to afford them protection from the falling raindrops. But the clouds soon dispersed, and they traveled on, the sun again shining from below the clouds, and before them lay luxuriant fields covered with a tapestry of green, meadows blooming with buttercups and daisies, sparkling in the recent falling raindrops. As they neared Poughkeepsie, the sun was sinking below the western horizon, the last rays were gilding the eastern hilltops, and the approaching shades of evening touched the landscape with inexpressible beauty. Mrs. Schank had been looking for their return for some time, for Mr. Vannist had informed her that if nothing prevented they would return before night on Tuesday. Presently she saw them coming down Main street, and her anxiety was relieved by seeing them once more safely ensconced in her house. Sanco took charge of the Dominie's horse, and Paul, who had just come from his store, saw that he was well cared for. Rebekah Schank accompanying Mr. Vannist to Fishkill, created considerable excitement among the matrons in Poughkeepsie, and they would congregate in each other's houses and discuss the subject. Some thought it was not right for the Dominie to take a girl with him when going to Fishkill to preach, and not return until Tuesday night; others said that they saw no harm in it, but they were all confident that they would make a match. "Don't you see," said one, "how often they walk out together?" "Yes," says another, "I saw them pass by our house one evening last week, going towards the river, engaged in close conversation." "Why," says an elderly lady, "I can see Paul's garden from our back window, and I have frequently seen them at twilight, sitting in Paul's summer house, and I heard Sanco say that Misses Becca and Massa Dominie were walking in the garden every night."

Rebekah did not communicate to her mother that Mr. Vannist had offered himself to her in marriage until some days after her return from Fishkill. She merely told her of the pleasant time they had spent among the people there, and the many acquaintances she had made. But Mrs. Schank had long seen that an ardent attachment had existed between them, which she hoped would ultimately end in marriage. This was a source of great anxiety to her, for she was fearful that he occupying a high position in society and the influence he had in his congregation and in the community at large, he might not condescend to marry Rebekah, but she also thought he would not win the affections of her daughter and then not marry her, but

she would wait and see what the future would bring
forth. A few more days had passed, when Rebekah
and her mother were in the sitting room alone. The
father and two brothers, Isaac and Cornelius, were at
the store, and Dominie Vannist had just left Poughkeepsie for Fishkill, and would not return until the
next Monday. Sanco was at work in the potato field,
clearing the hills of weeds. Juda and Fillis were at
work in the kitchen, and Mrs. Schank was busily
engaged in their household duties. Rebekah then
informed her mother of Mr. Vannist's offer to her in
marriage, when returning from Fishkill. Her mother
looked at her with some surprise, to think that she did
not communicate to her this information before, but
Rebekah said that she waited for a favorable opportunity, and then suddenly her father came into the
room, and she related to them the diffidence and agita-
tion the Dominie manifested under the large tree by
the wayside, when he gave her his heart. Her parents'
joy was unbounded, and the news soon spread through
the village, that Dominie Vannist was engaged to
Rebekah Schank, which now was the topic of conversation. Dominie Vannist promised Rebekah that he
would return on Monday from Fishkill, as he would
not preach at Hopewell until his next regular appointment there, and he arrived home on Monday at noon,
in time for dinner. After dinner, the Dominie and
Rebekah retired to his room, and an hour was spent
in close conversation. She related to him that she had
made known to her parents his offer to her in marriage,
and the pleasure it would afford them to see them
united, and, said she, the report is now circulated

through the village that we are engaged, and the wedding is appointed; and she farther said that Isaac told her that he overheard several young men, one a lawyer, talking over the affair at the Van Kleek House, wondering if they would be lucky enough to get an invitation, and several of her associates had hinted to her of her intended marriage. In the evening, Mr. Vannist entered the sitting room where Rebekah and her parents were sitting. The air was sultry, for it was midsummer, and Paul had just returned from his store, leaving his son Isaac there to attend to customers. As soon as the Dominie entered, Paul arose and seated himself close to an open window, to catch the summer breezes that were gently passing, when he remarked that he hardly had time to ask him if there was anything new at Fishkill, whether any of his congregation was sick, and where he remained over night. Such questions were usually asked when the Dominie returned from preaching or visiting his parishioners, and then the conversation ceased and a stillness pervaded the room for some time. Mr. Vannist knew that Rebekah had informed her parents of his offer to her in marriage, and the diffidency he expected he would have to contend with had subsided, and he proudly asked Mr. and Mrs. Schank for their daughter in marriage. "Yes," said Paul, "and I hope, with the blessing of God," but he could say no more; ecstatic joy pervaded his soul, and his mind was so absorbed with his daughter's marriage, that he could not find words to express himself. Mrs. Schank then remarked that Rebekah was their only daughter, and she could willingly consent to give her to him in marriage, and if she made him half as good a wife as she had been to her parents a dutiful and loving daughter, she would be worth to him more than all this world could give. Rebekah had been listening with intense interest, and when her mother related her filial affection and her consent for her to be united to him, until separated only by death, she could not refrain from weeping. Her love for her parents and their love for her presented to her mind vivid recollections. Their tender assiduities, the watchfulness over her in the helpless period of infancy, how they had guarded her heedless youth, and their increasing anxiety for her welfare in subsequent life, all tended to awaken emotions in her bosom which she could not suppress. Mr. Vannist remained calm and self-possessed, and the question which had so long lain next to his heart, had been decided, and now his mind was relieved, and soon all was tranquil in the room, when Mr. Vannist said it was time to retire, and bidding Rebekah and her parents good night, he went to his room, and seating himself by his window, his mind reverted to the events which had just transpired. He was only twenty-six years old, and what bright visions did the future unfold to him. He was soon to be united to one to whom he had given the warm gushings of his heart; her youth, her amiability, and her modest deportment, all tended to fill his soul with joy unutterable.

When it became generally known throughout the village that Dominie Vannist was engaged to Rebekah Schank, the excitement partially subsided, and the long expected event, when they were to be married, was looked for by the united congregations with interest.

Paul, who had the supervision of the parsonage, now began to look after the premises. It had not been occupied since it was vacated by the Rev. Benjamin Meynema, and the premises were in a dilapidated state. The villagers had trespassed on the grounds, and some of the outside fence was broken down; the window shutters were swinging, and the hinges of some were broken, caused by the fastenings not being secured. Paul had endeavored to protect the parsonage and he did all that lay in his power to keep trespassers off, but nights, boys and young men would go into the enclosure and commit depredations which he could not redress. He now employed a blacksmith at his own expense to make new hinges for the window shutters, and himself and Sanco repaired the outside fence, and Mrs. Schank set Fillis and Juda to work at the interior, cleaning the floors, scouring the huge timbers overhead, whitewashing the side walls, and cleaning the cellar and garret. Paul set out some apple trees in the lot that lay next to the Court house, and planted cherry trees, gooseberries, and currants in the garden, and when he went to New York to buy goods, he intended to purchase some nice furniture for his daughter, but the marriage had been postponed until Spring.

The winter of 1760 and '61 had been comparatively mild, and Mr. Vannist did not fail to go and preach at Fishkill every alternate Sabbath, for so little snow had fallen during the winter, that traveling was but little obstructed. Often times in severe winters the snow would block up the highways so that traveling would be impossible and Mr. Vannist could not fulfill his appointments regularly, but the present winter enabled him to attend to the spiritual wants of his people, and his leisure hours were spent in his study room with Rebekah, where they would remain for hours. Occasionally, when the weather was pleasant, they would call on some of the villagers, but Mr. Vannist was always attentive to the sick, and nothing would prevent his visiting the afflicted and imparting spiritual consolation at the bedside of the dying.

The first spring month had now arrived, and the migratory birds began to appear, and every indication of the breaking up of winter was now apparent. The blue birds were warbling on the house tops, and flocks of wild geese and ducks had collected on the river and swamps, which afforded plenty of game for the hunter. Paul had commenced making preparations for the wedding, which was to take place on Wednesday, the 5th of June, at his house.

Paul was making great preparations for that important event. The congregation from Fishkill had sent up to his house a large supply of turkeys and fowls. Madam Brett had sent a whole side of beef and a leg of mutton. Paul had received from New Hackensack and Hopewell large quantities of provisions, and when the morning of the 5th of June dawned, there never was a lovelier one. The spits in Paul's large kitchen fireplace, at an early hour, were hanging full of turkeys, fowls, beef, mutton, etc., for the wedding was to take place at twelve o'clock. The huge oven was crowded to its utmost capacity with pies, puddings, cakes, and other good things, and there was also sausages, souse and head cheese. A dozen or more colored girls were employed in cooking and baking. It was customary in those days, when weddings took place, to keep what then was called "open house," that is, to extend a general invitation a certain distance to every house, as the population was so sparse, and Paul gave a general invitation in the village of Poughkeepsie and a mile in the country, for all to be present. At ten o'clock the then village of Poughkeepsie presented a novel scene. The two congregations commenced to assemble and large wagon loads came pouring in Main street to Paul's house, some seated on chairs taken from their houses, some sitting on clean straw on the bottom of the wagon box; young men and women on horseback, all flocking to Paul's house. Paul seeing that it was useless to have the ceremony performed in the house, as he wished all to have an opportunity to witness it, concluded to have the marriage take place out of doors. He at once set several negroes at work erecting a platform in his yard, fronting Main street, and in an hour it was completed. As the hour of twelve drew near, the excitement became intense, and what added more to the enthusiasm was the appearance of Madam Brett, in her coach, drawn by four horses, coming down Main street, with two negroes in the front seat and one negro on the rear of the coach, whose business was to open the carriage door. It was always customary for the patentees to ride in a carriage drawn by four horses. The Van Cortlandts, Phillips, Verplancks, Beekmans, and Livingstons, always rode out for pleasure in carriages drawn by four horses. The Phillips, who owned the great Highland Patent, kept up that custom the longest. As late as 1816 they rode out with their carriage with four horses. The old carriage is still in existence. It was shown to the writer last summer by the foreman of the Phillips mansion at Garrison, in an out-building, where it had not been taken out for years. The wheels are as heavy as an ordinary lumber wagon used by our farmers at the present day, only a great deal more dishing. The carriage body rested on what was then called thorough-braces, which were used before the invention of the elastic spring. These thorough-braces gave the body a swinging motion, which yielded to the unevenness of the road. The carriage was more spherical and heavier than those used at the present time. The English coat of arms is emblazoned on the doors, and the interior was once beautifully tasselled. The page's seat in the rear is so arranged that he could either stand or sit to suit his convenience. If he stood up there were handles for him to take hold of so that he could keep his equilibrium.

In the carriage with Madam Brett was the Rev. Gualterius DuBois, from New York, who was to perform the ceremony, and two of her grandchildren. Her husband had been accidentally killed when comparatively young. Coming from New York on board of a sloop, the boom of the vessel struck him when entering the mouth of the Fishkill creek near Byrnesville, in 1721. It is said that his remains were interred in an old burying ground near there, where it is still to be seen. Dominie DuBois had come from New York by land on horseback as far as Madam Brett's, and remained there over night, and leaving his horse at the Madam's mansion, he came to Poughkeepsie with her in her carriage. Paul was pleased to see Madam Brett, for he was fearful that she would not be able to attend the wedding, for she was nearly eighty years of age and infirm. She only lived three years after, as she died in 1764. When the hour of the wedding arrived, the excitement became intense; the street in front of Paul's house was literally blocked with people. Every available space was occupied. The house tops near by were covered with people, and the forest trees in close proximity to Paul's yard were filled with half grown boys and negroes. Paul's barn roof and every window in his house; every pane of glass could be seen with a face peering through. Presently the bride and groom made their appearance, and walked gracefully on the platform, and Dominie DuBois confronting them. Over the platform swung the Dutch coat of arms, and on each end of the platform was fastened two banners, on one was large letters in Dutch, "Fishkill," on the other "Poughkeepsie." On the Fishkill banner was the representation of the Saviour's advent in the world, and the star which the wise men saw in the East, and beneath read: "When they saw the star they rejoiced with exceeding great joy." On the other banner was "Poughkeepsie," and that represented Moses on Mount Sinai receiving the law, and on it read, "And the glory of the Lord shone upon Mount Sinai, and the cloud covered it six days, and the seventh day he called unto Moses out of the midst of the cloud." While the marriage ceremony was solemnized the stillness of death pervaded the vast throng, and the heavens seemed to drink in with the assemblage. No waving cloud was seen, not even a ruffle was heard through the tree tops. The bride wore a trailing dress, and she held in her hand a boquet of choice flowers. The groom was dressed in small clothes, with silver knee buckles. After the ceremony was over, and the customary salutations passed, it was voted that Dominie DuBois should decide which banner was the prettiest, as there had been considerable strife between the two congregations which should excell. Dominie DuBois rather hesitated, but the ladies persisted till at last he consented. After paying an elegant tribute to the two banners, he said that if there was any difference, he should have to give Fishkill the preference. The Dominie had scarce finished, when quick as a flash cheers rent the air for Fishkill, the bride and groom, and the Dominie. Paul joined in the merriment with the Fishkillers. Some of the Poughkeepsie ladies were a little chagrined, but it was soon over. The table for the Fishkill people was set first, as they all wished to return home that afternoon. Precisely at one o'clock the table was all ready, and in the centre of it stood their banner. At the head of the table was seated the bride and groom, and Dominie DuBois sat next to the groom, and Madam Brett opposite, beside the bride. At the table was seated Colonel John Brinckerhoff, General Jacobus Swartout, Jacob Van Benschoten, Peter Monfort, Goris Storm, Robert R. Brett, John N. Bailey, Stephen Purdy, Cornelius Van Wyck, Johannas Terbush, and others. After the Fishkill congregation had finished eating, they invited the bride and groom to make them a visit, and then they dispersed to their homes. The Poughkeepsians then set their table and placed their banner upon it, and then the bride and groom took their place at the head the same as at the Fishkill table. By the side of the groom was seated Dominie DuBois, and beside the bride sat Katrine Van Kleek. Seated at the Poughkeepsie table was Hendrick Beekman, Bartholemew Cornell, Jacobus Vander Bogart, Boltus Van Kleek, Robert R. Livingston, Leonard Lewis, Paul Schank, and others. The last table was the negroes', which occupied the rest of the day, and at sunset it was all over. Madam Brett remained over night at Paul's, as he would not consent for her to return home the same day, for he thought it too great an undertaking. She and Dominie DuBois left the next morning. Before leaving she gave Rebekah twenty guilders to buy her furniture when she commenced housekeeping, but, alas, that happy day never arrived, as the sequel will show.

Dominie DuBois remained a week at Madam Brett's after the wedding, and preached on the following Sabbath at Fishkill before returning to New York.

Rebekah did not commence housekeeping as she first intended. Her father thought that the parsonage needed more repairs than he first apprehended, and he thought it advisable to defer it until the next Spring. The Dominie and his wife spent their Summer vacation visiting his friends in New Jersey, and before returning home they made a visit at Dominie DuBois's, who was then pastor of the Middle Dutch Church in New York, and had officiated at their marriage. The fall and winter they spent much time visiting among their people. Another Spring had now arrived, and about the latter part of March, Dominie Vannist got ready to go to Fishkill to preach, as it was the regular Sabbath to do so. He parted from his wife with a kiss, and set out for Fishkill.

The day was raw and chilly, and his progress was extremely slow. Every step his horse sank to his fetlocks in mud, and wishing to get to Fishkill before night overtook him, made no stop at New Hackensack. A damp snow commenced falling before he reached what is now known as Swartwoutville, and this added to the slowness of his journey; his horse at last was taken sick and he was obliged to dismount and lead him, and walking in the snow he felt a dampness penetrating his garments, and not reaching Fishkill Village until dark, when on arriving at Mrs. Terbush's, his clothes were wet and he was very much chilled. This place is now the residence of Lewis B. White; the house was demolished by his father, Dr. Barto White, in 1808, who then owned the premises. Mr. Vannist hitched his horse to a post and then knocked at the door for admission. Mrs. Terbush came to the door and expressed her surprise on seeing him covered with snow, which was melting and the water dripping off his clothes, and invited him into the house. He informed her that he had just come from Poughkeepsie, and at this time Mr. Terbush entered who saw his minister, who told of his exposure and the illness of his horse. Mr. Terbush had the Dominie's horse immediately put in his stable, and set one of his negroes to rub him and then cover him with blankets. Mr. Vannist unbuckled his shoes and then taking them off and laying them aside, a dry pair of stockings was given him, and also taking off his wet garments and exchanging for dry ones, he took his seat close to a large open fire, which had been replenished by one of the domestics. Mrs. Terbush now set to work preparing something for Mr. Vannist to eat, who had been exposed to the storm and eating nothing since he left Poughkeepsie. He, however, ate but little, and complained of chilliness and aching of his head and limbs. Seating himself by the fire until early in the evening, when he wished to retire. Mrs. Terbush had placed a warming pan filled with ignited coals in his bed, and when it had been sufficiently warmed, he took a glass of wine, diluted with milk, and retired for the night. Mr. Vannist had a comfortable night's rest and he awoke refreshed. Mr. and Mrs. Terbush, feeling very uneasy and anxious to hear from him, early inquired after him, who expressed himself very comfortable after refreshing sleep, and thought that he would be well enough to preach. At breakfast Mr. Vannist's appetite was much better, and after the family worship, he spent what little time he had left in collecting material, and looking over his sermon, which he had previously written. It was a clear, bright Sabbath morning, and the forests on the mountain tops were encased in snow and ice, which glistened in the rays of the sun. Every bush and sapling was bending under the weight of the new fallen snow, presenting a wintry appearance. As the day progressed, the warm sunshine began to dissolve the snow into slush and water, rendering the traveling very disagreeable. Mr. Vannist rode with Mr. Terbush in a phæton. A goodly number of his congregation were present, and he preached with his usual energy and zeal. His text was in Psalms, fifty-eighth chapter and last verse, "Verily there is a reward for the righteous, verily he is a God that judgeth in the earth." Mr. Vannist in the first place dwelt on the joys of the righteous, and in strains of heavenly wisdom he portrayed the joys that awaited them beyond the grave, but, said he, verily He is a God that judgeth in the earth, and all who will not put their trust in Him will eventually be judged with divine retribution. Mr. Vannist returned with Mr. Terbush from church, and after partaking of dinner, he remarked that he felt chilly and an aching similar to that of the preceding evening. He seated himself close to the fire, endeavoring to seek relief from the heat it produced, but the pain increased until he was unable to sit up, when Mr. Terbush helped him in bed. He had a very restless night, and Mr. Terbush thought it advisable to send for a physician, who, on visting him, found him suffering from a violent fever. He left medicine, with instructions as to how it should be administered, and said he would call again the next day. The physician was prompt as to time, and found his patient rather more comfortable, but his fever was unabated, and after giving instructions to Mr. and Mrs. Terbush as to care and treatment, he left him. The assistance of kind neighbors, who volunteered their services to help take care of their pastor, contributed much to alleviate his sufferings, but when the physician arrived the next morning and examined his patient, he was somewhat alarmed. His disease was typhus fever, which now had assumed a violent character, and he thought it advisable to dispatch a messenger to Poughkeepsie to procure a consulting physician and inform Mr. Vannist's people of his illness. He then wrote a note, addressing it to Paul Schank, informing him of the sudden illness of Mr. Vannist, and stating the nature and character of the disease, and if the fever continued as violent a few days longer he should consider him dangerous. The messenger arrived at the Van Kleek House at eleven o'clock, and informed the proprietor that Dominie Vannist was very sick at the house of Mr. Terbush, in Fishkill Village. He then gave his horse in charge of the hostler and proceeded to the store of Paul Schank, and handed the note to his son Isaac, his father having just gone to the house. Isaac immediately took the note to his father, who opened it and read the contents to himself, in the presence of his family, and while perusing it he betrayed considerable emotion, which was perceived by Rebekah, who anxiously inquired if anything was the matter. Her father then handed her the note, and she commenced reading it, but before finishing, it fell from her hand to the floor. Bursting into tears, she left the room, and there all alone she gave vent to excessive grief. Paul, too, had commenced weeping, and his wife and son stood gazing on the mournful scene, not yet having learned the cause of their sorrow. After recovering a little, Paul informed them of Mr. Vannist's illness, and then all wept, and after an interval of a few minutes, Isaac said that the messenger was at the Van Kleek House, and as soon as his horse was rested he was going to return to Fishkill with a physician who had been sent for in consultation. Paul then went to Rebekah's room and found her weeping violently. He informed her of what the messenger had said, and that probably the next news that they would hear from Mr. Vannist might be encouraging, but Rebekah wished to see him very much, and then her father offered to go with her immediately to Fishkill, which offer she accepted.

They did not set out for Fishkill until the next morning, for Paul had to look for a conveyance, he having none suitable, owning only one horse. Finally he procured a chaise, and they started early for Fishkill, and at eleven o'clock they arrived at Mr. Terbush's. Mr. Vannist was more comfortable, and he inquired of the physician from Poughkeepsie if Mr. Schank had been informed of his sickness, who replied in the affirmative, and then said that himself and daughter had just arrived, and they would be in presently. A gleam of joy illuminated the sick man's face, and in a few moments Rebekah and her father stood before him. Mr. Vannist had strength sufficient to extend his hand, and then said "Rebekah," who placed her hand in his, and the scene was so solemn and impressive that all present were overwhelmed with sorrow. Mr. Vannist expressed himself to her that his Saviour was precious, and with a feeble voice said, "Which hope we have as an anchor of the soul both sure and steadfast." Paul, after taking an affectionate leave of his minister, who trusted that if not permitted to meet here again they would meet in Heaven, returned to Poughkeepsie, leaving Rebekah at Mr. Terbush's, who watched almost incessantly at the bedside of her dying husband. He commenced sinking rapidly, and Rebekah soon saw clearly his approaching dissolution, and when the physician gave up all hope of his recovery, she calmly resigned herself and bowed in submission to the will of Him who doeth all things right. His last words to her were, "We will meet in

Heaven," and the 10th of April, 1761, he breathed his last.

Mr. Vannist's funeral took place at the church at Fishkill, the third day after his decease, and the whole surrounding country came to pay their last respects to one who held so strong an affection in the hearts of his people. His congregation from Poughkeepsie, New Hackensack and Hopewell, were all present. At ten o'clock the funeral procession commenced moving slowly from Mr. Terbush's to the church, headed by the clergy, physicians, and pall bearers, who were the officers of the church at Fishkill and Poughkeepsie. The floor of the church had been taken up from under the pulpit, and the earth removed and deposited on the floor beside the grave, and there the remains of the Rev. Jacobus Vannist were deposited. This custom of burying ministers beneath the floor, under the pulpit, in the Dutch church, died out in the year 1800. Rebekah, who had been with Mr. Vannist in his last sickness, and had stood beside his dying couch until his death, was now viewing the last mournful scene with her parents and brothers. It was not customary to preach funeral sermons in those days; a brief prayer and then an exhortation was delivered by the Rev. Hermanus Meier, of Esopus, who alluded to the short period Mr. Vannist had labored amongst his people. "Only two years and a half," said he, "since his settlement with them. God took him in the very Spring time of life, but his work is done, and the loss to his people is irreparable." During the address, the speaker alluded to the uncertainty of life and the necessity of a preparation for death, and the loss of their minister drew tears from many of the congregation. The coffin was then lowered into the grave, and the pall bearers commenced removing the earth from the floor, and as it sounded on the coffin, Rebekah's heart wrung with anguish, and when the grave was filled with earth, and the mournful throng slowly dispersed, she remained there with her parents for some time. At last they slowly left that hallowed spot and wended their way homeward. A tombstone was erected to his memory, and placed in the churchyard at Fishkill, bearing the following inscription in the Dutch language: "Jacobus Vannist, preacher of the Holy Gospel in Poughkeepsie and Fishkill, died the 10th of April, 1761, in his 27th year." This tombstone, in process of time had disappeared, but was accidentally discovered when digging a grave, where it had been placed. This stone is now placed against the rear wall of the church.

Until 1783, the old Dutch burying ground in Poughkeepsie remained undisturbed, and Paul Schank's burial plot was where Smith's restaurant is now located, and where the tombstones of Rebekah and her parents could be seen. The congregation then abandoned that ground and built their church on the opposite side of the street. Market street was then laid out through the burying ground, intersecting Cannon street, which then had just been opened. The remaining portion of the burying ground was leased for fifty years, in lots, to individuals. The leases prohibited the leaseholders from having cellars underneath the buildings erected thereon. These leases expired in 1833, when new leases were given, with the privilege of putting cellars underneath the buildings that stood on the old burying ground. The ashes of the dead were then all collected and placed in a vault prepared for that purpose, which is located in the rear of Smith's restaurant. There the remains of Rebekah and her parents lie, and there they will lie until summoned by the voice of the archangel, and by the sound of the trumpet of God. Then that vault will open its marble jaws, that grave will give up its dead, and Rebekah and her husband will come forth clothed in the bright vestments of immortality, and then they will all receive the joyful summons that will call them to their glorified home in Heaven.

THE SUBALTERN.

A TALE OF THE REVOLUTION.

The village of Fishkill Landing is comparatively of modern growth; including Matteawan, they have a population of some seven thousand inhabitants, and being in close proximity, they should be included in one village or city. They have doubled their population within a score of years, and they bid fair to vie with any city on the Hudson, between New York and Albany. Their locations are well chosen; the scenery of the Highlands, the majestic Hudson, and the valley of the Fishkill, all combine to make the place attractive to the capitalist and the pleasure seeker who wish to spend their summers in the quiet valley lying near the base of the mountains. Men of wealth and culture have already selected this place for their country residences, and several country seats have been erected, some at large cost. But what a change has taken place since the Revolution. Then, where these villages are located, there were only a few isolated dwellings. The mansion of Mrs. S. Verplanck, and of the Honorable Isaac Teller, deceased, built by Madam Brett, in 1710, and the old Pine house, east of Matteawan, on the highway leading to Fishkill Village, are the only relics now remaining of the Revolution, that we know of. The Teller house was then occupied by a gentleman named Depeyster, who came in possession of the mansion after the death of Madam Brett, in 1764, including the mill owned by her. Depeyster carried on the milling business, buying all the grain the country produced far and near, and after converting his wheat and corn into flour and meal, he would ship it to New York, where he had a brother engaged in mercantile business, who would sell it for him. Depeyster was a man of wealth, and occupying the Madam Brett mansion, he lived in the style of the patentees. His parlors were well furnished, and in the inclement season of the year, two blazing wood fires were constantly kept burning in them. His family consisted of his wife, son, several daughters, and a brace of negro slaves, for then slavery was tolerated throughout the country.

The Revolutionary war had broken out, and the battles of Lexington, Bunker Hill, and Long Island had been fought, and the American army had suffered a total defeat in the latter battle, and were obliged to retreat through New Jersey, which created great alarm throughout Fishkill, particularly the following Spring. when they heard that General Burgoyne, with ten thousand veterans, besides a host of Canadians and Indians, were marching from Canada, intending to force their way through the interior to New York city. General Washington hurried on Gates and Arnold, with an army collected from the New England States, and to these they joined the immortal Morgan, who had one thousand riflemen. Burgoyne was getting hemmed in near Saratoga, and the British commander in New York, hearing of his critical situation, sailed up the river with a large fleet to aid him, if possible. The inhabitants at Fishkill Landing, hearing of this large fleet coming up, were so terrified that most of them, with their families, decamped for the interior of the county, for a place of safety. Some sought refuge at Quaker Hill, in the eastern part of the county, others in the great Nine Partners, and some even in Connecticut. Depeyster's family, excepting himself, his daughter Katrina, and two negro slaves, Dinah and Pompey, removed to what is now known as the town of Pawling. Depeyster was a staunch whig, and he was determined not to leave his home, and flee, should the British fleet appear above the Highlands; and his daughter Katrina, and the two negro slaves, resolved to keep him company. A battle was expected to be fought in the immediate vicinity, and but few inhabitants remained at Fishkill Landing, and they kept a strict watch for the appearance of the fleet. General Washington supposed that the fleet might land somewhere near Cold Spring, and effect an entrance through the Highlands to Fishkill Village, and he accordingly stationed his army on the most advantageous positions in the Highlands, near the village. His headquarters were what is now the residence of Sidney E. Van Wyck, Esq., generally known by the name of the Wharton House. A heavy chain, supported by buoys, was stretched across the river at a narrow pass in the Highlands, but when the fleet struck the chain it snapped asunder like a reed, without injuring a vessel or obstructing the fleet, and onward they sailed up the river, and when the fleet hove in sight of Newburgh and Fishkill Landing, it created great consternation among the inhabitants. But to their great joy the fleet passed by without landing, occasionally firing off a cannon at the buildings on the shore, the balls whistling over the river's banks, striking sometimes near an isolated dwelling.

But the fleet sailed on, for they heard that a great battle had been fought, and Burgoyne was obliged to retreat, and his army greatly reduced and suffering for the want of provisions, and unless aid should soon come, he would be obliged to surrender. The fleet arrived opposite Kingston, then called Esopus, and there the commander learned that Burgoyne had surrendered with all his army to General Gates. The British commander, on hearing the sad news, ordered the village to be set on fire, and then immediately retired for New York. Arriving opposite Newburgh they halted, the fleet anchoring in the bay. Then Newburgh was located on the top of the hill, a small village containing only a few hundred inhabitants, and it was not until after the revolution, that streets were laid out on the descending slopes to the river. The main road that led to the river wound around the brow of the hill at the head of Colden street. North of Colden street, where Front street now is, the bank of the river was then skirted with gigantic forest trees and a large growth of underbrush. Some young men crawled through the underbrush near where Mailler's storehouse is now located, and fired upon the fleet, when instantly several cannon were brought to bear upon the spot. The cannon balls tore off some of the large limbs of the trees, which fell with a tremendous crash, demolishing the underbrush, and so frightened the young men that they fled for their lives.

A number of officers came ashore on the Fishkill side. Among the number was a subaltern, who took a stroll up the hill to near where the store of J. E. Member is now located, and casting his eye over the valley of the Fishkill, viewed the majestic Highlands, whose tops seemed reared to the clouds. The subaltern seated himself on a post-rail fence, which was then a favorite fence with the Dutch, which consisted of posts set in the ground, with holes made and posts inserted with a post-axe, when the rails were placed in and securely fastened. There sitting he fell into a deep revery, and while musing he was unconscious of aught that was passing around him, and time passed by unheeded, when suddenly he bethought himself, and looking toward the river saw that the fleet had disappeared from view. He hastened with all his speed to the river's brink, in hopes of seeing the fleet near enough to signal them, but the vessels were fast disappearing in the Highlands, and probably they had not yet discovered that he was left behind; and sailing under favorable wind it was impossible for him to expect to reach the fleet on foot. The first idea that presented itself to his mind was to take a horse from the pasture fields and mount him, and by putting him to the top of his speed, try to overtake the fleet, but that would be a hazardous undertaking, for he might be taken as a spy, and then his life would have to pay the forfeit. He next thought of disguising himself and trying to reach New York through the interior, but to pass the lines without detection would be almost impossible, and if taken prisoner his chance of life would not be as favorable as to surrender himself, and frankly state the truth. He walked slowly to the top of the hill where the village of Fishkill Landing is now located, but how different the scene appeared. Nothing greeted his eye but extensive fields, and now and then an isolated farm house. The main highway leading to Matteawan did not exist then, and where that busy street is now, was nothing but wild, uncultivated fields, covered mostly with forest. The subaltern left the highway and commenced slowly walking across the fields toward Matteawan, but the scenery which recently he had so much admired, had lost all attraction for him. His mind reverted to his native land, and the home of his childhood. The tender ties of a mother and sisters came rushing through his mind; how they wept when he enlisted to fight at the call of his country, and how their hearts would wring with anguish if they should hear that he was taken prisoner, and probably end his life on the gallows. Overcome by such thoughts the subaltern burst into tears.

Looking around he descried the Depeyster mansion. The day was drawing to a close, and no human being was in sight. The atmosphere was becoming chilly, and it reminded him of the necessity of obtaining lodging. He thought first of passing the night in an outhouse, but he at length concluded to try and gain admission to some house, not knowing what reception he would receive. He knew that it would be impossible for him to escape being taken prisoner in the heart of an enemy's country, unless he could exchange his military suit for a citizen's dress, and even if he could his chance then would be very precarious, and after reflection he concluded to try and find shelter for the night in some dwelling. He timidly approached the Depeyster mansion and gently knocked.

Depeyster had been much alarmed through the day on account of the British fleet stopping opposite Fishkill Landing, for he had a large supply of grain in his mill, and he was fearful they might seize the mill and take the contents, and he kept close watch through the day, and when the subaltern knocked for admission he was alarmed, for he had not heard that the fleet had left. He was revolving in his mind whether to obey the summons or not, but he finally concluded to go to the door and see who was there. Katrina remonstrated, for she was fearful something serious might occur. She supposed that the British fleet yet lay in Newburgh bay, and that some officers might make demands on her father, which, if not acceded to, their house might be sacked, their mill broken into, or something more dreadful happen. But Depeyster told Pompey to fetch him the gun from the armory, which was done immediately, and Katrina holding a light, for it was now dark, they cautiously approached the hall door and inquired who was there and their business. The subaltern replied that a friend in misfortune wished to obtain a night's lodging. Depeyster opened the door, and a richly dressed British officer stood before them. The subaltern introduced himself by saying that he belonged to the British fleet that had recently sailed up the river, and on returning the fleet had anchored off Newburgh bay, and several officers, with himself, came ashore, and he admiring the scenery of the Highlands had strayed from his companions, and falling in a revery had remained some time in deep thought, thinking of the future of this country, and that the colonies would eventually become free and independent, when suddenly recollecting himself, he looked on the river and not a sail was in sight. Retracing his steps with all haste to the river, he said he saw the last vessel disappearing in the Highlands, and he had probably not yet been missed by his companions. What course to pursue he did not know; he first thought of trying to make his escape, but upon reflection he concluded to abandon the idea, supposing that he would be taken for a spy, and then there would be but little hope of saving his life, and as night was close at hand, and the weather somewhat cold, he thought to try and gain admittance at some house, hoping some one would be kind enough to receive him.

Depeyster and Katrina listened very attentively to the young officer, and they could not help but admire the dignity that he possessed, as he was uniformed in the style becoming his rank. Depeyster politely invited him to remain for the night. The subaltern, after thanking him for his kindness, was ushered into a large parlor, Katrina leading the way. Depeyster informed him at once that he must secure his side arms and search his person, which the subaltern readily consented to, for Depeyster suspected some plot was being concocted by the enemy, and it was necessary for him to be very cautious as to who he received into his house.

The subaltern surrendered his side arms to Depeyster, and after a thorough search he discovered nothing that led him to believe but that he had given a true account of himself. Depeyster informed him that Gen. Washington, with a large army, was encamped at the village of Fishkill, a few miles east, and was awaiting the movements of the British fleet; and expecting that it would land somewhere near the Highlands, he had posted his army at Fishkill Village, in order to give them battle, and at the same time telling the subaltern that he must be taken to Fishkill on the following morning, and handed over to General Washington, and if he had given a true account of himself, he might be dismissed on parole or be remanded to prison until an exchange of prisoners, and he apprehended no danger of losing his life. The subaltern said nothing, but drew his chair close to the fire to warm himself, for he had been exposed to the cold. When he reflected on his situation, he covered his face with his hands, and commenced weeping. He was only twenty-three years of age, and was related to some of the first families in England, and occupying a position in the British army, his appearance commanded respect. As he sat there thinking of his dear mother and sisters at home, that they might never see him again, his whole form convulsed with agony. He could exclaim with Jonah of old, "Oh Lord, take, I beseech thee, my life from me, for it is better for me to die than to live." His appearance touched the heart of Katrina, and every cord there seemed to vibrate as she looked at the sorrow stricken officer, his hair falling in disheveled locks over his face, sparkling like gold from the light of the blazing wood fire, that shone so bright where he sat. It awakened emotions in her bosom which can better be imagined than described. Depeyster had sent Pompey to summon two of the nearest neighbors to his house immediately, as he had some business of importance with them, while Katrina and Dinah set about getting supper. The subaltern at length became more calm and collected, and partially recovering from his melancholy condition, he for the first time surveyed the room. He was struck with the splendor that he saw around him, for the house was most gorgeously furnished for those times. Splendid mirrors and paintings were suspended upon the walls, carpets of burning crimson, a massive mahogany side board in the corner of the parlor, loaded with plate and inlaid with rose wood, and tables of the same material. The windows, covered with costly hangings, greeted his eye, whilst Katrina and Dinah were busily engaged in preparing for supper. Soon everything was ready, and Depeyster politely invited the subaltern to partake with them. Soon they were all seated around the table, Katrina presiding, and ordering Dinah to attend to the wants of the subaltern, who was well cared for also by Depeyster, who bountifully supplied him with everything the table afforded.

Katrina then was only about nineteen years of age, and her person was peculiarly attractive; her countenance was always radiant with smiles, and down a finely curved neck fell her dark auburn ringlets in graceful disorder. Her well developed forehead, almost concealed by the rich tresses, portrayed a mind well stored with knowledge. She knew nothing of the false coquetry of the city belles, who pay their devotion to the shrine of fashion, and sport with the most sacred feelings of the human heart. She was open, frank, candid; her lips knew no guile, her heart whispered no deceit, she was the lovely Katrina. Her filial affection was unbounded, and when the British fleet sailed up the river and was expected to land at Fishkill Landing, and a battle was expected to be fought in the vicinity, and her mother, sisters, and brother fled, she could not think of leaving her father alone and unprotected; she would share with him all the privations and dangers that might occur.

After supper, the subaltern, wishing to retire for the night, for he was much fatigued and downcast on account of the misfortunes which had befallen him, Depeyster conducted him to a bedroom in the upper story, close to the roof, where he thought it was the safest place to prevent him from making his escape, and shutting the door and turning the key in the lock, securely locking the door, he left the subaltern alone. In the meantime Pompey had returned, accompanied by two neighbors that Depeyster had sent for, and whom he informed of the whole transaction; the manner that the subaltern came to his house and the account that he gave of himself. How the British fleet had left him in the heart of an enemy's country, and the anguish of mind he was now suffering, fearing when tried he might be found guilty and be imprisoned, or perhaps lose his life. Depeyster thought it would be necessary for each to take his turn and watch till morning, for the subaltern might make an effort to escape. This was acceded to, and each man stood sentinel in turn while the night lasted. But the subaltern had no disposition to flee; he lay quiet till morning, but his mind was restless. If he could be released on parole, he would be willing to accept the proposition, for he had no disposition to fight against the Colonies any more. He loved his country, it was true, but the kind treatment he had received softened his heart towards a people which his country branded as rebels, and now he was willing, if he could get his discharge, not to fight against the Colonies any more. Katrina he could not dismiss from his mind, and for one so young he had seen no one in all his intercourse with the world so interesting, and the tender assiduities he had received from her poured into his afflicted breast the healing balm of forgiving consolation. But the night wore away, and the rays of the king of day gilded the tops of the Highlands, and throwing his forked arrows through the glens and valleys that lay around the Depeyster mansion, summoning the subaltern to arise, that another day had dawned and ere its close a more terrible fate than he yet had experienced might be his. He had been up, and was walking to and fro across his room, when the noise of footsteps arrested his attention, and his bedroom door was unlocked and opened by Depeyster, who informed him that breakfast was waiting him, and at the same time the subaltern followed him to the breakfast room, where Katrina and Dinah had everything prepared. Soon they were all seated at the table, and before they had finished, the two neighbors who had remained with Depeyster through the night, drove in front of his mansion with a conveyance, which had been pre-

viously arranged to take him to Fishkill. Having
finished breakfast, Depeyster informed the subaltern
that it would be necessary for them to take him to
headquarters, and there he would be examined before
a military tribunal, and if nothing appeared against
him, he felt assured that he would be discharged on
parole. There was then but two roads that led to
Fishkill Village from the river. One went about north
as it passed the Depeyster mansion, and when the conveyance left there with the subaltern carefully guarded
by Depeyster and his two neighbors, Katrina from the
porch gazed at him until they disappeared from view.
She hoped that he would at least be set at liberty, for
she believed that he had given a true account of himself, and she felt an intense interest in his welfare, and
her father had promised to exert all his influence in
his behalf. Depeyster, with his prisoner, jogged along
towards Fishkill.

The country then wore a different aspect from the
present day. No smiling villages greeted the eye:
only now and then a solitary farm house was seen, and
large tracts of primeval forest skirted the valleys and
covered the mountain sides, in some places extending
up to the highway and looming up in all their grandeur where now is a busy thoroughfare, where the snort
of the iron horse is heard almost every hour, with villages, country seats, and opulent farm houses interspersed. But their journey was soon terminated, and
Depeyster, with his prisoner, was soon at the headquarters of Washington, and an interview was had
with him. After hearing all the circumstances from
Depeyster respecting him; how he came to his house

and surrendered himself, and now was safely handed over to his charge to be disposed of, Washington ordered the subaltern to be remanded to prison until he could summon a court martial to try him, which would take place in a few days.

The Reformed Dutch Church was then used as a prison, and it was a different structure from the present one. The building was four square, with a roof coming up from all sides to the center. From the apex of the roof ascended the cupola where the bell was suspended, and the Dutch coat of arms surmounted the top. The window lights were very small, set in iron sash frames, with port holes above for a place of defense against Indian incursions, which the early settlers were exposed to when the country was first settled. In front of the church was a large oak tree, whose giant arms extended over the street. One large limb came in close proximity to a window in the upper story. Among the prisoners confined in this church with the subaltern, was the celebrated spy, Enoch Crosby, who figured in Cooper's writings as Harvey Burch, who one dark stormy night crawled through one of the port holes and ventured to leap to a limb of this tree, which he succeeded in catching, and then softly letting himself down till he reached terra firma, when he was but a few feet from the sentinel, but the howling of the tempest drowned the noise that was occasioned by his descent, and he made his escape. Four years after the revolution this edifice was demolished, and the present church erected, which, for the want of funds, was not completed until 1794.

In the time of the revolution, there were two families whose names were Bailey living in Fishkill Village, one a great grandfather of the writer, who was born in the town of Westchester, Westchester county, N. Y., who purchased a farm in Fishkill containing 214 acres of land. The farm is now owned by Charles C. Rogers and William M. Baxter. The old homestead house was where Baxter now resides, and was replaced by the present edifice a few years ago. The other Bailey left the city of New York when the British took possession of it, and sought a temporary shelter in Fishkill in a small building near the highway close to where Mr. Rogers now resides. This Bailey was a cutler by trade, who made or repaired the sword of Gen. Washington while he resided there, and stamped his name upon it, "J. Bailey, Fishkill." Historians who have written upon the subject, have said that the Bailey with which family I am connected, made the sword, not knowing that there was another Bailey, whose name was John, living in Fishkill Village during the revolution. This cutler left Fishkill after the war, and returned to his home in New York.

The subaltern's trial took place in what was known of late years as the Union Hotel. The same building and room in which he was tried remained the same until the great fire in December, 1873, when the building was totally destroyed. In time of war trials of prisoners soon terminate, and the subaltern's case was quickly disposed of. As nothing further was proved than as above stated by Depeyster, the prisoner was released on parole. The subaltern, after thanking Washington for the kindness shown him, returned with Depeyster, who invited him to remain with him until he should get his final discharge, which invitation the subaltern gladly accepted. When Katrina saw him returning with her father, and learned from him that he was discharged on parole, she was much pleased, for her anxiety for his release was very great, and it afforded her unspeakable consolation to see him once more, not a prisoner, but a guest in her father's house. Depeyster's son, who fled with his mother and sisters when the British fleet sailed up the river, had not returned, and Depeyster needed his son's assistance very much, particularly in his mill, for he had the supervision of his books, and the accounts of all transactions in buying and selling was mainly done through him. The subaltern, learning this fact, volunteered to assist him. Depeyster soon found that his services were indispensable in the absence of his son, for he rendered him every assistance in keeping his accounts accurate, and being competent, he soon won the admiration of Depeyster and all who had intercourse with him. The subaltern began to feel more contented at his new home, and after business hours had passed, and seeing that the mill was safely locked, he always spent his leisure hours with Depeyster and Katrina, who tried to make everything pleasant for him, and long after Depeyster had retired for the night, Katrina and the subaltern would occupy the parlor alone, and their attachment for each other grew more ardent, and their love intense, as evening after evening glided away.

The winter of 1780 was the coldest that had ever occurred in this country. The cold weather set in early, accompanied with snow storms of such depth that the fences were buried under the snow, and the highways were literally blocked and impassable. For forty-two days it did not thaw on the sunniest side of a building, and the river froze to such an extent that loaded teams crossed the river at New York city to the opposite side, and the bay that extends to Staten Island, a distance of nine miles, was covered with ice strong enough to enable the British to transport their cannon across it in safety. The suffering through Fishkill was terrible, on account of the great depth of snow, rendering it almost impossible for the inhabitants to get to the mill. What little traveling there was through the country, was by roads on top of the snow, over fences, taking the nearest route to any given point. This road had to be beaten hard before it could be much used, and if the traveler deviated the least from the track, his sleigh and horses would instantly sink to such depth in the snow that he would have great difficulty in getting them again on the track. The difficulty in passing and repassing could only be overcome by detaching the horses from the sleigh and leading them singly by, then hitching them again to the sleigh with ropes, drawing the sleighs past each other on the beaten track. The snow hardened by the severe cold, formed a crust on the earth sufficient, with the aid of snow shoes, to bear the weight of the heaviest man. This gave the inhabitants the advantage to shorten the distance by taking the nearest route to Depeyster's mill. The frost was so intense that it was almost impossible for Depeyster to stop the ice from clogging the wheels of his mill, and enable him to grind for the suffering inhabitants, who came from far and near, crossing the river from Orange county with their hand sleds loaded with bags of grain. The subaltern and Pompey were constantly at work with their axes, cutting the ice that would form through the night, in order to start the mill as soon as possible the following morning, and often they would be assisted by many whose families were almost starving, so as to enable them to return home with their grist to satisfy the cravings of hunger.

But the long dreary winter gradually passed away, and the genial spring returned once more, dissolving the snow, and breaking the icy barriers which had so long held sway, and driving old Boreas to his icy den, covering the earth once more with verdure and beauty. Depeyster's family had returned, and the political horizon wore a more cheering aspect. The war cloud which had been so long hanging over Fishkill, had disappeared. Washington had removed his army to the South, where the war was now raging, and it inspired hope in Depeyster that the struggle which his country was passing through would finally terminate in her independence. The subaltern had received his final discharge from Washington, but he remained at Depeyster's. For two years he had resided there, and had shared with him all the dangers and trials when his family was away; had assisted him in his business transactions in the absence of his son; and now Depeyster felt under obligations for services rendered by him, yet he had not surmised that an attachment had been formed between his daughter and the subaltern, which would terminate in his asking for her in marriage. Depeyster's love for Katrina was most ardent; she had remained with him in time of peril; she had shared with him all the dangers and hardships which they had been exposed to; and with him was willing at any time to lay down her life on the altar of their country.

It was a beautiful summer's evening, and the roses and the violets were in bloom; the geraniums never looked more beautiful around the Depeyster mansion. The ivy and honey-suckles were climbing the porch, the terraces, and the ornamental trees. The silvery moonbeams stole softly through the narrow openings of the trees, and in the windows of the parlor where sat Katrina and the subaltern. The old family clock had long told the hour of twelve, when the subaltern had something to say to Katrina, and yet he delayed. The large candles on the centre-table had burnt down to the sockets in their sticks, and the light streaks of day were breaking up the dark clouds in the east. Pompey and Dinah were already up, preparing for breakfast, when the subaltern offered his heart and hand to Katrina, which was at once accepted. The subaltern, overburdened with joy, hastened to his bedroom, and threw himself on his couch, hardly realizing his situation. Ecstatic joy pervaded his soul, and with no inclination to sleep, it seemed to him that his life for the future would be one of continual sunshine. He had yet to get the consent of Katrina's parents. This he thought would be no easy task, for they were staunch whigs, and ardently attached to their country, while he was a British officer, intending soon to return to his native land. Would they be willing, thought he, for their daughter to leave her native land, her parents, sisters and brothers, and part with them, perhaps never to see them again in this world? Such thoughts occupied his mind when alone, and filled his soul with intense agony, and a dark cloud overshadowed him.

Sitting one evening in the parlor with Katrina and her parents, the subaltern, summoning courage sufficient, took the opportunity to ask them for their daughter in marriage. In doing this he betrayed considerable emotion, and Katrina perceiving it, was herself tearfully agitated, and when he put the question to her parents her whole frame shook with tremor. Her parents gave their consent readily, and Depeyster turned to the subaltern and said:

"If my daughter makes you half as good a wife as she has been to me a dutiful and loving daughter, she will be worth to you more than all the diamond mines of Peru. Perfect happiness is not to be found in this world; it remains inaccessible to humanity. Calm and temperate enjoyment is all that is allotted to men while sojourning here below." If any one in the world came near reaching that summit of joy, it was the subaltern, and when he took a retrospective view of his life for the past two years; how he had been left in an enemy's country, friendless and unprotected, expecting nothing but imprisonment and death, the tears he shed when thinking of his mother and sisters, his happy deliverance afterward, and the kind treatment that he received from Depeyster, and now a union with his daughter, which could only be separated by death, overwhelmed his soul with gratitude unutterable.

The dawn of the day of our country's deliverance had now arrived. Cornwallis had surrendered, and peace, blessed peace, once more smiled on our beloved country, which for seven long years had been drenched with blood and bedewed with the tears of widows and orphans. The joy throughout Fishkill at this event was unbounded, for now the inhabitants could beat their swords into ploughshares and their spears into pruning hooks, and cultivate their wasted farms, which had been so long neglected and impoverished during the war. But ere the joy had subsided, the marriage of Katrina and the subaltern took place in the Depeyster mansion, in the presence of the family, a few friends and the negro slaves. After peace, Katrina bid adieu to her parents, sisters and brother, and with her husband left for his native land, and here I will leave them, for what I have seen of the mutability of human affairs, of life's deceitful hopes and its fleeting and chimerical joys, I should fear, were I to follow them through life, and add to this narrative, I might be obliged to inscribe a misfortune there. But the Depeyster family, which then was so influential and wealthy, long since became extinct in the town of Fishkill.

VAN HORN.

A TALE OF HENRY HUDSON'S RIVER AND THE FISHKILL INDIANS.

The Hudson river was discovered by Henry Hudson, from whence it derives its name.. He was an Englishman by birth, and was employed by a London Company to make discoveries. A ship was fitted out by this company, and given in command of Hudson, to discover a northwest passage to the East Indies. This voyage, and another for the same purpose, proved unsuccessful, and the company suspended their patronage. Hudson then went to Holland and entered into the service of the celebrated Dutch East India Company. This company fitted out a small ship called the *Half Moon*, under the command of Hudson, with a crew of some twenty men. Hudson left Amsterdam on the 4th, and the Texel on the 6th of April, and arrived on the American coast on the 18th day of July, 1609, near Portland, in the State of Maine.

After this he sailed southward along the coast, making remarks on the soundings and currents, until he came to the entrance of Chesapeake Bay, about the 24th of August. From this point he returned northward along the coast, discovering Delaware Bay, and on the 3d of September, 1609, he anchored within

Sandy Hook. Here he spent ten days trafficing with the natives. The tradition is that his men first landed on Coney Island, which lies near Long Island, and now makes a part of Kings county. On the 11th of September he sailed through the Narrows, and on the 12th he entered the river which bears his name, and sailed up about two leagues. There the Indians visited the ship in great numbers, bringing with them corn, beans, tobacco and oysters in abundance, and exchanging them for such trifles as the ship's company were disposed to barter. Although they were civil, Hudson did not think proper to trust them, for he had lost one of his men before entering the Narrows by an arrow discharged by an Indian, which struck him in the throat, and by no means would he suffer any of them to remain on board during the night. From the 12th to the 22d of September, Hudson was employed in ascending the river, and when he arrived where the city of Hudson is now located, he considered it unsafe to proceed further. He sent a boat, however, with five hands, the mate, who had command of the expedition, being one, to explore the river higher up. They proceeded to where the city of Albany now stands, and returned, reporting to Hudson that the river in some places was not more than seven feet deep and the soundings very irregular, and deemed it unadvisable to attempt any farther progress. Hudson remained here several days, and his men frequently went on shore. The natives appeared very hospitable. An old Sachem took the mate to his wigwam, and entertained him with good cheer, and the savages flocked on board the ship in considerable numbers, bringing with them corn, tobacco, pumpkins and grapes, and some beaver and other skins, which they exchanged for hatchets, knives, beads and other trifles. Hudson and his men, for the purpose of making an experiment on the temper of the Indians, attempted to make a number of them drunk. They only succeeded in making one completely intoxicated. This phenomenon excited great surprise and alarm among them, for they knew not what to make of it, many supposing that he would die, but when he became sober, he expressed himself to his companions that he never felt better. This is the first instance recorded of intoxication by ardent spirits among the Indians on the American continent.

On the 23d of September, Hudson began to descend the river. On his way down his men went frequently on shore, and had several very friendly intercourses with the natives, who expressed a desire that they might remain among them. The ship anchored in the river off where the village of Fishkill Landing is now located, and a number of the crew went on shore there, and the previous kind treatment they had received from the natives, induced them to be very intimate with them. They visited them in their wigwams, and several of the crew ventured some distance in the country, following the Fishkill creek up to where Glenham now stands, plucking the wild flowers that grew on its banks and gathering grapes that hung in clusters on vines that had entwined themselves around the giant arms of the aged forest trees. While thus amusing themselves, they were suddenly surprised by a shower of arrows shot by a party of Indians who were ambushed. Unfortunately they had left their muskets aboard of the ship, and having nothing to defend themselves with but what materials they could hastily collect, such as stones and clubs, and being overpowered with numbers, they fled with all haste to the ship, the Indians closely pursuing them. One of their companions, whose name was Van Horn, received a wound in his knee from an arrow, which disabled him, and he was captured. The remainder made their escape to the ship. Hudson, on receiving this intelligence from his men, ordered a number of his bravest men, well armed, to proceed immediately ashore and take Van Horn at all hazards. The men were quickly rowed ashore, and then cautiously penetrated the country, which was covered with forests so dark and dense that they could not discover an object any great distance ahead. Suddenly a tremendous war whoop was sounded, and then the Indians sprung from their hiding places, and with tomahawks in hand rushed on their assailants. Hudson's men gave them a warm reception, and leveling their muskets they brought several of the foremost of them to the earth, which checked their advance. The Indians seeing the fate of their comrades, and the noise of fire arms so terrifying them, they fled precipitately into the woods, Hudson's men pursuing them, but being unacquainted with the country, they were obliged to give up the pursuit. Van Horn had probably been carried off to meet an ignominious death from the hands of savages, who seldom show mercy to a captive. The crew returned to the ship and reported to Hudson their unsuccessful attempt to rescue Van Horn. When Hudson received this sad intelligence, he immediately set sail. This was the second man he had lost by the Indians, and when the ship came between the Highlands, the natives again attacked them, repeatedly shooting at the crew with bows and arrows from several near points of land. Hudson's men discharged their muskets at them, and killed ten or twelve of them. In these conflicts, which were frequently renewed, none of the ship's crew appear to have been injured. On the 4th of October, just one month from the day on which Hudson landed within Sandy Hook, he came out of the river which bears his name, and without anchoring in the bay, immediately stood out to sea. By noon that day he was entirely clear of land, and steered directly for Europe.

Van Horn, who was taken prisoner by the Indians, was carried to the Indian village, which was located in Fishkill Hook, on the farm now owned by Charles Emans, and when the Indians arrived with their prisoner, curiosity became very much excited. The squaws, with their pappooses, flocked around Van Horn, all eager to get a sight of so strange a personage—admiring his light complexion, soft flaxen hair, and to them, delicate features. The Sachem took charge of his prisoner, and conducted him to his wigwam, and had his wounded knee dressed. He endeavored to make his situation as comfortable as it was in his power to do, for he valued his prisoner very highly. A bed of the finest robes was made for Van Horn to lie on, and some warm corn bread and bear's meat was placed before him. But he had no disposition to eat, for all hope had fled of his being rescued by his countrymen, and his heart sank within him. To think of his spending the remainder of his life among savages, perhaps never to see his countrymen, and never to visit his native land again, made his agony of mind indescribable. The thought of home, parents, sisters and brothers, came up vividly before him. How they would weep when the ship would reach his country, and the mournful intelligence would be conveyed to them that he was wounded and taken prisoner by hostile savages, who were represented as being cannibals, and that he was probably put to death by the most excruciating tortures. Such thoughts occupied his mind as he lay in the wigwam of the Sachem.

This tribe of Indians had made some progress in civilization. They had a little clearing on the farm now owned by Van Wyck and Johnson, where they cultivated corn, called Indian corn because it was unknown to the Europeans until discovered here. They had an apple orchard, which was located on the farm now owned by John Waldo, traces of which are still visible. Pumpkins and grapes were also found in the country. The government of the Indians was absolute. The Sachem is the great arbiter of law. His power, however, is rather persuasive than coercive; he is reverenced as a father rather than feared as a monarch. He has no guards, no prisons, no officers of justice, and one act of ill-judged violence would pull him from his humble throne. It will be recollected that Van Horn was captured about the 20th of September. The Indian apple orchard then was in full bearing, and was loaded with ripe fruit, and the Sachem dealt out the fruit to his tribe as he thought proper. None of his tribe would venture in the orchard without his permission, and the finest fruit he selected for Van Horn. Baked apples were placed before him in the wigwam, in the presence of the Sachem and his family, and every kindness was shown him. No pains were spared to make his situation pleasant and comfortable. The kind treatment that he received, revived his drooping spirits; his wounded knee was improving, and in a few weeks he was able to walk, and he ventured out of the wigwam for the first time to survey the country.

It was then the pleasant month of October, and the valley of Fishkill Hook presented to him a novel scene. In the rear of the Indian village was their apple orchard, in front was their cornfield, and the squaws were busily engaged in gathering the crops. Beyond lay interminable forests. The aged men and women were sitting near their wigwams, and the young men were all out on a hunt; the pappooses were playing in groups near the village, and the Sachem was superintending the doings of his people. He had erected a fort for a place of safety when attacked by tribes who were at war with him, and when obliged to retreat they would flee to this fort, and barricade themselves in, and keep the enemy at bay. This fort was located on a hill near the residence of H. D. Sherwood, and is known as Fort Hill to this day. In a few months Van Horn had entirely recovered the use of his limb, and the Sachem gave him permission to go a hunting with his tribe and fish in the Wiccapee, a small creek that runs through the valley of Fishkill Hook and discharges its waters in the large creek near Johnsville. During the long and severe winters the tribe would fish in the large creek with nets made of thread twisted from the bark of Indian hemp, by cutting holes through the ice with stone axes or hatchets. In this manner they would catch large quantities of fish. Van Horn was not allowed to go alone any distance from the Indian village, the Sachem being fearful he might attempt to make his escape, but this was almost impossible. Hudson was the first European that had sailed up the river, and probably there would not be another expedition sent to make discoveries for some years. Hudson had been given the command of the *Half Moon* by the Dutch East India Company to discover a northwest passage to the East Indies, and as he was unsuccessful in discovering such passage, they probably would not soon attempt a second voyage. Under circumstances like these, Van Horn's chance for returning to his native land was almost hopeless, yet he did not despair. He could not entertain the idea for one moment of spending the remainder of his life among savages whose living was precarious, oftentimes suffering from hunger and cold; their little stock of provisions some times consumed before Spring, and then a scanty subsistence could only be procured by hunting and fishing.

Van Horn had been accustomed to all the comforts and luxuries of civilized life, but he fared with the Sachem and his family, which was poor enough. If any of the hunters succeeded in killing a bear, the Sachem selected the choicest part of the beast for himself, the remainder he divided among his tribe ; and if a buffalo was killed, which was seldom, as the animal was scarce in this part of the country, he always rewarded his hunters, and there was great rejoicing whenever such an event occurred, and a great feast was provided on the occasion. That the buffalo existed in Fishkill when Hudson discovered the river, there is not the least shadow of doubt, although Hudson did not see any. He penetrated but a little way into the country, and tarried but a few days in one place, and spent only one month in exploring the country adjacent, when he returned to Europe, and nearly a century elapsed after Hudson discovered the river, before any permanent settlement was made in Fishkill, although it was the first town settled in the county. Our early historians have mentioned animals that existed in this county when first discovered, that have long been extinct. They have mentioned that lions abounded on the high mountains along the Hudson, and there was seen sometimes a kind of a beast which had some resemblance to a horse, having cloven feet, shaggy mane, one horn just on the forehead, a tail like that of a wild hog, and a deer's neck. From the description given of this strange beast, it resembled exceedingly the unicorn. An animal bearing this description has been recently seen in the mountains in Colorado.

Van Horn was kindly treated by the Sachem, but he was very careful not to let him have too much liberty, for he was the first prisoner he had taken who was of a race that he had never seen before. He had learnt all the facts of Hudson and his crew when they ascended the river; the description they gave of the great ship, which his tribe looked at with wonder and amazement; and he regarded Van Horn as a great personage, and he expected when he had imbibed their manners and customs he would marry his daughter Manteo, who was then in the bloom and beauty of youth, only twenty years of age, whom the Indians regarded with great esteem. Her head was adorned with beautiful feathers, and a mantle of deer skin, embroidered with white shells, hung gracefully over her shoulders; her waist was encircled with a crimson scarf, and moccasins of soft furs encased her feet. Her appearance was expressive to Van Horn, and he had learned the Indian language sufficient to understand the design of the Sachem, and his mind revolted at the idea of marrying a savage; but he soon perceived that it would not be advisable for him not to appear to reciprocate the affection of Manteo, trusting in Providence for a way of escape before he would be obliged to yield to the wishes of the Sachem. Van Horn had already learned the character of the Sachem, and if he showed any dislike for his daughter his life might pay the forfeit. He showed her every respect, and often they went to the Wiccapee alone to enjoy a pleasant sail in her little canoe, made of light birchen bark, which her father had given her, and how delighted she was to glide it swiftly, with the splash of her oar, over the smooth and limpid waters which Van Horn feigned to admire. At times they would practice with the bow and arrow, and Manteo was proud in showing her skill to White Feather, which name the Indians gave him, in shooting the arrow at a mark. Manteo became ardently attached to Van Horn, and his presence was to her sweeter than nectar, and for hours they would remain in the forests alone, sitting under some broad armed tree, and drink in, as the flowers drink the dew, those tender accents so musically low; to catch his burning glances, showing that his affections were entwining themselves around the secret recesses of her soul, which to her was now the glorious dream of her being. How hard it is to unwind the tendrils of love gathered around the heart, to cast off that passion that we have nursed when its roots are interwoven with the fibers of our life. Such love did Manteo cherish for Van Horn, and such love he could not help but admire. As Van Horn showed much respect and affection for Manteo, the Sachem gradually extended his privileges. If he went out a hunting with his tribe, and strayed off alone in the forests, he returned, and often Van Horn did this to try the temper of the Sachem. At length he remained out all night in the woods without creating suspicion. He yearned for his native land, and when alone in the forests, would give himself up to serious reflection, thinking that soon he would be obliged to marry the Sachem's daughter, and then all hopes of his seeing his country again would be forever obliterated, and he would have to be contented to live the remainder of his life with the Indians. Under circumstances like these, Van Horn's situation was peculiarly afflicting, but he was learning more and more every day the geography of the country, and he had learned the way to the river, and found the spot where he had landed with his countrymen and was taken prisoner by the Indians.

One day Van Horn went with the Indians to hunt in the swamps which lay along the large creek near where Johnsville is now located. He took a different route and reached the river where Hudson's ship first anchored. He then sat on the river's bank, thinking of his misfortunes. He burst into tears. A year had now elapsed since he was captured, and no tidings had he received from his country, and no hope of his ever leaving this savage wilderness. His friends perhaps had abandoned all hope of ever seeing him again. His heart was torn with anguish. How it gladdened his heart when Hudson enlisted him to go on a voyage to discover a north-west passage to the East Indies. What bright visions were then before him, and how his parents wept at his departure; but the anticipation of seeing countries heretofore undiscovered and unknown to the civilized world, and the fame and glory that he would win if successful, would more than compensate him for all the toil and dangers to which they might be exposed. One of the crew had lost his life from an arrow shot by an Indian, before Hudson entered the river, and Van Horn wished that might have been his fate, choosing rather to die than to eke out a miserable existence here with the savages. With such painful reflections he retraced his steps towards the Indian village, where he arrived about sunset, after being absent nearly two days. The Sachem had become very uneasy about him, for he was fearful that something might have happened to him, and Manteo, too, ran to meet him, and expressed her great joy at seeing him, and accompanied him to her father's wigwam, and there provided the finest robes for him to rest on, and then she made some warm bread and broiled some venison for his supper. Van Horn ate heartily, for he had not tasted any food since he left the village, except some grapes which grew wild in the woods, he having made but little effort to shoot any game, for he had no inclination to hunt. His mind had been occupied in devising some way which, through Providence, might carry him back to his native land, and to that river where he was taken prisoner, he looked for a ship that might be sent out to make discoveries and trade with the natives, and if he should be so lucky as to see her when ascending or descending the river, an opportunity would be afforded him to escape. The Sachem was pleased to see Van Horn or White Feather so attentive to his daughter, and he looked forward with great pleasure to the day when the marriage should take place, and Van Horn read in him the desire that he cherished in having him become his son-in-law. He always manifested a great deal of affection for Manteo, especially in his presence.

The following winter was dreary enough; the snow fell early and deep, and the weather was often severely cold. Game had become scarce, and the Sachem's best hunters were constantly out in search of game or something to satisfy the cravings of hunger; and they often returned without anything. What little stock of corn they had, the Sachem dealt out sparingly to his tribe. Those that were not so well skilled in hunting, employed their time in fishing on the Wiccapee or the large creek, and the quantity of fish they caught helped to drive away famine. When the winter broke up, wild geese, ducks and pigeons appeared in great numbers, and the swamps that lie along the Fishkill creek appeared alive with them, and the hunters returned home loaded with fowl. Van Horn and Manteo, with their bows and arrows, would go out in quest of squirrels and pigeons, which then were plenty in the adjacent woods, which they shot in large numbers, and Manteo was delighted in spending so many happy hours with White Feather, hunting in the forests and sailing in her canoe on the Wiccapee. She anticipated that the day was not far distant when she would be united to him whom she looked upon as one far excelling her own people, and the love she cherished for him penetrated her inmost soul. As the Spring advanced, the song birds appeared, and the forest trees were bedecking themselves in their brilliant garments. The wild flowers were expanding their leaves, the apple trees in the Indian orchard were unfolding their buds, and some of them were tossing their snowy banners to the breeze. The valley of Fishkill Hook never appeared more beautiful in its primitive state. On a pleasant morning, Van Horn, the Sachem, and his daughter, were enjoying themselves sailing in their canoe on the Wiccapee. The warm zephyrs of Spring were gently wafting its waters; all was still in the surrounding forests except the singing of birds and the barking of squirrels, when the Sachem appointed the time when White Feather should marry his daughter. He intended to make a grand feast on that occasion, but as the marriage would not take place in several months, he would delay preparations for the present. The Sachem now placed the utmost confidence in Van Horn, and he allowed him unlimited freedom to rove whereever he liked, and sometimes he would be absent from home several days, lying out nights in the woods when the weather was pleasant, subsisting on wild fruit, which abounded. One day, when near the river, he heard the report of a musket. It was the first noise of fire arms he had heard since he was taken by the Indians. He hastened to the spot from whence the noise proceeded, and there beheld one of his countrymen, who was greatly surprised on seeing him. Van Horn was completely overcome with joy, and related his whole history from the day when he enlisted under Henry Hudson to the time he was captured by the Indians, and his subsequent life. He informed the stranger that the Sachem lived several leagues in the country, and that if he did not make his escape soon, he would be obliged to marry his daughter. The stranger informed Van Horn that he belonged to a ship that sailed from Amsterdam, and had arrived on the American coast several weeks before, and that they had been trading with the natives, and the ship lay out in the river nearly opposite. Van Horn thought that no time should be lost, for if any of the Indians should see him attempting to escape, he probably would lose his life, so they hastened with all speed to the river, and entered the small boat and rowed with all speed to the ship. The captain and crew were all his own countrymen, who had been sent from Amsterdam to trade with the natives and explore the country. The Captain received Van Horn kindly, who related his adventures in a country heretofore unknown to the civilized world, and how long he had remained there, and his living with savages, which was listened to with thrilling interest. When the Sachem received the intelligence that another ship had ascended the river, and Van Horn had got on board of her and made his escape, he was mortified and chagrined, and he regretted he had not made a slave of him, as it was customary with the Indians to make slaves of their prisoners or put them to death.

When Manteo was informed of White Feather's escape, and that he had betrayed her, a wild cry of agony came up from the very depths of her soul, and she was so overwhelmed with grief that she remained for months in her father's wigwam, excluding herself from the world and continually weeping. The intense mental agony that she endured, told fearfully on her constitution, and the tender assiduities of her father and friends to make her happy once more, all proved unavailing. Death came at last to her relief, and terminated her existence, and ended her sufferings. Her remains were interred in the burying ground of the Sachems, which was then on the farm now owned by Charles Burroughs.

Soon after, other vessels were sent out by the Dutch East India Company to trade with the natives, and trading posts were established at Fort Orange, now Albany, and on the island of Manhattan, now New York, and the Dutch commenced permanent settlements in those places which they purchased of the Indians. The Dutch settlements commenced extending up the Hudson, and a trade was carried on with the Indians in Fishkill, and large tracts of land were purchased of them in Westchester county, and finally, in 1683, the Indians in Fishkill sold their tract, comprising the original town and a portion of the town of Poughkeepsie, to Francis Rombout and others. Rombout was a distinguished merchant in the city of New

York. His only daughter, Kathrina, inherited her father's right in the Patent, and with her husband, Roger Brett, came and located on the Patent, and built the house now known as the old Teller Mansion, at Matteawan, in 1710.

Van Horn arrived at Amsterdam after being absent from his native country two years. The joy of his parents on seeing their son once more, was indescribable, for they supposed, from the intelligence they had received from Hudson, he was cruelly put to death by the savages. Van Horn then related to his parents his two years adventures, the manners and customs of the Indians, and his happy deliverance, for which he felt grateful to a kind Providence, in conducting him safely back to his parents and friends.

But Hudson was reserved for a more terrible fate. He soon discovered the great Northern bay which bears his name. There, after an unwise delay, he was compelled to pass a distressing and dangerous winter. In the spring, in addition to all of his other misfortunes, he found a spirit of dissatisfaction and mutiny growing among his crew, and at length manifesting itself in open violence. They proceeded so far that on the 22d of June, 1611, a majority of the crew arose, took command of the ship, put Hudson, his son, and seven others, most of whom were sick or lame, into a boat, turned them adrift on the ocean, and abandoned them to their fate. This was the last that was ever heard of Henry Hudson.

THE SQUATTER'S DAUGHTER.

A TALE OF THE EARLY SETTLERS OF PUTNAM COUNTY.

Putnam County was formed from Dutchess County, June 12th, 1812. This county was originally the great Highland Patent granted June 17th, 1697, to Adolph Philipse, a merchant of New York city, who died in 1743, without issue, leaving his estate to his nephew, Frederick Philipse. The latter had five children, Frederick, Philip, Susannah, Mary and Margaret. This patent was divided into nine lots, three each four miles square, bordering on the Hudson, and denominated water lots; three each four miles wide by twelve long, extending north and south of the patent, and denominated long lots—and three each four miles square upon the east border, and denominated back lots. This patent was considered the most unproductive of any purchased on the Hudson, and large portions of it were then considered of little value, embracing all the rough, rocky and mountainous portions of Putnam county. In those mountainous districts the squatters would locate, and the first patentee, Adolph Philipse, who then resided in New York, and was engaged in the mercantile business, did not molest them, and during his life he received but little from the sparse population that was located there.

After the patent was divided, as above stated, Philip Philipse became heir by will to one-third of the patent, and during his life his estate enhanced in value, and he had agents to collect the rents of his large landed estate. He, like his predecessor, allowed those tenants denominated squatters, who inhabited the mountainous portion of the patent, to remain there rent free, thinking they would have to struggle hard enough to gain a livelihood without exacting any dues from them.

A squatter, whose name was Nazareth Austin, located on the south part of the patent, now known as Canopus Hollow, one of the roughest parts of it. Amongst his neighbors he usually went by the name of Ned. The patent was originally covered with forests, and Ned was there some years before the patentee discovered where he had squatted. Ned then had made some progress in clearing a little spot to plant some corn and potatoes between the rocks and stones, which literally covered the earth. He had erected a log hut, raised a yoke of steers, two cows, and a dozen sheep, and was so situated as to keep soul and body together. Horton pond, which is now known as Canopus lake, was but a little way from Ned's hut, and there he would resort evenings, and sometimes on rainy days, to spear the pickerel and bass which abounded in the water. Ned's family consisted only of his wife and daughter, and Pompey, the dog; they were the only inmates of his cabin. The few neighbors that lived near him, like all settlers, were fond of the chase and spent much time in hunting. Ned having no sons, his daughter Jane would sometimes accompany them through the forests in quest of game and wild animals, which then inhabited those mountains. The wolves, sometimes, during the long severe winters, when driven by hunger, would come out of the mountains and make great havoc amongst the squatter's sheep and cattle, which was attended with a loss more or less severe to them. The squatters, too, were very eager to destroy the wolves more than any of the beasts of the forests, for the county had offered for every wolf's head five shillings English currency.

During one very cold winter the wolves became more troublesome than usual in the neighborhood, and some one would lose a sheep or other stock almost every night, and the settlers at length came to the conclusion to try to rid themselves of the wolves which infested the neighborhood. If a light snow had fallen during the night it was easy to track them to their dens. Such an opportunity soon presented itself to the squatters. A light snow had fallen, and the wolves had again committed depredations, carrying off and destroying several sheep. The squatters lost no time in pursuing them, and Ned, with several of his neighbors, including even his daughter, were eager in the pursuit. They followed the track with the help of Pompey, the dog, and soon found where a wolf had entered his den. It was a precipitous ledge of overhanging rocks, with an apartment underneath sufficiently wide for the wolves to enter. At the mouth were discovered partial remains of the head and legs of sheep and calves. The company concluded that there must be a number in the cave, but how to force them from it was a difficult task. Ned had lost several sheep by the wild beasts. He made several flambeaux out of birchen bark and pitch, which he obtained from the pine trees which the forests abounded in, and cautiously ventured into the mouth of the cave. The ingress was wide enough for him to proceed with gun in hand, with Pompey close at his heels. The wolves, seeing the approach of Ned, retreated out of the cave from the opposite side of the ledge. But Jane, who had been watching the movements with a double-barrel rifle, brought two out of three of them to the ground. "Bravo," cried Ned; "daughter, we will have the bounty now," and he soon had their heads hanging in his cabin.

Ned, during the winter season, spent his time principally in hunting, and in the spring he would take his wolves' heads to Poughkeepsie, to obtain the bounty, and when he received the money he would divide with his wife and daughter, and this was the only money that his family received. It was carefully treasured up, for the farm supplied Ned's family with the means of subsistence. Although it was mostly covered with rocks and large forest trees, Ned, with the help of his wife and daughter, felled the lofty pine, the sturdy oak, and removed large stones and piled them into heaps, and reared walls around the little clearings they had made. At length Ned had a dozen or more acres enclosed where he could keep his sheep from straying out into the gloomy forest.

In this manner Ned's daughter grew up accustomed to labor, helping her father on his farm, and during her leisure hours she would take her rifle and Pompey and go to the forests in quest of game, and oftentimes the sharp crack of her rifle would stop the bounding moose and start the elk, which then were inhabitants of those mountains. At other times she would amuse herself in fishing in her little boat in the Canopus lake, taking the trout and the pickerel which abounded in the waters. Sometimes she would shoot the eider duck, for large flocks were often seen sporting on the surface of the lake. She could also manage the steers equal with her father. In this manner she grew up to womanhood, away almost from civilization. But Ned's wife was a woman of different tastes, and in her youth she had enjoyed polished society, and had received advantages of education, and although living there in the rude wilderness, where civilized man hardly entered, yet her appearance bespoke that she had seen better days. Her daughter Jane was her only hope, and it grieved her to think that she was shut up there in the wilderness secluded from the world, with no society but squatters to associate with, and no school but her father's cabin to educate her. During the winter season, when the weather was too cold to help her father cultivate his little plantation, or hunt in the forest, or fish in the lake, Jane would sit in their little cabin receiving the teachings of her mother, who had brought with her from Europe a neat library, which she had carefully preserved when she settled in this country with a colony of French Huguenots. Here in their log cabin she had taught her daughter the first rudiments of education, and all the useful branches of learning that she was capable of. Ned's pioneer life had formed habits of necessity in his family, like all the first settlers of a new country, and although his daughter had been accustomed to this mode of living, yet the instruction she received from her mother gave her a polish which otherwise she could not receive, for education then in this country was confined to the few.

As the country became settled, the lands on the patent enhanced in value, and Philipse had come to the conclusion to make every man who was located on the patent pay rent or leave. Accordingly an agent was sent to accompany his son, a young man of twenty-two years of age, to ferret out the squatters. The old Philipse homestead then was at Carmel, on the south side of the lake. The agent and young Philipse set out on horseback, for the country then was too rough for wheel carriages, and they occupied several weeks in finding the number of inhabitants on their vast domains.

At length they came through Canopus Hollow, the roughest portion of the patent. It was in the month of December and the wintry winds were sweeping through the valley of Canopus, and they were cold and fatigued with the journey. It was late in the day when an opening was seen in the forests, and a log cabin was presented to their view. They rode up to the door and knocked for admission, when Ned opened the door and asked what they wanted. The agent replied that he was the authorized agent of the great Highland Patent, and he was sent out to look up the number of settlers that were upon it. He said the patentees had come to the conclusion that every man that was located on the patent should pay rent or vacate the premises; at the same time pulling a paper from his pocket showing his authority as agent for that purpose. Ned invited them to come in and he would have a talk with him. The agent and young Philipse accepted the invitation, and they immediately dismounted. Ned had constructed a temporary shed of logs, and had covered it with a bark roof, and took their horses and led them under the buildings and gave them provender, and then they entered his cabin, Ned leading the way, and introducing them to his wife. The agent and young Philipse surveyed the interior of the cabin. The furniture was simple, consisting of one table, a few chairs, a looking-glass, one bureau and a bed in the furtherest corner of the cabin. On the bureau they noticed a number of books and an atlas hanging directly over the bureau. A pair of stairs led to the garret. A December storm was about setting in. A drizzling rain had already commenced, and Ned's wife remarked that it was time that Jane returned. She had only gone to the lake to fish a little while, and she expected her home ere this time. At that instant Jane opened the door of the cabin and was at once in the presence of the strangers. In one hand she held a basket filled with fish, and in the other she held some game, which consisted of two ducks and a number of black squirrels. Black squirrels were numerous in this country when it was first discovered by the Europeans, and they were plenty in all of the river counties as late as the Revolution. In the last half century they have entirely disappeared. They are yet found in western New York. The sudden view of the strangers, so entirely unexpected to Jane, caused her to be deeply agitated, but quickly recovering herself she showed the fish and game to her parents. Her mother then introduced her to the strangers, and after the usual ceremonies had passed, Ned spoke and said that the gentlemen would remain over night and that they wanted supper. Ned's wife and daughter set about to get the repast, Ned, in the meantime, building the fire. The fire-place occupied one side of the cabin, and was large enough to take in long wood. Ned soon yoked his steers and hauled a large log to the door, and with the help of his wife and Jane they rolled it in the large fire-place, and then placed a smaller one on the top with the aid of hand spikes; then Ned and his wife lifted a fore-stick in front and then filled the space with small wood. Soon the fire commenced blazing up the mouth of the huge stone chimney, and lighted up the cabin sufficient to read without a candle, as darkness had now set in. Ned's wife and daughter were now busily engaged in getting supper; they had prepared the game which Jane had taken that afternoon. The December wind was blowing with frightful gusts through the valley of Canopus, and whistled around Ned's cabin, whirling the snow, but the agent and young Philipse heeded not the storm, for they were comfortably quartered. As Ned's wife and daughter were preparing the supper, their appetites were becoming sharpened. The fire threw out such heat that the agent and young Philipse retreated to the furtherest side of the cabin. Ned said that he would go out to see how the horses fared, and replenish their racks; and on returning he said the storm was increasing and the snow was falling fast. Supper was now ready, and the guests were soon seated with the family around the table. After supper the agent informed Ned that he must know something about what rent he would be willing to pay, commencing with the new year, and at the same time showing him a written instrument, which were the laws of the patentee. Ned handed the paper to his daughter, telling her to read it. Jane then read the contents aloud. During the reading their observation was fixed on Ned's daughter, and they were surprised to think that a squatter's daughter should possess such advantages here in the wilderness, because there were as yet no schools on that portion of the patent. Jane then informed the agent that her parents came there penniless, and endured incredible hardships to gain a livelihood, and that her mother and herself had taken their turn in the forests, had shouldered the axe and helped her father fell the gigantic oaks and hemlocks, and remove the rocks and stones and place them in walls; that they had helped him protect his cattle and sheep from becoming a prey to the wolves and panthers that nightly surrounded them. They had hewed the logs for his cabin, and helped her father haul them to the spot and rear his cabin, and now after struggling for years to get a comfortable shelter and a few sheep and cattle to drive famine from their door, would they be so ungenerous as to demand rent in a country where the land was covered with rocks and stone. Each word took effect, and for some moments not a word was spoken. She had resumed her work again in clearing the supper table. Her hair, which was long, lay in clustering curls over her neck and shoulders, and her sleeves were rolled above a pair of arms perfectly rounded. The agent said nothing more that evening to Ned about paying rent, and the conversation turned to other subjects. Ned gave a history of his pioneer life, how long he had lived there, and the difficulties he had to contend with in that rough country to gain a subsistence, and how his wife had emigrated to this country with a number of French Huguenots, the severe labor his family had undergone, and now he was getting things in shape to get a little pay for his labor.

Philip listened very attentively to the agent as they talked over the matter; his eyes were fixed intently on the large fire, occasionally casting his eyes at Jane and her mother, for the squatter's daughter had made an impression which he could not easily forget. The manner in which she expressed herself in defending her father, in saying that he ought to go rent free, how hard they had toiled and helped clear the forests, and removed the rocks and stone and reared their cabin, made a deep impression on him. It appeared to him that she had more than an ordinary mind. The evening at length wore away. The agent and Philip occupied the bed in the lower part of the cabin, but Philip could not sleep, for the squatter's daughter occupied his mind. The December storm was howling around the cabin, but the cold north-easter they did not feel. The large fire exhibited nothing now but a heap of ashes and embers, but the room was yet comfortably warm. The long December night was irksome to young Philipse, for he was restless, so much so that he disturbed the agent, who asked him if he was unwell. He replied no, only he had no disposition to sleep. "That is queer," replied the agent, "after a long day's journey without anything to eat till night." "True," replied Philip; "I am sometimes afflicted with nervousness after eating a hearty supper, which sometimes causes me to be wakeful nights."

At the dawn, Ned went out to look after the strangers' horses, while his wife and daughter were preparing breakfast, which consisted of roast ducks and good corn bread. After breakfast young Philipse requested the agent not to say anything more about paying rent, saying he had toiled hard enough to get a living, and as he was getting old he had better pass him by. This the agent said he was not authorized to do. "If he will not pay any rent, I shall have to notify him to vacate the premises." Philip remonstrated, saying that he himself was one of the lawful heirs, and that he was willing that Ned should remain there rent free for life. This was the first time young Philipse had dictated to the agent in regard to what should be done to those squatters that were located on the patent who refused to pay rent. Ned brought the horses to the door, and when the agent and young Philipse were ready to depart, they informed him that he would remain there for the present without being molested. The same time the squatter's daughter listened very attentively to what passed between the agent and her father. As the agent and young Philipse departed, Philip cast a lingering look at the cabin before they plunged in the forests. The valley of Canopus presented a wintery appearance, for the new fallen snow had whitened the summits of the mountains, and loaded the tree-tops in the valleys. Every bush and sapling bent under its weight, and the weather wore a wintry aspect. The agent and young Philipse wended their way through the forests, looking up the next squatter. Sometimes the underbrush would reach the stirrups of their saddles, again their horses would have to pass through deep ravines, where there would be small streams to ford, where the ice had formed through the night with thickness sufficient to hold the weight of their horses; anon they would emerge into an opening where a squatter had erected his log house, when they would dismount and tarry a while and make known their business; then they would proceed to the next squatter, and so continue until they arrived at the end of the patent. Having finished their business they proceeded direct to Carmel.

Then the agent reported to the patentee the situation of his patent, the number of inhabitants that had squatted upon it without paying rent, and the improvements they had made and the compensation they would receive if they chose to vacate their premises; they all complied with the exception of one, Nazareth Austin, who was squatted in Canopus valley, whom he permitted to remain there for the present, rent free. "And why exempt him," inquired the patentee. "Through the persuasion of your son," answered the agent. "Then you have disobeyed my orders." "Yes, but it can be easily rectified, if you say so." "But I will consult my son, and then inform you what to do." Here the conversation ended, and the patentee wondered what object his son could have in granting the privilege to one squatter to remain on the patent rent free. Philip then informed his father where Nazareth Austin was located in the valley of Canopus, on the roughest section of the patent, how they remained there over night, and the history he gave of himself and family in locating there, the hardships they had undergone in settling the wilderness, the privations and sufferings they sustained for years, the rocks and stones they had removed, and that he had no son, and his wife and only daughter each in turn shouldered the axe to help clear the forests and rear the stone walls to protect their sheep and cattle from straying in the forests and keep them safe from beasts of prey; and his daughter too had helped hew the logs with a narrow axe to build his cabin, and that now Austin was far advanced in life, and soon would be incapacitated for labor, and he hoped he would be willing for Austin and his family to remain there free of rent for life. Mrs. Austin, young Philipse continued, had seen better days, and had emigrated to this country with a colony of French Huguenots, and had advantages of birth and education which she had obtained in Europe, and had been accustomed to polished society, and now he felt interested in the welfare of the family, and he thought they had a duty to perform, and that it would be gratifying for him to know, in the decline of life, that he had bestowed charity where it was in reality needed. The father made no reply, but told the agent to make out a deed, which was immediately signed by the patentee, for a certain number of acres where Austin lived, and young Philipse was permitted to present it as a gift to Nazareth Austin.

The new year had commenced, and the month of

January had passed, and Austin sat with his family in his cabin. The snow had covered the valley of Canopus for more than two months, and the wintery blasts yet prevailed, with no indication of the breaking up of winter. Austin was thinking whether it would be better to remain there if the patentee should demand rent, or leave. All the squatters that he had heard from had concluded to pay rent, or leave in the spring. Austin was revolving in his mind what to do if he should receive notice to pay rent the ensuing year or vacate the premises, when the barking of Pompey warned him of the approach of something, and taking a lighted candle and opening the door, young Philipse on horseback was before him. Austin recognized him at once, and asked him to dismount, to which he readily assented. Austin soon had his horse in comfortable quarters, and young Philipse was soon sitting in the cabin warming himself before the large fire. Philip had rode from Carmel that day, and he felt the severity of the cold. Austin's wife and daughter rendered every assistance in their power to make him comfortable. Having finished his meal he took a seat with Austin in front of the large fire. The conversation soon turned to the occupation of the premises another year, whether he would be willing to pay rent or leave. Austin replied that he would be compelled to leave unless the rent was very small. Young Philipse pulled the deed from his pocket and gave it to Austin, who handed it to his daughter to read. Jane immediately read the contents. During the reading Philip's eyes were fixed on Austin, who was listening with intense interest to his daughter, and when he learned that a deed was presented to him by Philip's father, his joy was unbounded. He could not express to Philip the happiness it afforded him, and how grateful he felt towards the giver; and he wished that he might live to see the day that he would be able to repay him. Philip said nothing further on the subject, and before an hour had passed away he was busily engaged in conversation with the squatter's daughter. Presently they were alone in the lower part of the cabin, for Austin and his wife had retired for the night. Before retiring Austin had taken the precaution to have a large supply of wood to replenish the fire when necessary, and Philip and the squatter's daughter sat there alone. Austin's silver watch, which hung up over the fire-place, told the hour of twelve, yet young Philipse was not disposed to sleep, nor was he tired with the fatigue of the day's journey, for he was so deeply interested in conversation that time passed away unheeded. The night wore along and the hour of two had passed, yet Philip had something to say which he could not delay any longer, and then he offered his heart and hand to the squatter's daughter, which was readily accepted. Philip sat there till the light streaks of day were breaking up the dark clouds in the east, and Austin was up seeing to his horse and foddering the sheep and cattle. After breakfast Philip reminded Austin of the remark that he made last evening, how grateful he felt toward his father for presenting to him a deed for this farm, and he hoped he would live to see the day that he could bestow so great a favor; and now he had it in his power to return it to his son. "How?" inquired Austin. "Give me your daughter in marriage," said

Philip. "Yes," said Austin, "and this affords to me more happiness, if possible, than the deed you presented to me last evening."

When Mrs. Austin learned that the young patentee had offered himself to her daughter in marriage, she could hardly realize it, and she learned from her husband too that Philip intended to take her immediately to Carmel, and Austin and Philip soon were constructing a sledge for that purpose sufficient to hold two persons. Having finished it, Philip attached his horse to the sledge, and Jane, bidding her parents farewell, they set out direct for Carmel. On arriving home, Philip introduced Jane Austin to his parents as his betrothed wife. His father was thunderstruck, and was greatly incensed against his son for some time, but having learned the history of Mrs. Austin, that she fled from her own country from persecution with a colony of French Huguenots, and that she belonged to some of the first families of France, and had come to this country to enjoy her religious freedom, and that, too, she had had the advantages of birth and education, which few in this country enjoyed, he at last made no objection to the marriage. A few months elapsed before the squatter's daughter became the wife of the young patentee. Shortly after their marriage, Austin's death took place, and Mrs. Austin left her log cabin and went to live with her daughter, who then was beautifully located on the patent, living in affluence and enjoying all the luxuries a new country afforded.

THE HAUNTED TAVERN, AND WITCHCRAFT IN NEW HACKENSACK.

THE HAUNTED TAVERN.

In the town of East Fishkill stands an old dilapidated dwelling-house, known in the early history of our county as the Haunted Tavern. It is an ancient structure, built more than a century and a quarter ago, and now has the appearance of great antiquity. This house would hardly arrest the attention of the passer-by, for there is nothing attractive to the stranger or tourist. The old sloping roof, the huge collar-beams, and oaken rafters, have not been molested, and the same covering and weather-beaten siding, have withstood the storms and winds of more than a hundred winters; but the tradition which has been handed down to us of robbery and murder perpetrated there, if true, would awaken in the mind scenes that would startle every reader of this narrative, and cause a shudder that would fill the very fibres of the soul. The old house was first occupied as a tavern, and dates back to the first settlement of the town. Then there were no thoroughfares like those of the present day, and in every neighborhood the pioneers would collect in certain localities, where there was a tavern, and spend their leisure hours in taking a social glass, playing at cards, and in other amusements. This old tavern was the headquarters of the people of the surrounding country, where the early settlers would congregate on training and holidays, particularly Christmas and New Year, and would have what then was called "shooting matches," which consisted of different varieties of poultry, such as turkeys, ducks, geese, and domestic fowls, being set up as a mark to be shot at. The owners charged a groat for the privilege of shooting once, and the first blood that was drawn from the bird by the marksmen, won the prize. The highway in front of the tavern was straight and level for a mile, and this was the great race course for the pioneers to try the speed of their horses. The landlord was a very penurious man, and his object was to make all the money he could out of his customers. If an exciting horse race was to come off, he provided for the occasion. His bar was well stocked with liquors, and meals were served, and often many imbibed freely at the bar. A large collection of people could be seen along the highway where the horses were brought out, standing in groups, or sitting on the road fence, anxiously waiting for them to start, and a number of small bets were frequently made in what in those days were called "treats," on which horse would be the winner, and the loser would pay at the bar. No temperance societies then existed, and prohibition was unknown; the use of intoxicating drinks was the prevailing custom of the country, but the reader must not infer from this that all were intemperate, far from it. There were those who were never under the influence of ardent spirits, but occasionally took a glass.

The old tavern was located some distance from the nearest settler, remote from any village, surrounded with forests dark and dense, and if a traveler was overtaken there by night or weather bound, the landlord would extort all the money he could out of him. When our country was new, traveling was difficult; the utility of steam for propelling vessels had not been discovered, and steamboats and railroads were not known, and the traveling through the country was by a lumbering stage-coach or in a private conveyance over roads that were rough and uneven, consequently the traveler made slow progress, and taverns were more or less benefited and the business lucrative. This old tavern had its share of business, but startling stories at length were circulated throughout the settlement about the landlord—that travelers were often robbed when remaining there over night, and that the landlord always managed to escape detection, denying any knowledge of theft being committed in his house. Many believed that he had large sums of money buried in his cellar, others said when frequenting the tavern unexpectedly, they saw piles of johannas, pistoles, doubloons, and crowns, which then was the currency of the country. But notwithstanding the stories that were current about the country, that the landlord would rob and cheat, he paid strict attention to his business. He encouraged horse racing and card playing, and those who were habitual visitors at his tavern left all their money there. But eventually the landlord was in reality rich ; whether he made his money by foul means or out of his business, the community were divided.

A story was circulated throughout the country, that a peddler with a pack was traveling on foot, and night had overtaken him at the old tavern. It was in the month of December, and a severe storm of rain, sleet, and hail, had set in, and the night was dark and gloomy. So unpleasant was the weather that what few there were at the tavern, left early for fear they would not be able to reach their home, and before nine o'clock no one occupied the bar-room but the landlord and the peddler. The following morning the storm was unabated, and so dreary was the weather that none ventured to the tavern for several days, and when the storm had subsided, the peddler was almost forgotten. One or two persons appeared to recollect a peddler stopping there the night the storm commenced, but all traces of him had disappeared. Fearful stories were told that the peddler never left the tavern, and strong suspicions against the landlord were indulged in, that the peddler was murdered in his tavern. Others again doubted, and the landlord appeared ignorant of what was said against him. Stories like those related, would form the gossip of the surrounding country during the long winter evenings, and children would listen to their parents for hours, telling them stories of robbery and murder perpetrated there, and that his accomplices in those deeds of horror were the inmates of his tavern, consisting of his wife and domestics, who carefully concealed their guilt. It was said that there were secret rooms in the tavern, where none were allowed to enter, and if a traveler stayed there over night, who was unacquainted with any one, the landlord would conduct him to one of those secret rooms to lodge for the night, and those rooms were the theatre of atrocious crimes perpetrated on such, which, if true, would make humanity shudder, but as nothing definite was known, the landlord lived there the remainder of his days, and there we leave him.

Whether the stories above related about robberies and murders, perpetrated in the tavern, were true, I know not, we leave the reader to judge. After the death of the landlord, many believed that he had buried large sums of money in the cellar or somewhere on the premises, but the difficulty was to find it, and so superstitious were many at that time, that they believed if they should dig for the hidden treasure, the ghost of the old landlord would appear, for they believed the old tavern was haunted. After the death of the landlord, the tavern was unoccupied for some time, and a story was told of some one passing it in the night, who saw the landlord in the bar-room, holding a light and looking out of the window, and he knowing that the tavern was vacated, and no one had lived there since his death, became so frightened that he put his horses to the top of their speed, and the noise of his old wagon reverberated through the neighboring woods, and might have been heard for a mile. But the desire to obtain the money that was believed to be buried in the cellar of the old tavern, overcame the fear of some of the most courageous, and accordingly two men who professed not to be afraid of anything, neither ghosts nor witches, not even the old Nick himself, determined at all hazards to make the attempt to get the hidden treasure. Squires and Payne, for those were their names, who had been good customers of the old landlord when he was alive, thinking he had got their money wrongfully when they were a little under the influence of liquor, while sitting in the bar-room, thought that a fine opportunity to get some of it back. These two men lived near neighbors, their farms joining. They possessed rough exteriors, like all pioneers in the wilderness, and it is not until such men level the forests, open roads, bridge the streams, and erect comfortable dwellings, that a new country is a fit habitation for the more refined. They were accustomed to toil and the use of ardent spirits, which they thought was necessary to enable them to endure the hardships of settling a new country.

Squires and Payne would meet in a secluded place, and talk over their plans how to get access to the old tavern. They carefully concealed their design, and a dark night was selected to carry it out. They provided themselves with everything necessary, their tools consisting of a shovel and spade, a pickaxe, two tallow candles, an iron candlestick, a tinder-box filled with tinder, a flint and steel, which was the ancient method of striking fire, and when the appointed night arrived, as soon as darkness set in, shouldered their tools and wended their way to the old tavern, where they arrived near midnight. They had provided themselves with a flask of liquor to cheer them in their labor and drive away fear. The old tavern looked deserted, particularly at the dread hour of midnight, for no human being had entered it since the landlord's death, and Payne and Squires began to think of the story their neighbor told of seeing a light in the bar-room, and the landlord standing near the window, while he was riding past there in the night, but they thought it was no time now to think of ghosts. Squires took the flask from his pocket, and drank off some of its contents, and then handed it to Payne, who partook freely of its potations, and then they commenced operations. They found but little difficulty in gaining an entrance through a window. After this was accomplished they struck a light with their flint and steel, which emitted sparks of fire in the tinder box, which adhered to the tinder, and then Squires lighted their tallow candle, which they put into the iron candlestick. They picked up their tools and proceeded carefully to the cellar, where they believed the money was buried. Squires already began to quake with fear, although he had boasted of his courage before leaving home, saying that he cared not if the ghost of the old landlord did appear, the money they were bound to have, and no ghost, no, not even Satan himself, could frighten him. Payne, too, possessed courage before he left home, but fear began to take hold of him; but taking another draught from their flasks they off with their coats, and seizing their shovels and pickaxe, they commenced digging. The old tallow candle threw out a flickering light as they plied themselves to their work, and stimulated with the hope of finding money they indulged in little or no conversation. The old cellar walls, and the huge timbers that supported the building, and the doleful looking surroundings of the cellar, added to the dark and dreary hour of midnight, created in Payne and Squires fears which can better be imagined than described. Presently Squires remarked that he heard the noise of footsteps in the bar-room overhead. Payne replied in the affirmative, and inquired what can the noise proceed from. Squires replied if the ghost of the old landlord or the old Nick was coming they would not scare him, if the money was buried there, he was determined to dig till they should find it, although both were terribly frightened, when Payne was so overcome with fear that he dropped his shovel and started on a run for the cellar stairs, saying that the landlord or the devil was standing in the corner behind him. Squires never stopped to look, but dropping his pickaxe, he scrambled up the stairs after his companion. In the confusion they knocked over the old iron candlestick and extinguished the light; leaving their coats and tools in the cellar, they groped through the dark passages, sometimes striking themselves violently against the door-posts as they emerged from room to room, half frightened out of their wits. They at last succeeded in finding the entrance, and imagining that a ghost was close to their heels, they plunged headlong out of the window. They lost no time in trying their speed, and reached their homes completely exhausted. After Squires and Payne had recovered from their fright, which took several days, and suffering from severe bruises which they received in making their hasty flight from the old tavern, they now concluded to keep their adventure there a secret. Payne probably saw no ghosts when he was digging for money in the cellar of the old tavern, but his imagination was so powerfully wrought upon, from his superstitious belief in ghosts, that he imagined he saw something in a corner of the cellar when digging. Squires and Payne had left all their tools in the old tavern cellar, and how to get them they did not know, for they had not the courage to go to the tavern after this event, so they concluded to keep quiet at home. The following Spring the old tavern, including two hundred acres of land, was rented to a man whose name was Dundee, who came from Long Island, who on examining the house discovered that an excavation had been made in the cellar and the tools which had been used to open the excavation were left by parties who, to all appearance, had fled precipitately. He discovered an iron candlestick with a tallow candle partially consumed, a tinder-box, one shovel, a pickaxe and spade, two coats, one containing a flask of liquor, &c. Dundee wondered what object could have induced any one to make this excavation, but on hearing that the former occupant had, as many believed, buried money there, he concluded that some one had made the attempt to find it. But who could the parties be, thought he. The tallow candle, which was partially consumed, led him to believe that the earth had been removed in the night; but when he was informed that probably robbery and murder had been perpetrated in the house, he thought that the landlord might have removed the earth with the intention of burying money, or it may be some one that had been murdered, he was at a loss to conjecture. If he should undertake to dig for money, he might find instead of money, some one that had been buried there, and that would alarm him, and rather than run the risk of getting money by this method, he concluded to fill up the excavation. But

Dundee had been informed that the house was haunted; he occupied it as a farm-house; he was a firm believer in ghosts and witches; under circumstances like these we should imagine he could see a ghost or a witch very easily. He would vacate the premises at once, but he had just begun to occupy them, and it was the first of April, and the season for commencing farming had now arrived, and it was too late in the season to look for another farm, and if he should it would be very difficult to find one, and he concluded to remain there for a year, and say nothing to his family respecting his fears, not wishing to alarm them; for if he communicated to them that the house was haunted, he would have to vacate the premises at once. This would subject him to great inconvenience, as there was no farm far or near that he could rent. The farm he occupied was owned by one of the patentees, which included the Beekman and Rombout purchases. His rent was small, only forty skipples of wheat a year—a Dutch measure containing three pecks—and he concluded to commence farming immediately, not deeming it prudent to dig for money, nor allow any one to search for the hidden treasure, believing that ghosts would appear whether any money was found or not. Stories of robbery and murder were often the conversation in the neighborhood, believed to have been perpetrated in the old tavern, when occupied by the landlord, and that money was buried in the cellar or on the premises, but Dundee strictly forbid any search to be made, and the stories that were related about seeing ghosts, he feigned not to believe.

A century and a quarter ago, when this old tavern

was occupied by the landlord, mankind was superstitious, education was confined to the few, and witchcraft was more or less believed in, and sometimes the delusion broke out in communities. In 1690 it spread to such an alarming extent in Salem, Massachusetts, that nineteen were executed, and hundreds imprisoned. In Boston, Springfield, Charlestown, and Dorchester, many were executed, merely for being suspected of witchcraft. Even in England, the learned men in that time believed in witchcraft. The learned Baxter, who flourished then in England, where the same notions on witchcraft prevailed, pronounced the unbeliever in witchcraft an obdurate Sadducee, and Sir Matthew Hale, one of the brightest ornaments of the English bench, repeatedly tried and condemned those as criminals who were accused of witchcraft. The human mind is prone to superstition, and it more or less prevailed in every country two centuries ago, and even in those countries which were civilized and refined, and upon which divine revelation had shed its light, the learned as well as the unlearned, were subject to the prevailing power of popular delusion, and the code of laws framed in Hartford, Windsor, and Wethersfield, in Connecticut, reads, as may be seen at the present day: "If any man or woman bee a witch, that is, hath or consulteth with a familiar spirritt, they shall bee put to death." The Rev. John Brown, one of the greatest divines of the age, who lived as late as 1787, says: "A witch is a woman, and a wizard is a man, that has dealings with Satan, if not actually entered into formal compact with him. That such persons are among men, is abundantly plain from Scripture, and that they ought to be put to death." He then quotes passages from Scripture: Deuteronomy, 18th chapter, 10th verse, and Exodus, 22d chapter, 18th verse. He then proceeded to say: "It is plain, however, that great caution is necessary in detecting and punishing the guilty, lest the innocent suffer, as many instances in New England and other places show. To me it appears obvious that for one to regard with anything like fear, persons suspected of this infernal power, is nothing less than indirectly rendering homage to Satan." Thus, we think we have shown sufficient proof that in the most enlightened countries they believed in witchcraft less than a century ago. Can we wonder then that stories of ghosts even in the haunted tavern, as related in this narrative, were believed in?

Dundee pursued his vocation, mingling little with society, and whatever he heard respecting ghosts being seen in his house while unoccupied, after the landlord's death, he said nothing. He had resided there about three months and had not seen anything to create in him any fear, and he concluded that the stories of robbery and murder perpetrated there were more or less exaggerated. Squires and Payne, who figured so conspicuously in this story, expected to hear some startling news from Dundee before this, that he had found some of the landlord's money secreted somewhere, or some ghost had appeared to him or his family, but not hearing of any such thing, they concluded to pay him a visit. They set out one morning for that purpose, and soon arrived at Dundee's. They found him in his barn busily employed unloading hay from off his cart and placing it in the mow. They introduced themselves, and then explained the object of their visit, saying they expected to hear of his finding money ere this, as the house he had rented was occupied as a tavern for many years prior to his renting the premises, and the landlord was very penurious and his business lucrative, and it was believed he had buried large sums of money in the cellar or somewhere about the place, for they said that no doubt he had often robbed travelers when they put up there for the night, and stories, too, were circulated that murder had been perpetrated there. Dundee replied that he had not attempted to dig for money, nor allowed any one to search the premises, believing if he should allow any digging, they might find, instead of money, some one buried, and that would frighten his family, and he would have to vacate the farm at once. Dundee informed Squires and Payne that when he came there last Spring, he discovered an excavation that had been made in the cellar, and that he had made enquiries respecting who the parties were, but was unable to obtain any information, and the tools were left, and it appeared to him they must have been terribly frightened. The tools, he said, he had not used, and they were in the barn, at the same time showing them to his visitors, who saw their coats, one containing the flask of liquor; also their shovel, pickaxe and spade, the old iron candlestick, and tinder-box. Payne and Squires feigned ignorance as to how the tools came in the cellar of the old tavern, and carefully kept to themselves their adventure. Payne and Squires would not claim their property; choosing rather to lose it than let Dundee know they were the identical persons that owned the coats and tools, and had made the excavation in the cellar of his house, and as Dundee had informed them that he would not allow any digging on his premises for money or anything else, they left for their homes rather disappointed. Dundee lived on the old tavern farm one year, and not seeing anything nor hearing of any ghosts, he leased the farm for a number of years, and lived there quiet till his death, without being alarmed about seeing any ghosts. The stories of the old tavern being haunted gradually died away, and the recollection of its early history as "The Haunted Tavern," is at the present day almost entirely forgotten.

WITCHCRAFT IN NEW HACKENSACK.

In 1786 witchcraft broke out in an adjacent neighborhood, in a family who then resided in New Hackensack, one of the most influential and wealthy in the town, living in a brick mansion known as the residence of Doctor Stephen Thorne. In the gable of the mansion was the name of the owner in large letters, and the date of its erection. The Doctor and his wife, and one or two of the older children, were on a visit to a neighbor, leaving the smaller children home in charge of a domestic, who went to the cellar about eight o'clock, accompanied by one of the members of the family, a girl of fourteen years of age, to get a bowl of apples and some walnuts. While the domestic was filling a small basket with walnuts, a fearful knocking commenced close by her, and so frightened were they, that both ran with all haste up the cellar stairs, the knockings following the domestic. The alarm increased, for the knockings continued in rapid succession. When the Doctor arrived, he found his family in the wildest state of excitement, and all were weeping. After enquiring the cause, he quickly perceived that a knocking was distinctly heard beneath the floor where the girl stood. The Doctor supposed that he could soon explain the cause, believing that some trick was performed by some person or persons, merely for amusement. He examined every room in the house. If he stood close by the girl, the knockings appeared beneath the floor; if he went into a lower room, the knockings sounded from above; if he went in an upper room, the knockings were distinctly heard below. The Doctor was not frightened, for he was one of the most eminent physicians of the age, and he had great experience in his practice and intercourse with mankind, but still he could not divine the cause, and he finally told her to retire for the night. The knockings followed her to her bedroom, and continued without intermission on the headboard where she lay. That night brought no sleep to the Doctor and his family, and the following morning the news spread rapidly through the neighborhood, that strange knockings were heard continually in the house of Doctor Thorne, following his domestic wherever she went, day and night. Hundreds came to see and hear, and were satisfied that it was not the work of man; that no stratagem of his could produce what they saw and heard. The news soon spread over the whole country, far and near, and it attracted the attention of learned men.

A number came from Poughkeepsie, New York, Philadelphia, and the New England States. These men tried to solve the problem. They placed her in different positions, sometimes sitting her on a timber, held by two persons, several feet from the earth; the knockings then sounded from the timber. Not only were the knockings continually sounding wherever the girl went, but the knives and forks would fly from her hands when she partook of her food, and furniture, such as chairs, would overturn when she had occasion to take hold of them, and tables would move from her. If a person sat close beside her, on a chair, the chair would shove from her. In one instance the grandfather of the writer of this article, who then lived in the neighborhood, whose weight was two hundred pounds, took a seat close to her, and his chair immediately shoved away. Curiosity became excited, and editors of leading journals, few in number in those days, published accounts of this remarkable case in their newspapers, which created intense excitement. The New York Mercury of that day, noted at some length this mysterious affair, from which we had intended to take a few extracts, but at the present writing we are unable to lay our hands on the paper, but all came to the conclusion that it was either witchcraft or some mystery which they could not explain. The Doctor was obliged to seek relief from his numerous visitors, and the writer's grandfather kindly volunteered to take the girl into his own house, and he distinctly recollects hearing his father, who was then a boy some twelve years of age, say that he had sat for hours beside the cot on which the girl rested, with his hand on her forehead, in order that she might sleep. The moment he placed his hand on her forehead, the knockings would cease, but the moment his hand was removed, the raps would be resumed on the headboard, and what added singularity to the case, he was the only person who could exercise the influence. Finally she went to live with a relative, the knockings followed, but eventually they became less frequent, and not so loud, and at last they ceased entirely. Some years after this event, the girl paid a visit to Dr. Thorne's, and was received kindly at his house. When she left, the Doctor lost a fine cow. Soon after she visited him again, and when she left he lost another cow. She then paid him a third visit. The doctor's son owned a fine colt, which he thought a great deal of, and when the girl left, his colt was taken sick and died. The doctor's son was enraged, and said she must not enter there again; if she paid them another visit he would show her the door. His father tried to convince him that such losses would occur, and probably they would have lost their cows and colt if the girl had never paid them a visit, but his son would not believe him, and he was determined to keep his resolution; but the girl never came there afterward.

These facts have been collected by research, and they may help fill up a vacuum in the history of our county. I would say in my closing, that I am proud of being a descendant of one of the families who first settled the original town of Fishkill; the first settlement in the county began in that town. Their names will be remembered long after the history of our county shall have been published, and their last resting places overlooked and forgotten. Our county has had her superstitions, and I would ask what country is exempt? Then let us draw a vail of filial affection over the delusions of our forefathers, for they have all passed away, and a brighter day has dawned on the whole civilized world.

THE BROKEN-HEARTED.

The scenery of the Highlands is very rich and sublimely beautiful. The mountains, mantled with evergreens, the rivulets dashing playfully down in cascades, entice, with resistless temptation, the attention, and excite the admiration of the beholder. The noble Hudson, winding its way through the mountains, whose projecting peaks peer thousands of feet above it; here and there waves the hemlock, in solitary, yet princely splendor; the huge pine, whose limbs have nodded to the winds of an hundred winters, proud of age, in the grandeur of its own sombre hue, changeless and eternal; the deep valleys, almost encircled by high and continuous ranges of hills, covered with the deep colored and exuberant foliage of the forest.

Just north of the Highlands, more than forty years ago, not far from the banks of the noble Hudson, stood a handsome country seat. Its situation was on an eminence commanding a beautiful view on every side. To the south the eye could rest with delight on the blue tops of the Fishkill Mountains, peering one above another in emulous strife, and to the north for many miles the beautiful river could be seen winding its way through the country, covered with vessels, which floated like motes in the sunbeam. In the east could be seen the sloping and still extended valley and Matteawan creek, washing the mountain at its base, to the beautiful village of Fishkill, then the largest in the town. Art had not been wanting in garnishing the exterior with every decoration which could render it handsome. The observer would at once conclude that its inhabitants were of no small importance in the community, nor wanting in this world's wealth. It was the mansion of Mrs. S., a widow of forty. Her husband had fallen a victim to that most fearful scourge, the yellow fever, in 1822, while in the city of New York on business, leaving his wife and only daughter to the care of a kind Providence, and the inheritance of his vast wealth. This sudden bereavement afflicted her heart severely, and for months she abandoned herself to sorrow and grief. As these wore off, her affections intuitively fastened themselves upon her child with greater tenacity, and she devoted all her care and attention to the idol of her soul. Under the auspices of her kind parent, Cordelia grew up a lovely and accomplished girl, and was admired by all who knew her.

As Mrs. S. wished to spare no pains to educate her daughter, she accompanied her to the city of New York to complete her education, and procured board in State street, which was then one of the most fashionable streets in the city, the wealth and fashion of New York then being below the Park. Broadway, Greenwich and State streets were among the leading in the city, and the Battery formed the principal place of resort. Mrs. S.'s boarding house was so situated as to have a commanding view of the Battery and Bay, and every pleasant evening Cordelia and herself would walk on the battery, and sometimes up Broadway as far as Trinity Church. During these walks they would meet the most gay and fashionable people in the city, and Cordelia, then in the bloom and beauty of youth, intelligent, educated and handsome, her hair a sunny brown, and falling in luxuriant ringlets over her graceful neck, often attracted the attention of the passer by.

One fine afternoon in September, Cordelia took a walk alone on the Battery. It was one of those pleasant days that often occur at that season of the year. The air was balmy, and the beautiful Bay was covered with ships, steamboats, and small vessels, plowing their way through the water, and dashing the silvery spray upward, as they moved gracefully to and fro. The tall masts, with their snowy canvass, were waving to the breeze, and glistening in the sunbeams. Cordelia stood close to the iron railing, looking out upon the Bay, and admiring the sparkling craft dancing upon the water, when a richly dressed young man, who had been standing unnoticed near her for some time, introduced himself to her by saying that "he had been viewing the scenery for hours; that he had traveled in foreign lands; had seen the Bay of Naples, and had sailed in Dublin Harbor, but he thought New York Bay, and the surrounding scenery of Long Island, Staten Island, New Jersey, and islands in the harbor, with the numerous ships, steamboats, and smaller vessels that were constantly departing from the port, presented a scene more beautiful than he had ever witnessed abroad."

The sudden interview with the stranger drew from her a look of surprise, and for a moment she was agitated, and betrayed considerable emotion, but recovering herself, she mildly replied "that she had been admiring the scenery so intensely for some time, that she was unconscious of aught that was passing around her."

The stranger was the son of one of the wealthiest merchants in the city. He had been to Europe, and had but recently returned, and had come out on the Battery that afternoon to spend a few hours pleasantly, when he saw Cordelia, and as he gazed at her when she was looking out on the Bay, admiring her glossy hair, which flowed in ringlets over her neck and shoulders, he ventured to address her, and her mild reply made an indelible impression on his heart. Cordelia immediately retraced her steps to her boarding house, and hurriedly threw off her hat, for the manner of the stranger who had so unexpectedly addressed her, had awakened emotions which she could hardly suppress. This was perceived by her mother, who inquired if anything had befallen her. Cordelia made no reply, but immediately left the room to evade an answer.

The young man eyed her with intense interest as he saw her leave, and following at a distance, unperceived by Cordelia, he saw her enter her boarding house, and then taking a pencil and a piece of paper from his pocket, he noted down the number, and then returned to his home, which was located on the west side of Broadway, near the Battery. There, alone in his room, his mind reverted to the place where he had seen the beautiful girl. He drew the paper from his pocket, looked at the number, and then walked the room in deep meditation, his mind fastened on her who was now the object of his affections. He cast his eye out of the window that looked into State street, for he thought with the aid of his glass he could see the number; but in this he was mistaken, for State street is shaped like a bended bow, and Cordelia's house was located beyond the curve. He seated himself in a chair, and burying his face in his hands became absorbed in deep thought. He was the son of wealthy parents, and now he was unhappy, for the young lady whom he had seen on the Battery having left him so abruptly, he thought he had done wrong in introducing himself to her; but he thought if he could be united to her for life, he would be perfectly happy. The young man was dissipated, and his parents, to reform him, sent him on a tour to Europe, hoping it would benefit him, but on his return he soon became associated with his old companions, and every evening he would join them in their places of resort, and return home in a state of intoxication. But now he had formed the resolution to spend his evenings at home, abandon his old associates, reform his habits and live a temperate life. The following evening he remained at home, and his old companions in guilt met as usual, but one of their number was absent, and they thought he had drank to excess the night previous. But when they met the second night and found their companion still absent, they supposed him sick, and the following day one of his old comrades met him in the street, and thus accosted him :

"Why have you not been with us these two evenings ?"

He replied that he intended to lead a different life.

and dissipate no longer, and that he would meet with them no more. His old friend tried to dissuade him from his purpose, but it was useless, and they departed. When the club met again they were informed of his decision.

William now spent his evenings at home, to the surprise and joy of his parents, and every pleasant afternoon he would take a walk on the Battery, casting a wistful look in State street, as he walked leisurely to and fro. Occasionally he would look out on the Bay, but the scenery had lost all of its former attractiveness. He often looked at the multitude of people that were constantly passing and repassing, hoping that he might meet the beautiful girl again, but all efforts to see her were unavailing. He took the note from his pocket, and looked at the number. He could not be mistaken, and knowing no person residing there, he hoped to meet her again on the Battery, but in this he was disappointed. Weeks had now rolled away, but he could neither see nor hear of her. He smothered his feelings, and said to himself, "Must I lose her forever—must I return to my dissipated habits, mingle with my old associates, and die a drunkard?" Such were the thoughts that occupied his mind.

The interview between Cordelia and the young man alluded to had taken place on the last day that her mother and herself were to remain in the city, and the following morning they took passage on board the steamboat for home. After remaining there for several weeks, her teacher wrote a letter informing her that she would be very happy to have her spend a few days with her. With the consent of her mother, Cordelia set out alone, by steamboat, for New York. On her arrival she was received by her teacher, and was soon safe in her old boarding house in State street.

William continued his promenades on the Battery, every pleasant afternoon and evening, wondering what had become of the lovely girl, and while pondering the subject in his mind one day, to his great surprise he met Cordelia. So sudden and unexpected was it to him, that he betrayed considerable emotion, and Cordelia was no less agitated and confused. It was late in Autumn, and the Indian Summer lay quietly slumbering over the landscape, and the red sun was just dipping its weary form in its western grave, and its rays tinged the top of the tall trees on the Battery and reflected brightly their scarlet leaves. William introduced himself by saying that he remembered speaking to her some time ago when walking on the Battery, and asking her at the same time if she recognized him. Cordelia replied in the affirmative, and taking his arm, they leisurely walked till they came to a resting place, when they sat down together. William remarked that he was in the habit of spending an hour or more on the Battery every pleasant afternoon, and as he had not met with her, he supposed that she seldom walked out. Cordelia replied that she did not live in the city, that her residence was on the Hudson river, near Fishkill Landing, and that she had recently been boarding in State street with her mother, and attending school. After completing her studies they returned home, and only a few weeks had elapsed, when she received a letter from Miss A., in State street, saying that she would be pleased if she could make her a visit, and with her mother's permission she set out alone for New York, and arrived the day before, and as the afternoon was so very pleasant she thought she would take a walk on the Battery, and on the following Saturday she intended returning home. William listened attentively to the young lady, as she explained to him the reason he had not seen her since their first interview on the Battery. They remained there for some time in close conversation, and time passed away so pleasantly that the shades of evening began to thicken before Cordelia was aware it was so late, when she remarked that she must leave him, for she had promised Miss A. that she would return before sunset, and that she had staid longer than she intended. William accompanied her to Miss A.'s, and before leaving her remarked that as she intended leaving the city on Saturday for home, he would be very much pleased to accompany her. Cordelia replied that it would also afford her much pleasure, and accepted the offer. William went home with a buoyant heart, such as one feels when leaving the object of his love. After Cordelia left the young man, she began to reflect on what she had been doing. She had consented for William to wait on her home without her knowing anything about him further than his own statement. He had informed her that he was the son of a wealthy merchant living in Broadway, and doing business in Pearl street, and she thought she had been imprudent in accepting his offer. Yet she admired him, yes, loved him, and if he had an unblemished reputation, she would be happy in receiving him, and she was fearful, too, of introducing a stranger to her mother, and one

with whom she had had so short an acquaintance.
Such thoughts occupied her mind during the few short
days that she remained in the city. But the hour
arrived. William, with a carriage, awaited her in
State street, and they were soon aboard the steamboat sailing up the majestic Hudson.

It was a beautiful morning and the rays of the sun
gilded the domes and spires that loomed up over the
city, and it presented a beautiful prospect to the travellers, as the steamer ploughed her way through the
water. Steamboats then did not sail as fast as at the
present day, and they were usually six hours in sailing from New York to Newburgh, when the passengers for Fishkill were landed and conveyed thence by
the ferryboat to Fishkill Landing. Time passed away
very pleasantly with Cordelia and William, and they
were safely landed, and a stage was in readiness to
convey them to their place of destination. A short
drive in the stage brought them to Mrs. S.'s and William was soon introduced to her. She gave him a
cordial reception and he was soon seated in the parlor.
William admired the situation, for it was one of the
finest country seats on or near the Hudson. The parlor
was most gorgeously furnished, and the sun shone
through the large windows, and shot its fiery rays
across the crimson carpets, and reflected upon the
splendid mirrors and paintings that were suspended
upon the walls. He had been accustomed to fashionable life, and he had seen the gaiety and splendor of
both hemispheres, but he had seen but few situations
in his own country that surpassed it. The beautiful
view of the Hudson at the north could be seen to

High Point, and to the south the majestic Highlands, whose towering peaks rise one above another in grandeur. William was delighted with his visit, and everything, he thought, was there to make him happy. He thought nothing hindered him from securing Cordelia, for he knew she loved him, and they had formed an ardent attachment for each other. Mrs. S. had treated him kindly, and he promised Cordelia when he left that he would soon visit her again.

Mrs. S. was much pleased with William, and had no objection to his marriage with Cordelia, provided his character was stainless, and when she questioned her mother, therefore, respecting him as a companion for life, she replied favorably. As soon as William left Mrs. S., she immediately wrote to Miss A., in New York, relating all the circumstances of Cordelia's visit to her house, of her acquaintance with William, at the same time giving her the statement he had made respecting himself, and requesting her to get what information she could respecting him. Hardly a week had passed when she received a letter from Miss A., stating that she had obtained the information desired; that he was the son of a wealthy merchant doing business in Pearl street, and living in Broadway; that he was a dissipated young man, and that his parents had done everything in their power to reform him, but to no purpose; and as a last resort had sent him on a tour to Europe, with no better results. Mrs. S. had not informed Cordelia of her inquiries respecting William, and when she read the letter to her she burst into tears, and her agonies of mind were indescribable. She could not abandon the idea of marrying William, and she was greatly incensed at Miss A. for writing such a letter to her mother. But she was fearful that it might be true, and she shuddered to think that he was immersed in dissipation, for the image of his loveliness was now stamped where no hand but that of death could efface it, and during her short acquaintance with him she had seen nothing to indicate the truth of such a report, and she thought his character pure and unspotted. But William was soon to make her another visit, and then she hoped that he could prove the report untrue.

William, on his return home, kept aloof from his old companions, and his mind was occupied in thinking of Cordelia, and he was impatient for the time to arrive when he was to visit her again. When the time came, he was soon again at Mrs. S.'s, and after he was comfortably seated in the parlor, he perceived that Cordelia was agitated. He thought she had been laboring under mental inquietude, and it alarmed him. She treated him with her usual kindness, and yet he thought there was something lurking in her heart which made her unhappy. Cordelia knew that her mother intended making known to him what she had heard respecting his character, and she hoped that he could prove it untrue, and this encouraged her; but when her mother introduced the subject, he lost his self control and frankly confessed it, and then Mrs. S. read the letter which she had received from Miss A. During the reading William was deeply moved, and the tears soon found their way to his cheek, and Cordelia was so overcome that she was obliged to leave the room. She soon returned, weeping, and resumed her seat on the sofa. Her face was suffused with tears, as she listened to her mother, while she informed William that he must leave the house forever. When he bade adieu to Cordelia, the tears were rolling down his cheeks, and his heart was swelling with sorrow. He hurried to the city, joined his old companions in guilt, became a confirmed inebriate, dragged out a miserable existence, and died a wretched death. But the shock was too great for Cordelia. Isolated and alone, she shunned all society, and became melancholy. Her mother saw the fatal mistake that she had made, and she made every effort in her power to render her happy, but all proved unavailing, for she saw, when it was too late, that she had destroyed the peace of her daughter, and it penetrated the very chamber of her soul. She had inflicted a wound which no medicine could heal, no tears wash away! Secluded from the world, Cordelia's grief was unmitigated, and during the few short years that she lived, she was never more seen to smile. She died of a broken heart. Mrs. S. regretted very much the manner in which she treated William, and after the death of Cordelia, she had no desire to live. Her cup of sorrow was filled to the brim, and she was compelled even to drain it to its very dregs, for the trouble and mental agony that she endured soon terminated her existence.

Kind reader, Cordelia and her mother now sleep in the village churchyard at Fishkill Landing, beneath the stately branches of the cypress, and there will they slumber until the arch-angel shall lift his trumpet and sound the summons for all to appear at the Judgment Seat!

THE HIGHLAND FARMER VS. THE WESTERN FARMER.

What a contrast there is in the circumstances of mankind, often engaged in the same occupation, more particularly those who are engaged in agriculture. This may be in a measure owing to the difference in the management of their farms, and the productiveness of the soil. Often do we witness the rough and sterile land on the mountains, while in the valleys below lie beautiful farms, unobstructed by rocky knolls or worthless swamps, and when brought under cultivation affording rich returns to the husbandman, while the farmer on the mountains, practicing the most rigid economy and industry, often has to contend with poverty through life.

We may inquire why is this so? why are some portions of the country so rough and broken, when a few miles in an opposite direction it is almost destitute, if not entirely, of rocks and stones? The only answer that can be given is, infinite wisdom has made it so.

Situated on one of the highest elevations of the highland mountains, is a farm-house that was owned by one family to the third generation, and the occupant was called the highland farmer. From his doorsill he could look down on the rich valleys of the Fishkills, and in Summer he could see the golden harvests, and in Autumn the ripening fields of corn stretching through the valleys, interspersed with mellow orchards and flocks and herds. He often inquired of himself why his forefathers settled on the mountains and entailed on their posterity poverty, when land was so cheap in the valley. The highland farmer now was in straightened circumstances, for he had a large family to support. The large forests which covered the farm when his grandfather settled there, had now nearly disappeared, for they were obliged to market a number of cords of wood yearly to help maintain their families. This privilege now was denied him, for he had hardly sufficient fuel to supply his own fire. He was obliged to turn out every haying season, to help the farmers in the valleys get their hay in, in order to obtain a few loads of coarse fodder to enable him to keep his few cattle through the winter, and often he would feed them so scanty that he would lose one or more from starvation. Under circumstances like these, the highland farmer was often depressed in spirits. His old dilapidated dwelling was getting leaky, for the shingles and clapboards were falling off, his children were poorly clad, and his rocky farm produced less every year.

It has often been remarked that man conforms to the country in which he lives. If it is rough and unproductive, he is generally unpolished himself, for he has not the advantages of those who live in countries where wealth and refinement prevails. The highland farmer's opportunities were limited, and often would he go to the village in the valley to purchase some necessaries for his family, and the rich farmers would congregate at the village store to converse on the topics of the day, when the highland farmer would listen very attentively to their conversation, and he often contrasted his situation and opportunities with theirs, which often times made him very unhappy.

The highland farmer had a well balanced mind, and he often regretted his living there, in that rough and broken country. Had he left there when he was young and emigrated west and purchased new land, he might now have been a wealthy and influential citizen, and his children would have had better opportunities and occupied higher positions in society.

The highland farmer had now arrived at the meridian of life, and the prospect of his ever bettering his condition was by no means flattering, yet he could submit to all this if he could only improve the condition of his family, for this was his greatest trouble, and this no one knew but himself. His wife and children often discovered that he was unhappy, for he would sit hours with his family, during the long winter evenings, without attempting any conversation, and at times he could not refrain from weeping, and they often inquired the cause of his sorrow, but he would not inform them.

The winter of 18— was a very severe one. The snow had fallen the latter part of November and remained till spring, and during the winter months it covered the earth four feet deep on the mountains and more than three feet in the valleys, and at times the wind would whirl it into eddies and pile it up in huge masses along the wayside, rendering the roads often impassible, which caused much suffering among the poorer classes. It was difficult for those living on by-roads to get to mill or store, or even to the woods for fuel. The highland farmer had to cart his fuel on his back, beating a path to the woods with the aid of snow shoes to keep him from sinking through the snow to the earth. The nearest mill to him was in the Highlands, and there too he was obliged to go on foot. The snow had formed a crust on the surface sufficient, with the aid of snow-shoes, to hold up the weight of the heaviest man. This enabled the highland farmer to take a bag of grain upon his back to the Highland mill and return in safety. The emigration West the following Spring was so rapid, to Chicago and Milwaukee, that produce was shipped from Ohio to those western States to supply the emigrants with food. This rendered the price of grain in the eastern States very high, and enhanced the value of land in our river counties. Land speculation had caused good farming lands to sell for one hundred dollars per acre, and farms on the mountains even were sought after.

A mechanic living in the village in the valley, having a little money, wishing to invest it in land, and not having enough to purchase a farm in the valleys, turned his attention to the mountain. In reviewing the farms there, he concluded to try to buy out the highland farmer. They were not long making a bargain. The mechanic made him an offer, which he readily accepted. An article of agreement was soon drawn up and signed by both parties. After the highland farmer had sold his farm, he began to reflect on what course to take. Everything to him now appeared different. He and his parents and grand parents had been reared there.

The place where we have been born and reared, often causes an attachment which we carry with us through life, however uninviting it may appear. Every particular spot calls up before us some tender recollection. Parents, brothers and sisters, all have been born there. The highland farmer now experienced the tender ties which were about to be severed forever. Every rock on the farm he loved, every stick of timber in his dwelling was dear to him, the brook that meandered through the back yard, where he had played with his associates from his earliest recollections, seemed now to him a lovely spot. He had often prayed that he might not end his days on the highland farm, and now his prayer was answered, and he had often wept over his misfortunes, and now could he leave without any regrets, thought he to himself. Oh, no. The highland farmer was yet in the prime of life. He had not reached his forty-fifth year, and he concluded to emigrate to one of the Western States. Accordingly he set out on his journey. Being unaccustomed to travel, the distance alarmed him. The canal and stage-coach were the only means to convey passengers west from Albany, for the railroad from Albany to Buffalo was not then completed. The highland farmer took passage aboard the canal boat to Buffalo, and after reaching Niagara county he concluded to go no further. Lands then were comparatively cheap in Western New York, for the farmers had but recently commenced removing to new States further west, and the country yet was the favorite resort for emigrants. The highland farmer purchased a good wheat farm, containing two hundred acres, for a few hundred dollars more than he sold his rough and rocky farm for. The farm was partially improved. The dwelling house was built of logs, like those of most of the first settlers, but the barn was a large frame building, recently built, and the land was mostly cleared, new and productive. The highland farmer lost no time in getting his family to his new home, and the following Spring they were all comfortably settled, and ready to commence farming. The mode of working now was entirely different, for the highland farmer had no rocks and stones to contend with. His farm would vie with any in the rich valleys of the Fishkills, for not a boulder or cobble stone could be found, and he put his crops in the earth in season, and in the fall he had a golden harvest. He soon canceled the debt he had contracted when he purchased his farm, and yearly he raised large crops of wheat, for which he received when in market, prices which enabled him to have a surplus of money sufficient to build him a substantial farm dwelling house, which when completed added greatly to the happiness and comfort of his family. The highland farmer now was in affluent circumstances, and he paid great attention to the education of his children. When he lived on the highland farm his house contained no reading material but an almanac, a Bible, and Webster's spelling book. Now it was furnished with a neat library. He had never subscribed for a newspaper until after he settled in Niagara county, for his means were too limited, and now it was to him one of the greatest of blessings. Rich and prosperous in his old age, he was perfectly happy, and no more can we apply to him the appellation of the highland farmer, but now we will call him the western farmer.

He had a desire once more to see the place of his nativity. If he could visit his birth place once more, he thought he could die contented, for truth compels me to say that when he first removed to his western farm he was home-sick for months. And can we wonder at this? No, for he had lived in no other place, hardly spent two consecutive nights from home, and he wanted to revisit it before he died. Accordingly he set out, accompanied by one of his sons, for that purpose. They soon arrived in the valley of the Fishkills, and made a stop at the village store. The rich farmers had congregated there as usual, and were discussing different subjects when the western farmer and his son entered. His old neighbors did not recognize them. They whispered to each other, asking who the strangers were. Some remarked that they appeared to be men of wealth and eminence. Curiosity became excited to know who they could be, and what their business was. The western farmer and his son knew them all, and for a while kept themselves at a distance, leaving the villagers in suspense. At length he introduced himself to one of the company, informing him who they were.

The villagers surveyed the western farmer and son from head to foot, for they were clothed with costly apparel, and in conversation they were well posted with the events of the day. He gave a brief history of his situation in Niagara county, and what a beautiful farm he owned, and he had now come once more to see the old homestead. From the villagers he learned that the mechanic who purchased his farm was sadly disappointed. He went there with bright anticipations, expecting to better his condition, but being unacquainted with farming, and owning land covered with rocks and stones, he went behind hand every year. Becoming disheartened, the mechanic at last got discouraged. He had been accustomed to economy and industry, but severe labor amounted to nothing. It was true that the products of the land were dear, but he could earn more working at his trade than toiling on a rough worn out mountain farm. The mechanic at length found a customer for his farm, and selling out at less than cost, and glad to come off so, he purchased a small farm at the base of the mountain, where there were less rocks and stones, and was now comfortably situated there. The western farmer and son called on him. The mechanic had not yet entirely recovered from his reverses, and the western farmer's and son's appearance made an indelible impression on the mechanic's mind. He saw the fatal mistake he made when he purchased the highland farm. Had he then gone west and located on a good wheat farm, he might now have been in like circumstances with his friend who had called to see him. The western farmer ascended the mountain, where lay the farm, the place of his birth. How his heart beat as he neared his old domicil. With what intense interest did he view every surrounding object, and when he reached the farm his eye scanned the mountain. How different every thing appeared to him, for he had been accustomed to live in such a beautiful country that his old highland farm appeared more uninviting than ever. Every rock appeared to have grown larger. The scenes of his childhood came up before him in vivid recollection. The brook where he had so often played with his brothers and sisters still meandered through the landscape. The old chestnut tree from which he had so often gathered the fruit in his childhood, and which had been beaten by the storms of a hundred winters, was still there. The few aged hemlocks which he had been accustomed to see from his infancy, were still clinging to those elevated mountain peaks, bidding defiance to the tempest that howled around them. The exterior of the old homestead wore a more cheering aspect, for it had been newly roofed and sided, but the interior looked more gloomy and dismal than ever. The low ceilings, with timbers uncovered, the small dark windows, and huge stone fire place and old oaken floors, were the same as when he left there twenty years ago. The western farmer scrutinized the old homestead with peculiar interest, for it was the last visit he expected to make to the highland farm. He had now arrived at the age of more than three score years, and the few remaining years that would be allotted to him here he intended to spend quietly at his western home. He cast his eye again over the valleys of the Fishkills, and every thing arose in perspective view before him. Not a cloud obstructed the horizon. The hazy atmosphere that so often hung upon the adjacent mountains and over the valleys had now disappeared, and the view from the highland farm never appeared more beautiful, for there was nothing to interrupt it. Numerous small villages, stately mansions and farmhouses, dotted the earth on every hand. The Matteawan creek lay sparkling in the distance, with its tributaries winding through the valleys like threads of silver. The majestic Hudson could be distinctly seen, and with what thrilling interest did he gaze at the splendid craft—dancing upon the water. The western farmer's mind reverted to those days when he lived there on the highland farm, struggling with poverty, and he was obliged to labor for the rich farmers living in the valleys in order to maintain his family, and how he envied their situation; and now he owned a farm in Niagara county, rich and productive as theirs. The transition from poverty to wealth within the last twenty years he could hardly realize. With such impressions he bid adieu to the highland farm, and was soon again at the residence of the mechanic.

The western farmer and son tarried several days with the mechanic, who made every effort in his power to make their visit pleasant. The mechanic related to him his experience in farming on the highland farm; that when he purchased the farm and had consummated the bargain he thought his money was well invested, and early in the Spring of 18— he commenced operations. Toiling through the seasons nearly fourteen hours out of twenty-four, among the rocks and stones, and being unaccustomed to such physical labor, his constitution began to give way. With all the exertions he made he hardly brought the year around. The second year he exercised the same patient and stubborn industry to improve his condition, but all to no purpose. With his health impaired and no fences on his farm, his house open and leaky, with no means to repair them, he sold the highland farm at a sacrifice, and purchased the farm he now occupied, and having partially recovered his health and improved the condition of his family, he intended, as he was now far advanced in life, to spend the remainder of his days there.

The western farmer listened very attentively as the mechanic related his story, and then he related his experience living on the highland farm; how many years he had there to contend with poverty, and his family uneducated, and now he owned a good wheat farm in Niagara county, containing two hundred acres as productive as any in Old Dutchess, with a dwelling which he had recently built, large and commodious, and he owed no man a cent, and he had spared no pains to educate his children.

The western farmer and son paid a visit to a few more of his old acquaintances, and then set out on their journey home. Very friendly was the parting between him and the mechanic. He rode through the valleys of the Fishkills, and the highway which he had so often traveled in early life. The alterations and improvements which had been made since then, the last time he ever expected to see them, were scenes deeply interesting. An hour and a half's drive, brought him to the Hudson, and as he gazed upon the river from Newburgh, a view unobstructed for many miles either way, the numerous sails, towering highlands, whose tops seemed to pierce the very clouds, adding a zest to the surrounding scenery. Soon the steamer hove in sight that was to convey him to Albany, and bidding adieu to all the scenes of his childhood, the western farmer and son sailed up the noble Hudson. Taking a packet from Albany, they soon reached their home in Niagara county. There the western farmer lived to a good old age, rich and happy, enjoying himself in the bosom of his family, and dying, as I trust, in the hope of a blessed immortality beyond the grave.

DEACON JONES;

OR, THE PIONEER.

In the year 1790, the State of Connecticut contained nearly 240,000 inhabitants, and so rapid was emigration from the Eastern States west, that it was half a century afterward before the population of the State reached 300,000. Western New York and Ohio, then a wilderness, was the favorite resort of the emigrant from the New England States. So great was emigration from Connecticut to Western New York and Ohio about the year 1800, that her population for several years was almost stationary. A large number of families would sell their rough and rocky farms and prepare themselves with a covered wagon and leave for the beautiful and fertile valley of the Ohio, and so large a share of emigration did Connecticut contribute to that state, that that portion lying south of Lake Erie was called New Connecticut.

In the county of Fairfield, in that state, lived a man whose name was John Jones, having a large family and owning only sixty acres of land, the most of it rough and broken, and under the best of cultivation it hardly supported his family. Having heard of the wonderful stories told of the rich lands lying south of

Lake Erie, he concluded to try his fortune there. Hard, indeed, was it for him to leave the home of his childhood, the school-house where he had received his first rudiments of education, the brook in the meadow where he had so often played with his associates, ever since his first recollection, the church where he had so often worshipped the God of his fathers, and the churchyard where his ancestors had slept for several generations. He had for nearly a quarter of a century been a pillar in the church. When it became known that he intended to leave for Ohio, the church and neighborhood were deeply affected. The church would lose one of her main pillars, the neighborhood one of her best citizens. Deacon Jones having sold his farm and with the proceeds purchased a large tract of land in Ohio where Cleveland is now located, then a vast wilderness, inhabited by savages and beasts of prey, and a distance, too, of nearly five hundred miles, a great journey in those days, for then there were no steamboats nor railroads, and traveling was a toilsome occupation. Deacon Jones had a large lumber wagon made sufficient to hold his family, and covered so as to protect them from the storms, and to rest in during the night. The time was drawing near when he was to bid farewell to those he had held most dear. The last Sabbath had arrived when he was to meet those with whom he had communed in the church from his earliest years to the present time; his pastor who had so faithfully delivered the warnings of inspiration, and had been instrumental in winning him to the Saviour. All these tender recollections of by-gone days clustered around him, and as he sat in his seat in that sanctuary probably for the last time, and was to leave on the morrow for a country where the herald of the cross had not yet been proclaimed, his heart was wrung with anguish. But the prospect of bettering the condition of his family was a great inducement for him to leave the home of his birth, and live the few remaining years which might be allotted to him away from friends and society; for he anticipated the time would come when the large tract of land which he had purchased would be very valuable, and would be the means of placing his family in comfortable circumstances, if not making him rich. Flushed with such expectations, Deacon Jones, on the first Monday in May, in the year 1800, bid adieu to his native place, and with his family, consisting of his wife, four girls, one son whose name was Lewis, started for his new home in Ohio, where Cleveland is now located. Deacon Jones had used all possible means to make his family comfortable during the long journey, which he knew would occupy thirty-five or forty days. His large covered wagon was sufficient to hold his family and the few necessary articles of furniture he knew he would want in a new country. Drawn by a good sturdy yoke of oxen, he pursued his course. Ohio then contained only about 25,000 inhabitants, and where Deacon Jones had purchased was a boundless forest, for then Western New York was considered the out-post of civilization, and beyond there Deacon Jones would find only a few isolated settlers. But he was aware of this. To shun the Alleghany mountains he proceeded north through Columbia county, in the State of New York, following the Hudson river to Albany, and there for the first time Lewis beheld a city, for he was then only ten years old, and had been but a few miles from his native place. Albany then contained about 1500 buildings and upwards of 6,000 inhabitants. Although a small city compared with its present magnitude, the curiosity of Lewis was excited when passing through the principal streets. The public buildings, the tall glittering church spires, the people, the vehicles, the large stores and shops, all were new to him. But Deacon Jones soon emerged from the city, and was on the state road leading west and as far as Whitestown, situated on the Mohawk, one hundred miles west from Albany. The roads were passable for heavy loads. Going along at the rate of twelve miles a day, sleeping in his wagon nights, he was eight days reaching Whitestown, then a flourishing village.

On leaving Whitestown the country wore a different aspect. It was more sparsely settled, and the roads in many places almost impassible, and in the low wet places the pioneers had rolled in logs and covered them with a thin layer of earth. The heavy rains that had recently fallen had washed the earth away, leaving the logs uncovered, and as Deacon Jones rode over the logs the joltings of the wagon made it more fatiguing to his family than performing the journey on foot. His son Lewis was a mere youth and unable to walk, being of a feeble constitution, and with his mother seated in the covered wagon, pillowing his weary head upon her bosom, he began to experience the hardships of the wilderness. Deacon Jones never was discouraged. Always cheerful, and often speaking words of encouragement to his family, and urging his ox team through the long listless day, stopping only to refresh himself and family, turning his oxen nights in the forests, and in the morning hunting up his team, and then pursuing his journey. Sometimes a deer would cross his path, which afforded his family much pleasure. Arriving at Geneva, which then contained sixty families, Deacon Jones tarried a few days to refresh himself and family. An Englishman named Powell kept a hotel there, and the kindness that Deacon Jones and family received made them once more happy.

Passing through western New York from Geneva to Canandaigua and to the Genesee river, the scenery was picturesque, the country beautiful, and very open in many places. The openings were free of timber, then appearing to contain at least two or three hundred acres, beautifully variegated with hill and dale; sometimes composed of a range of gentle ridges of land running most frequently from north to south, between each a run of water and considerable bottom on each side. It was again in some places timbered chiefly with hickory, oak, basswood and pine. Then again on the open flats on the Genesee river were ten thousand acres lying in one body, not even encumbered with a bush, but covered with grass of such height when full grown that the largest bullock at thirty feet from the road would be completely hid from view. Deacon Jones passed through the country and crossed one of the prairies, where there were a few scattering trees interspersed, in the latter part of May. The weather had been delightful for some days, not a cloud obstructed the horizon and the rays of the sun in the middle of the day were uncomfortably warm. He halted at noon, as usual for himself and family, and turned his oxen out on the prairie to graze; of a sudden he heard distant thunder, lifting up the cover of his wagon he saw a dark angry cloud skirting the horizon. The first appearance gave him little alarm, but it gradually increased and gathered strength as it rose. The flashes of lightning followed each other in rapid succession, and the continued peals of thunder reverberated through the air. Presently the rain fell in torrents and the wind blew violently, and the falling water beat against his wagon, in places driving through. Deacon Jones, sitting in his wagon, watching the storm, discovered a flame of fire bursting upward, caused by the lightning striking a dry tree and which had kindled with amazing rapidity. At length it appeared like columns of fiery red, surmounted by a crest of flame. Lewis had never witnessed such a sight before, and it filled him with terror. The tree stood more than one hundred feet in perpendicular height, and the flames soon reached the top. The wind blowing a perfect gale, the fire caught in another tree but a short distance from it, both forming a burning arch over the road and falling at last with a crash, one over the other, like so many burning pyramids, similar to those funeral piles of old, in which were collected by pagan piety the ashes of departed heroes. Deacon Jones' family were very much frightened by the storm, particularly little Lewis, lying close to his mother, and her arms folding him close. Deacon Jones betrayed no fear, nor was he discouraged, for he thought that he could scan the future history of Ohio. He prophesied that in a half a century hence she would be the third State in the Union in wealth and population. How beautifully has his prophecy been verified, for just half a century elapsed from Deacon Jones' settling in Ohio, when she was the third State in the Union in population, containing two millions of inhabitants. The storm had abated just as the sun was setting in the west, and being some miles from any habitation he did not resume his journey till morning. It was the beginning of June before Deacon Jones discovered the shores of Lake Erie, and following the Lake he was soon in the State of Pennsylvania. The forest now had became so thick and dark that it was often difficult to proceed, and it was forty days before he reached the State of Ohio. And yet he was fifty miles from his destination. His progress now was extremely slow, mostly beyond civilization, and surrounded by aborigines of the country, with no road but an Indian path, and often the trees standing so close that his wagon could not pass without his chopping down a tree, making his journey painful in the extreme. His family, too, worn out with the fatigues of the journey, were becoming disheartened. Arriving within twenty miles of his destination the road was entirely ended, and now he had to cut his way through the forest. Then for the first time Deacon Jones showed signs of discouragement, for he was in an interminable wilderness, with no one but his family, surrounded probably by hostile tribes of Indians, with an only son but ten years old, and through sickness unable to assist him in the least. His wife and daughters each in turn shouldered the axe and helped clear a road through the forest, till at last he arrived at his farm, located on the shores of Lake Erie, where Cleveland is situated. His oxen, tired and worn down with the long journey, were unable to perform much labor, and it was necessary that he should provide some shelter for his family. Weak and exhausted himself, and his family prostrated, they began to experience hardships heretofore unknown. No house but his wagon, provisions getting scarce, he had to begin to live by the chase. But mustering courage he commenced felling trees and thinking how he should build a log house.

A tribe of Indians was located near Deacon Jones, and he often heard that kind treatment towards them was never forgotten, that the attachment they cherished for a friend was greater than those formed by civilized nations. Those Indians often paid him a visit, and he treated them kindly, his family giving them some little article of luxury which they could conveniently part with. They volunteered to assist him in building his house. He was far beyond churches, schools, stores, mills, and even roads, and many miles from the nearest settler. He of course could not get nails nor boards to use in flooring his log house. The Indians assisted him in getting his logs on the ground, and when he had a sufficient number he commenced building. As he advanced, with his axe he flattened the logs and laying one above the other, chinking the crevices with earth, making it perfectly tight, and with his oxen, assisted by the Indians, he soon had it of sufficient height to commence the roof. Having no material but logs for the roof, he hewed them with his narrow axe, and by laying them close to the ends of the timbers resting on the gable ends of the building, and gradually drawing them together until the two opposite sides met, at the same time carrying them up very steep, a roof was formed perfectly tight. Having floored his cabin with logs flattened on both sides, his family was soon comfortably settled in their new home.

Having obtained some provisions from the Indians, Deacon Jones commenced clearing the forest, for he wanted to put in as large a crop in the fall as he was able to prepare the ground for. His wife and daughters, and even little Lewis, helped fell the trees, for it was now the middle of July. After felling a large number of trees he would haul them together with his oxen and when dry set fire to them. In this way, by the last week in September he had ten acres ready for wheat.

Deacon Jones and family had toiled hard during the Summer, living mostly by the chase, often destitute of bread and fearing famine might overtake him before Spring, and having no wheat to sow his fallow ground, his anxiety was indescribable. But he had taken the precaution before leaving his native place to include in his stores a half bushel of early corn, which he planted as soon as he had cleared a little spot, and although it was the twentieth of June before he had finished planting, the crop was maturing. Sitting in his cabin one evening, tired with the fatigues of the day, his face buried in his hands, thinking where he should get wheat to sow his field, a stranger darkened the entrance. On looking up he saw one of his own race, the first he had seen except his family since he came there. He learned from him that a large number of families had left their homes in Connecticut, and had made all necessary arrangements for the coming winter. Deacon

Jones soon made known his wants. The stranger informed him that they were located about eight miles distant, and having heard that he lived there, he had resolved on paying him a visit. He informed him that they could supply him with wheat to sow his fallow ground. Early the next morning Deacon Jones yoked his oxen, and with his friend in his large wagon they proceeded on through the woods, cutting their way through. They soon reached the pioneers. Deacon Jones received a few bushels of wheat from each settler. He went home rejoicing, and before the second week in October had elapsed he had finished sowing. His crop of corn, too, had sufficiently matured, for frosts do not come as early as in Connecticut. This supplied his family with corn bread through the winter, and the abundance of venison which he shot afforded him plenty of provisions. In the Spring of 1801 Deacon Jones' wheat, which he had sown in the Fall, looked very promising, for the soil where he had located was very productive. Emigration was coming in from all of the New England States, and the sturdy pioneers soon commenced opening roads and bridging the streams. Some of the emigrants settled near him, and soon churches, schools, stores, and grist mills were erecting, and Deacon Jones had an abundant harvest.

The next year Ohio was admitted in the Union, and only ten years had elapsed since Deacon Jones settled there, when the State had increased from 45,365 to 230,760 inhabitants.

In the year 1810 we find Deacon Jones living in a substantial frame house overlooking Lake Erie, with comfortable out buildings, within call of the school house and in the sound of the gospel, a prominent member of a christian church, and an interesting family around him. His son Lewis had grown to manhood, and occupied a high position in society. But Deacon Jones did not live to see his family in possession of a large fortune, for he had passed the meridian of life. He had seen three score years, yet he had lived to see all his children married except Lewis, who was the youngest, and comfortably settled around him. But the forest was fast disappearing, and in the year 1820, only ten years further in the history of Ohio, the State contained nearly 600,000 inhabitants. But look further in the history of that State. Ten years again passes by and the State has 938,000 inhabitants. We behold a city springing up where Deacon Jones had settled. Cleveland then contained one thousand and seventy-six inhabitants. But thirty years more had passed and Ohio was the third State in the Union in population, and Cleveland contained nearly fifty thousand inhabitants. Deacon Jones' family is living in that beautiful city, and Lewis is now one of the most wealthy and influential citizens, living at the advanced age of eighty-four years. Deacon Jones did not live to see the future glory of Ohio, but his prophecy was fulfilled. Before that time had arrived his spirit had taken its flight.

THE FARMER'S DAUGHTER.

Who that has traveled through New England does not admire the scenery. Its rugged hills, fertile valleys, cragged rocks and lofty mountains greet the eye, and those valleys are dotted with thriving villages, beautiful country seats, and stately farm houses, with farms well cultivated and occupied by a population whose industrious habits are handed down from their puritan fathers. Their religious zeal and the diffusion of knowledge has made the name of New England known throughout the civilized world. Her people have been always remarkably industrious and economical, owing probably to the sterility of the soil, the long dreary winters, the rough and broken country.

But, reader, did you ever visit a New England farm house, and see the industry, the economy and contentment, which makes every rational household happy. The thrifty farmer of New England and his family rise before the sun, and after an early breakfast, he and his sons go with their workmen to the field, and his daughters attend to the dairy, making butter and cheese, and doing all work usually required in a farm house. This places himself and family beyond the reach of want, and education being diffused among the masses, New England has produced many distinguished men. Their colleges have flourished beyond any others in the United States. The illustrious characters they have produced, who have distinguished themselves in politics, law, divinity, the mathematics, and philosophy, national and civil history, and in the fine arts, particularly in poetry, evince the truth of these observations.

Near one of those lovely villages which lie scattered throughout the valleys of New England, stands a substantial farm house, reared about the beginning of the present century. To the eye of the traveler it would attract no attention, for it has none of the improvements of the present day.

No beautiful lawns nor handsome evergreens surround it, but there is a beauty that one can not fail to admire. It is the thorough cultivation, that denotes the hand of industry rather than taste. The practical horticulturist had not been there, but rank pastures, heavy waving fields, and luxuriant meadows, indicate rich returns to the husbandman. The small clump of trees left here and there in the fields to afford fuel in the winter, and lend a grateful shade in the summer, diversify the scene, and render it still more beautiful.

It was the home of Lucy Knapp, the farmer's daughter. She had never been beyond the boundaries of her native town, and had never received an education beyond what the village school afforded. Taught from her infancy the puritan habits of her ancestors, the strict observance of the Sabbath, their economy and industry, she was reared up an utter stranger to the gaiety and fashion of city life. In her childhood her delight was her filial duty to her parents, and attachment to her associates, and after school hours she would roam with them over the fields and pluck the wild flowers that budded and bloomed, and gather berries that grew on the hillsides of her father's farm. As Lucy was the only daughter of Joseph Knapp, and having many brothers, when she became old enough she had arduous duties to perform; for the labors in a farm house years ago were more toilsome than at the present day. The saving of labor by modern inventions has done away with the spinning wheel and the loom, which in those days to the farmer's daughter was a laborious task. But the products of her loom and wheel clothed the family in winter, and the butter and cheese which were used at their plain board was made by her. Industry and fresh air had given Lucy strong health, and if she was beautiful while engaged in her labors of love during the day at home, or twining the hill flowers among the tresses of her hair, in the afternoon shade of the maples and elms that were standing near the house, she was doubly so to her parents. Her steps had now come up through life's bright sunshine to her eighteenth Summer, and she had lived in the quietness of her rural home. To say that she was lovely, was not enough. She was eminently beautiful, and many an eye was directed to the gallery, as every Sunday she quietly took her seat in the choir of the village church, and waited the giving out of the opening hymn. Her voice was sweet and full, and mingled like an angel's with the melody which went up in praise to the Author of all Blessings. Her eyes were the reflection of the softness and purity of the summer's heaven, and the tinge of the early morning rested on her cheek. Although she must have known that she was beautiful, by the smiles that lit up the faces of all she spoke to; she did not show it by a single appearance of vanity. She plaited her shining auburn hair in simple folds upon her forehead, and her father and mother regarded her with pardonable pride.

In the village lived a lawyer of large wealth, which he had accumulated by his profession. He had a son Robert, who had been to the village school with Lucy from infancy, and often they had played together, and rambled through the meadows, and sported by the brook which flowed through the orchard behind her father's house. Robert was designed for the profession of his father, and after passing through college, his father sent him to a law school in the distant city of Boston. Robert made rapid proficiency in his studies, for he was a young man of quick parts, good perceptions, retentive and ready memory. But ah, there was something dearer to him than life. It was the love he cherished for Lucy, the attachment he had formed for her when going to the village school. That love had grown more ardent as he advanced in years, and when he was to leave his native village for the city of Boston, the last Sabbath he met with her in church, he waited on her home from meeting, and betrayed emotions more easily imagined than described.

There is something holy in such first early love, so unselfish and pure. How the man of the world, in his musing hours, looks back upon it, after years have glided by, even with tears, though it be not sorrowful, except in contrast with the present. That eye which to the world is so cold, as it scans the crowd, is sometimes moistened with such remembrances, and the knitted brow relaxes for a moment, forgetful of its pride. Lucy regarded the attention that Robert had shown her as nothing more than friendship. One afternoon her father returned from the village and handed her a letter. Seeing that it was mailed at Boston she retired to her room, there alone with trembling hands she opened it and perused the contents. It was from Robert, and the letter portrayed his feelings when leaving his native village, the affection he cherished for her from his earliest recollection to the present time, the many happy hours they had played together on the gentle slope of the hills beyond the brook, which flowed through the orchard beyond her father's house. That love had now become interwoven with the fibres of his heart. It had grown with his growth, and strengthened with his strength, and now after completing his studies and getting into business for himself, he would be very happy to link his earthly career with her through life. Oh, who can imagine the feelings of Lucy, the emotions she betrayed while reading the letter, for she too had loved Robert, but she had smothered that love in the secret recesses of her heart. She knew that he was attentive to her; but she thought the intimacy he had manifested toward her when going to the village school, the happy hours they had played together in their childhood, were the causes of his attachment in riper years. Who can fathom the depths of a woman's love? More priceless than the gems of Golconda, more devout than the idolatry of Mecca, is that unquenching love that flows from the gushing fount of the female heart. Lucy returned from her room, and read the contents of the letter to her mother, who was highly pleased, for her parents regarded Robert with esteem, one born and reared among them, and who had always borne an unblemished reputation.

Lucy soon answered his letter; and she alluded to bygone days, the tender recollections of the past, the happiness it afforded her when thinking how they used to roam over the fields in quest of flowers and berries with her brothers, and now that he had offered to unite himself to her, to share with her the joys and sorrows through this vale of tears, nothing would add more to her happiness than to tread life's journey with him.

Robert, the reader may imagine, was at the post office when the mail arrived, and how it gladdened his heart when he received an answer to his letter. He was perfectly happy, for he was making such progress in his studies that he expected soon to be admitted to the bar, and he hoped then to get some lucrative employment, for he did not wish to apply to his father for support. Little did Robert suspect that his father would be angry when informed of his intention of marrying Lucy Knapp, the farmer's daughter. He was impatient to visit home, to see his parents and the object of his affections.

It was on Saturday afternoon when he arrived at his native village, and with what joy he was received by his parents, for they were proud to learn that he was so far advanced in the study of law that he would soon be admitted to the bar, and his examination would shortly take place. Robert informed his parents that evening of his intention of marrying the farmer's daughter. They were sitting in the room and his father was busily engaged in reading. As he related to him his engagement, the village lawyer dropped his book, and his countenance denoted anger, for he thought that the learned professions occupied a higher position in society than plain, industrious, substantial farmers. He had sense enough to respect them, but for his son to marry a farmer's daughter was something that his proud spirit would not brook. After sparing no pains for his education, he would look forward for him to marry the daughter of some one liberally educated. He endeavored to dissuade him from marrying Lucy, but all to no purpose. He said he must then leave the house, and he threatened to disinherit him as the last resort.

Robert passed a sleepless night, for he saw that he had displeased his parents, and now he must abandon the idea of marrying Lucy, or the doors of his father's house would be forever closed against him. His parents the next morning said nothing to him on the subject, but they looked at him with a frown of disapprobation. It was the Sabbath, and as quiet stillness pervaded the village, and the sound of the church bell reverberated through the valley, calling the people to the house of God, Robert directed his steps there alone, for his parents had no wish to attend church that day, and he occupied the family pew alone. Who can describe his feelings, when casting his eyes in the gallery he saw Lucy sitting there! Oh, what an hour that was to him! The faithful pastor delivered the warnings of inspiration to his flock, but every word to Robert passed by unheeded. After the services were ended an opportunity was soon offered to him to speak to Lucy, and Mr. Knapp politely waited on him and invited him to accompany them home and dine with him, to which he readily assented. When the village lawyer was informed that his son did not return from church, but went home with Mr. Knapp, he became melancholy. Retiring to his parlor, and half reclining himself on the sofa, he sat buried in thought. It was a pleasant Sabbath afternoon in September, and the sunshine looked in that gorgeous parlor and lay in rosy flakes about the crimson drapery of his palace home, as it entangled itself with his gray hairs. Presently starting up he walked to and fro through the room with a hurried step, and thinking over what he had said to his son the night previous, his anxiety of mind was indescribable. He was in hopes that his son would return home before leaving for Boston, and then he might reconcile matters, but early the following morning Robert took the stage for that city. He had had a pleasant visit at Mr. Knapp's and the Sabbath evening he spent with Lucy alone. He then informed her that his parents were displeased when he made known to them his intention of marrying her, but his mind was made up, and it was useless for his parents to attempt to thwart him. Robert now tried to dismiss his troubles, for he was to be examined with other students, and he bent all his energy to prepare himself for the examination. From early morn till late at night he was perusing his studies. The day at length arrived, and the students went through a rigid examination, and Robert won laurels that day, for he won the prize. An eminent Judge of the city wrote to his father, and informed him of the honors his son received. He was now admitted to the bar, and had commenced practicing law in that city. As the village lawyer read the letter to his wife he betrayed considerable emotion, for he had driven his only son from his house—for what, he inquired of himself. Only because he would marry a farmer's daughter. Robert had not written home since his last painful interview with his father, which distressed his parents very much; and his father resolved on writing to him, for he regretted very much the manner in which he had treated his son. He would rather he would marry the daughter of some learned professional man, but as Lucy was his choice, he would object no longer. He then wrote to his son and informed him how unhappy he had been since the evening they had last met, how cruel he had treated him, and the threats he had made him, and what agony of mind he had endured since then, and now he admitted that he was in the wrong, and he hoped that he would forgive him, for he was his only son, and what a cordial balm it would be to him if he would return once more to his parents. He had been successful through life, and had amassed a fortune, and now he had arrived to the age of three score years, and life to him, with but few exceptions, had been one continual sunshine; and now, a dark shadow dropped over the sunshine. His heart was proud and self-willed, but there was a fountain there very far down whose waters would never dry up. It was his love for his son.

Robert was busily employed in his office one afternoon, tired with the fatigues of the day, and laying aside his pen, he was filing some paper which had been mislaid on his desk, when a carrier handed him a letter. A glance at the superscription revealed the hand writing. As he read the letter and saw that the love his father cherished for him burned brighter than ever, asking his forgiveness and humbly imploring him once more to return to his parents, he burst into tears, but they were tears of joy which none but a son could feel. The stern heart of the father had at last yielded, and the following morning he took the stage for his native village.

What a happy day that was to Robert as the stage rolled along, and when he drew near his early home and could catch a glimpse of the church spire, his mind reverted to the scenes of his childhood, his parents, his Lucy, all were to him tender recollections. It was the early part of March, and the night air was chilly and raw, and the wind swept through the village with short and frequent gusts. The village lawyer was sitting in his own room alone late in the evening, for the family had retired for the night. All was death-like silence around him except the whistling of the wind which he heard through the tops of the tall trees that stood around his stately mansion. Throwing himself back in his arm chair he was restless, for he was laboring under mental trouble. "I wish Robert" just escaped his lips, when a loud rap was heard at the door. Starting suddenly from his revery he caught a light, and opening the door his son rushed in his arms and said "Father." A happy night that was to that household, and as the village lawyer saw the light of another day, he had experienced happiness to which heretofore he had been a stranger.

Delightful June had come with its roses and balmy breezes; and deeper green upon the trees of the upland had succeeded the tinge of spring. The wild flowers were again in bloom, and every thing was brimming with delight to the ear and eye. Deep in the leafy solitudes the robin warbled its low sweet notes, and the swallow was passing and re-passing over the daisied meadows, lightly dipping its wing in the ripples of the stream as it caught up the insects hovering over the surface. All was joyfulness, but none were more joyful than Lucy and Robert, for the wedding day had arrived, and the village lawyer's son became the husband of the Farmer's Daughter.

A TALE OF THE REVOLUTION.

The village of Fishkill at the commencement of the Revolution, had comparatively few dwellings. The inhabitants were mostly of Dutch descent, and they retained the manners and customs which their ancestors had brought with them from their fatherland.

The most prominent person who resided at that time in the village, was John Swart, who was a staunch Dutchman, and one of the most wealthy men in the country. He went by the name of Captain Swart. The Captain's farm contained several hundred acres of land, and his dwelling was the most expensive edifice of any round about. It was a large double mansion, with spacious hall, and extensive piazza in front. The hall contained a set of hickory arm chairs, a great ornament at that time, for, reader, you must remember there was no costly furniture then as at the present day. Some of the most wealthy families had no carpets on their floors. The house of Captain Swart, except the parlor, was destitute of carpets, and regularly once a week the cleaning and sanding of the floors was performed by the negro slaves, for at that day slavery was tolerated throughout the country.

The Captain had a daughter whose name was Amelia, who was at that time in the bloom and freshness of youth, being eighteen years of age, and her countenance shone in peerless beauty. Her complexion was soft and delicate, while down a finely curved neck fell her dark auburn ringlets in graceful disorder. Her well developed forehead, partially concealed by the tresses, presented strong indications of a powerful and well regulated mind, which had been improved and disciplined by a thorough course of studies, and through her own assiduity and perseverance in acquiring knowledge. She knew nothing of the false coquetry of the city belles, who pay their devotions at the shrine of fashion, and sport with the most sacred feelings of the human heart. She was open, frank and candid, her lips knew no guile, and her heart whispered no deceit.

The Captain, too, was one of the most influential men in the county, and held a prominent position in the Dutch Church. The clergyman who officiated at that time was Dominie Reysdyck. The church was but an indifferent structure, a very unpretending four square building. The entrance was on the main street, and it had a barrack roof, with a sort of cupola and bell, while the old Dutch coat of arms surmounted the same. In front of the church was a large oak tree, that was necessarily taken down when the present edifice was about to be erected. The upper story had port holes in the walls, to enable the inhabitants to defend themselves, as in a fort, in case of an attack by the Indians, to which they were constantly subject, when the country was first settled. Four years after the close of the Revolution, this old church was taken down and the present edifice was erected, though it was not entirely completed until near the year eighteen hundred.

The Revolutionary war had now broken out, and the battles of Lexington, Bunker's Hill, and Long Island had been already fought. The inhabitants of Fishkill were at this time greatly alarmed, as the American army had suffered a total defeat, and was retreating through New Jersey. General Washington encamped that winter at Valley Forge, and in the spring General Burgoyne with a large army, was on his way from Canada to New York, while Generals Gates and Arnold had collected a body of men to oppose his advance. Burgoyne was getting hemmed in at Saratoga, and the British commander from New York sailed up the Hudson river to reinforce him, and they burned dwellings along the shore as they passed up. The Americans, supposing they would doubtless effect a landing, collected an army at Fishkill to give them battle. The British passed on up as far as Hudson, when hearing that Burgoyne had surrendered, they immediately returned. General Washington's headquarters were at that time at Derrick Brinckerhoff's, near Fishkill Village, where he was accompanied by Lafayette and staff. Washington about this time sent one of his aids, whose name was Dixon, to a cutler's, then doing business in the village, to get his sword repaired, and in going thither he passed the residence of Captain Swart. Amelia was sitting on the piazza, engaged in reading the paper. The tragical death of Miss McCrea, who had been murdered by Burgoyne's savage allies, and the British army on the river being expected to land every moment, she reflected as to what might be her fate should a battle take place in or near the village. She therefore ventured to speak to the officer as he passed, and inquired of him if the British had yet landed. His reply was that they had not, and probably they would not, for they had probably by this time passed down below the Highlands.

Dixon was struck with the appearance of the young lady. Her dark hair was all dishevelled, and her eyes were red with weeping, as she held the newspaper with trembling hand, and her plaintive voice was subdued and faltering, as she expressed her dread of the battle field. Dixon hurried from the trembling girl, as her presence caused him to be deeply agitated. He completed his errand, and soon returned again to his post of duty, but the beautiful girl he had met with was constantly on his mind. He had thirsted for military glory, and he was rejoicing to think that he would soon be able to show his valor on the battle field. But the strife of the warrior to him was now nothing. The lovely girl that he had seen he felt assured could afford him far more happiness and joy than all the laurels that he might reap from the crimson field of battle, and he desired an opportunity to have another interview with her. He accordingly got permission of his commander, Washington, to attend divine service at the old Dutch church on the following Sabbath, which was then expected to be held there.

It was not customary, during the troublous times of the Revolution, to have preaching regularly on the Sabbath. The Dutch church was sometimes used as a prison, and when it could be dispensed with for that purpose, the pastor would give notice that service might be expected. Dixon, as might be expected, was early at church, and seated himself in a conspicuous position. The congregation was fast assembling, and he looked with intense interest as they seated themselves. Presently entered Captain Swart and his daughter, who walked to the pew that Dixon had already occupied. He opened the door, and was about to leave, but the Captain beckoned him to remain, and he was soon seated between the Captain and Amelia. Dixon at that time was but twenty-two years of age, and was related to some of the first families in Virginia, and through the influence of friends had succeeded in getting to be an aid-de-camp to Washington. He was a person of pleasing manners and amiable disposition. Health and humor shone in his countenance, while his locks of golden hue shaded his ample forehead, and the sparkling fire of his eye was softened by becoming modesty. A deep crimson suddenly suffused his manly cheek as he thus found himself beside the fair Amelia, and the deep emotions of his bosom may be better imagined than described.

At that day, divine service was performed morning and afternoon, with but a short intermission, and the congregation tarried until both sermons were concluded. The same custom is still prevailing in some sections of the Eastern States. During the intermission Dixon ventured to speak to Amelia, and introduced himself by asking her if she recollected having spoken to an officer a day or two previous, who passed her residence, and she at once recognized him as the person. They slowly walked around and near the church, beholding the army quietly reposing in and around their tents, while the American flag was floating gracefully to the breeze. A Sabbath stillness pervaded the quiet village, and Amelia anxiously inquired if they expected an engagement with the foe. He assured her they did not, as the latest news they had received was that they had safely landed at New York, and that Washington would probably move his troops in a few days. They soon seated themselves together beneath a large forest tree that overshadowed the highway, and Amelia was delighted to think that there would be no battle fought in their peaceful village, while she fondly hoped that the difficulty between the two nations would soon be brought to a happy termintion. Dixon spoke of the trouble that existed between the colonies and the mother country, and believed the breach could not be healed, and after a short struggle the colonies would be free and independent. Amelia hoped for the best, and while thus discoursing the bell announced that the afternoon service was about commencing, when Dixon and Amelia were soon seated again, as before, with the worthy Captain.

After church the Captain politely invited Dixon to accompany them home and dine with them, to which he readily assented. It was customary with the Dutch in those days, to have their best dinners on Sundays, and as it came late in the day, it created an appetite with the Captain, and he always relished them. Upon their reaching home, the servant soon announced that dinner was in waiting, and little time was lost before they were all seated at the table. After dinner, the day being nearly spent, Amelia and Dixon were soon alone in the parlor, with nothing to disturb their happiness, and time passed so pleasantly with Dixon, that it became later than he was aware, when he intended to leave. Amelia kindly asked how long he should remain at Fishkill, but he could not say, though he supposed Washington would remove the army as soon as there was no prospect of a battle being fought in this vicinity. He said, however, that he would endeavor to see her again before leaving, and then bade her a good evening.

Dixon now retraced his steps towards headquarters. The villagers had all retired to rest, and nothing was heard but the sentinel pacing his nightly round, and the howling of the wind that was sweeping through the village, with short and fitful gusts. As he passed the large tree under which he and Amelia had sat that day, during the intermission, his mind reverted to those happy moments passed together there. He cast his eye around and saw his country's flag floating in the moonbeams, and waving to the breeze, and as he gazed upon the spot that but a few hours since had found him so happy, he felt an anguish beyond all expression. He was now an officer of rank, yet he would cheerfully resign his commission, and leave for his native State and home, if he could possess the lovely object of his affections, from whom he had just parted. The kind reception he had met with at Captain Swart's, and the treatment he had received that day, awakened new emotions in his bosom. It encouraged him to repeat his visit, and at the same time inspired him with fresh hope, and he quickly retreated to his resting place at Derrick Brinckerhoff's. Scarcely had he got to sleep when the startling cry of fire awoke him from his slumbers. The Mills belonging to Mr. Brinckerhoff were now enveloped in flames, and the fire had made such progress before it was discovered that all efforts to extinguish it proved unavailing, and the morning light witnessed a heap of smouldering ruins. How the fire originated was never ascertained. The troops had liberty to leave the encampment every day at certain hours, and they had committed many depredations. The Presbyterian church, near Brinckerhoff's, was considerably damaged by the soldiers, who had taken the siding off as far up as they could reach, to boil their camp kettles, and they had also destroyed most of the fences along the highway, from the headquarters to the village. General Washington ordered every soldier into the encampment, and gave strict orders to the sentinel not to let one pass without a written order from their officers. He at the same time offered gratuitously a sufficient number of men to rebuild at once the mills destroyed. Accordingly a large number of soldiers were immediately set to work, some in hauling timbers, some as carpenters, hewing and framing, and in a short time the present Mills were ready for occupation.

The country at that time was comparatively new, and wore a different aspect from the present. Dark, dense forests were interspersed from the village down to Fishkill Landing, some of them extending along the line of highway, and not enclosed. No smiling village greeted the eye of the traveler by the way, and the now beautiful Matteawan was nothing but an extensive field, while the village of Fishkill Landing had but a few isolated dwellings. Johnsville could boast of but one solitary dwelling, and Stormville had but two, including a tavern. From Stormville to Fishkill Village was an extended forest. The mode of traveling was mostly with heavy lumber wagons, having a coarse box resting on the bolster, the seats in which were chairs taken from the house. The lines and traces of the harness were of rope, and the dress of both sexes, was of home manufacture, coarse and cumbersome. Education was not by any means as universally diffused then as at the present time, and school houses were scarce throughout the country. There was an academy east of the village, near the present Presbyterian parsonage, which was under the supervision of Rev. Chauncey Graham. It was a small building, with a cupola and bell, and was taken down shortly after the Revolution and re-built at Poughkeepsie. The Episcopal Church in the village of Fishkill was built prior to the Revolution, and was surmounted with a tall steeple, which was taken off about the year eighteen hundred and ten, as it was considered dangerous. The small-pox broke out about this time in the army, and this church was then used as a hospital. The soldiers' graveyard was at the foot of the mountain, near the residence of Isaac I. Van Wyck. There was a newspaper printed in the village at that time, which was the only one in the county. It was edited by Samuel Louden, who had fled from New York city when the British took possession of it, and he here established his press at the place now the residence of John C. Van Wyck. Before Washington left Fishkill, Dixon had an opportunity to make another visit at the residence of

Captain Swart, and as he knew he would be obliged to take leave soon, he resolved to lose no time in making his business known; and as a favorable opportunity offered, he addressed himself to his dear Amelia, telling her the object of his visit, that he had come to offer himself to her, and desired to know at once her conclusion, as his time would not admit of any delay. Amelia admired the appearance of the young officer, for he was uniformed in a style becoming his high rank, and he had letters from his native State showing that he belonged to some of the first families. Amelia was much agitated at the sudden proposal, and her whole frame was convulsed with tremor. She hesitated for a time, deeming her acquaintance so very short, though he was unquestionably an officer of rank and related to distinguished families in Virginia, and she at length suggested that if he would resign his commission and retire to his plantation, she would consent to marry him, to which he readily assented. Dixon lost no time in tendering to Washington his resignation, which was accepted, and the marriage ceremony soon took place, Dixon and Amelia soon leaving for his native State. They settled on his large plantation, where they lived the remainder of their days in peace and happiness.

Captain Swart had several sons, who as they grew up became intemperate and great spendthrifts, who wasted his property, and at the close of the war of 1812 he died. His family soon spent the remainder of his property, and left for parts unknown, and the name has become extinct in the town of Fishkill.

FARMER JONES;

OR, THE DISCONTENTED MAN.

All mankind are in pursuit of happiness, and how many different ways do men pursue it. Some pursuing one vocation, some another. "How few, alas, possess it in this world," thought farmer Jones, as, he returned home from the labors of the day. It was the season of haying and harvesting, and farmer Jones had been swinging his scythe all day through his big meadow, as he called it, with his workmen; for he wanted to finish his haying that week. He had been a long month engaged in his harvest and hay, and he was worn down with the severe labor of that busy season. Mowing was then done with the scythe, for it was before the invention of mowing machines, and the labor of getting hay was more laborious than at the present day. Farmer Jones' home was always made pleasant to him, for his wife was industrious, and she knew that her husband was tired and she had supper ready as soon as he and his workmen arrived. She, too, was tired of the busy season of haying, for her husband employed several extra workmen, and as soon as the haying season was over they would be discharged. Farmer Jones had never been engaged in any business but farming. Born and reared a farmer, he thought it a laborious life. He often contrasted his situation with the glove-handed, learned professional man, and the broadcloth merchant, and thought if he had studied for a profession, or was engaged in the mercantile business, how pleasant life would be to him. Mr. Jones was one of those thrifty farmers who tended strictly to his business, and his farm being under thorough cultivation, rewarded him. He seldom contracted a debt, and he always had a surplus at the end of the year. Placed as he was beyond the reach of want, and never necessitated for money, he knew but little of the harrassing cares of the learned professional man and the merchant. Mrs. Jones, too, was frugal and careful in the management of her household affairs. In her dairy and poultry yard large profits were realized, and her daughters were taught the lesson that industry and economy is the road to wealth. But the times were changing, for farmer Jones and his wife thought that labor was getting disreputable. Their neighbors, Mr. Smith's sons and daughters, lived without work, and his son John had a fine carriage and horse to ride out, and he had just purchased a piano for his daughter Mary, and Jacob had gone into the mercantile business. Mrs. Jones thought they could purchase a carriage for their son James, and a piano for Sarah; and could afford those luxuries as well as their neighbors. Farmer Jones was pleased with the idea, and he thought to himself that he had been successful in farming; but his life had been one of incessant toil, and not occupying a position in society as he thought with the learned profession and the merchant, he concluded not to let his children follow his honest and honorable calling. Farmer Jones' means were sufficient to purchase a carriage for his sons, and a piano for his daughter, nor was there any wrong in so doing. But he concluded not to bring them up to toil on the farm as he had been. Accordingly he sent his eldest son, Nathan, to the city of New York, having procured him a situation as a clerk in an old established firm then doing business in Front street. Nathan was the youngest clerk, but his duties were neither arduous nor many, and he had many leisure hours which he spent in reading, and writing letters to his parents, contrasting the difference between the farmer and the merchant, stating what drudgery and physical labor the farmer had to undergo which the merchant knew nothing of. Nathan had not yet learned the risks of mercantile life. He little knew that instances had often occurred, of the merchant being worth his thousands and tens of thousands to-day and a bankrupt to-morrow. Farmer Jones, too, was wholly ignorant of the mercantile disasters that so frequently occur. He had often read of failures, but he thought they were only a few isolated cases compared with the number that were successful. He was happy to think that his son was so well pleased in his new situation, for he thought that he had a business talent, and now he would be soon on the road to wealth and happiness. Nathan studied to please his employers, for he did not wish to lose his situation. He attended strictly to business, and in a few years he was advanced to first clerk in the establishment, with a salary of one thousand dollars per annum. Farmer Jones was highly pleased with his son, when he was informed by letter that he was first clerk in the firm, and he anticipated that he would live to see the time that Nathan would be one of those merchant princes living in Fifth Avenue, or occupying a country seat on the noble Hudson. Nathan had been only one year first clerk when the senior partner of the firm wishing to retire from business, an opportunity presented itself to Nathan to become a partner in the firm, which the junior partners gladly accepted. Nathan wrote home to his father, relating all the facts of the dissolution, and that an opportunity was now offered which ought not to be lost. Only $10,000 was now wanting for him to become a partner in an old established firm doing business in Front street. Farmer Jones read the letter with avidity, for he thought his expectations would be realized. He had that amount of money invested in bonds and mortgages on farming land, yielding him seven per cent. per annum. It would, thought he, take all my surplus, but my farm I have, which will afford me a good living, and farming is a calling which my sons shall not follow. I will not have them drudge for a living as I have done, and Nathan offers to take James as a clerk in the firm. He is old enough, so he says, and I will advance him the money. Farmer Jones found no difficulty in raising the money, for his personal property was all first class mortgages on unincumbered real estate, and he wrote to his son Nathan that the money would be forthcoming as soon as the new firm was established. Nathan soon received his father's letter informing him to make all necessary business arrangements, and the new firm commenced under favorable auspices the first of February.

Farmer Jones now experienced that happiness which most men do at some period of their lives who have lived to the age of three score. Through all the troubles which we pass in this turbulent world there are times when we are happy, when every sorrow is banished, and every trial ended. But alas! how little do we think that happiness is often evanescent and transitory. The phantom that farmer Jones sought with such unremitting assiduity eluded his grasp; and when he reached his hand to take the cup she extended, he found the long expected draught strongly tinctured with the bitter dregs of disappointment. If he and his family had been contented when engaged in this rural occupation, how much more prosperous and happy they would have been, as the sequel will show. Contentment will blunt the arrows of adversity so that they can not materially harm us. That, with religion, will smooth the rough paths, and tread to earth those thorns that we must expect to meet as we journey onward to the appointed goal. She will soften the pains of sickness, and she will be with us even in the cold gloomy hour of death, cheering us with the smiles of her heaven-born affection. Hope leads us triumphant to a blissful eternity. Farmer Jones had several sons and daughters, and he knew that he could not give his son Nathan $10,000, and all his children the same, for he was not worth that amount of property, but he thought that Nathan would soon realize a fortune, and then he could refund part of the money, for his income now depended wholly on his farm, and that barely supported him. Farmer Jones was now living in fashionable life. His two sons that lived home had their carriages and fast horses and lived without labor. His daughters had long ago despised the labors of the kitchen, and their time was mostly spent in the parlor receiving calls and in spinning street yarn. The poultry yard was neglected, and the large dairy which he formerly kept was so diminished that they hardly made butter enough for their own consumption. The farm was worked on shares, and the crops were scanty and sometimes a total failure, and farmer Jones began to feel the want of money. He now began to think that farming was a poor business, and the money that his farm would sell for he thought would be worth more to him if safely invested, and then himself and family could live at their ease, and his two sons that lived home might get in some genteel business which would be far more respectable than farming. His son Nathan was doing a good business in New York, and James was a clerk in the same house, and he hoped that his two sons home would find some lucrative employment which would elevate them above the farmer. Nathan often wrote home to his parents, informing them of the amount of business they were doing, and the large profits realized. They had sold west on credit, goods amounting to some hundred thousands of dollars. But a financial crisis at last came. The money due them west could not be collected. They had sent agents west and they informed them by letter that most of their creditors were insolvent. Their notes were becoming due, and they had no money to meet them. Nathan wrote home to his father, informing him that on the goods they sold west the money could not be collected, and that their notes must be met or they would have to make an assignment. If he would endorse their paper it might save them, and there would be no immediate danger, and if there was they would certainly secure him. Farmer Jones now began to experience trouble. His $10,000 was in the firm, and now they wanted him to endorse their paper, probably to a large amount, and he thought it a hazardous undertaking. He now felt the want of money, for his bonds and mortgages were all gone, his farm, his fences and buildings were in a dilapidated state. He thought of the time when he was working in his fields, toiling through the heat of summer, enduring the labor on his farm, and often would see the learned professional man and the merchant, the dandy and the professional loafer, dressed in their fine apparel, and he was unhappy. But now his mind had changed. Ten years ago he did not owe one dollar, and he had his thousands out at interest. Now all his money was in his son's possession in the city of New York, and he thought under present circumstances, it would be lost. Oh, how he regretted that Nathan went to the city. If he had only purchased a farm, thought he, and settled him on it, and pursued that course with his children, and trained them up to useful labor as he was, and commenced life as he had, how much better would be his situation now. To endorse for the firm might make him a bankrupt, and could he think of being destitute in the decline of life, when only a few years ago he had, exclusive of his farm, $10,000. Such thoughts gave him many sleepless nights. Farmer Jones had spared no pains or expense in giving his family a good education in the English branches, which fitted them for every qualification in life. If he had stopped there, if he had not taught them that labor was disrespectful, he would have escaped the mental agony that he was now suffering. He finally wrote to Nathan that he had done all for him that he could without incurring the risk of losing all his property, and they must expect no more favors from him. If the firm could not survive without his endorsing their paper, if they could not get help from some other source, and they should be obliged to make an assignment, they must try to save enough out of the wreck to pay him his demands.

When Nathan received his father's letter and read the contents to the firm, they abandoned all hopes of sustaining themselves. The money due them west was nearly all irrecoverably lost, and their notes were becoming due which they could not meet, and they finally made an assignment. The failure proved to be a bad one, and Farmer Jones' $10,000 went with the rest; and when he was informed of the failure, and that the money that he had let Nathan have was lost, he was melancholy. His family now was earning him nothing, and he had contracted debts with the merchants, mechanics and laborers which he was unable to pay. His house and outbuildings needed repairs, and when he thought of the time when he had an income of $700 exclusive of his farm, and did not owe one cent, his anguish of mind was indescribable.

Farmer Jones now began to think that the merchant, with all his fine exterior, was often times, if his debts were paid, worth nothing, and his opinion of the learned professions was but little better, and that the farmer, situated as he was ten years ago, was the happiest being in the world. Farmer Jones now perceived that he had mistaken ideas of the happiness of man and of his calling. He was now in the decline of life, for he had passed the age of three score years, but he was determined to retrace his steps, to go back to the old primitive landmarks of living. That industry which had been taught him by his father he now began to instill in his children. Farmer Jones never showed a miserly disposition in his most prosperous days. His friends and neighbors that paid him a visit were received with kindness, and he always had leisure to entertain them, but himself and family in those days never eat the bread of idleness.

The firm that Nathan was a partner in, closed up their business, and he and James remained in the city as clerks, receiving a salary sufficient for their support. Farmer Jones and his two sons at home commenced business anew. They applied their industry to the farm, and his daughters attended to the duties of the household. The dairy was enlarged and the poultry yard was not neglected. The buildings and fences were repaired, and soon farmer Jones began to have a surplus. He was too far advanced in life to have the supervision of his farm, but his two sons, John and Cyrus, managed the farm so economically, that at the end of the year there was a handsome dividend. Farmer Jones was happy in his old age, envying none of the learned professions nor the broadcloth merchants. He could sit under his own vine and fig tree, none to molest nor make him afraid. Not depriving himself and family of anything that was necessary for their comfort and happiness, they had their carriages and fine horses, and the girls their piano and fine furniture, but it did not embarrass him, for the industry that he taught his family purchased these articles, and when a friend called to see him, every effort was made by the family to make him happy. Farmer Jones lived to see the day that he was in affluent circumstances again, and his two sons married and settled around him on substantial farms. His daughters, too, married farmers who were industrious and thriving, and they eventually became wealthy.

THE MECHANIC'S WIFE.

It was the gloomy month of November, and a drizzling rain had continued for several days, with a chilly wind from the northeast making everything look dreary without. Mrs. Strong was sitting close to the window in her little room, watching the people who were obliged to be exposed to the weather, for the traveling was very unpleasant. The falling rain had made the streets wet and slippery, for the atmosphere had now become freezing, and Mrs. Strong was happy to think that she was so comfortably situated. Her infant was lying in the cradle close by a warm stove, sleeping soundly. Yet anxiety was depicted in her countenance, which showed that she was laboring under mental inquietude. Her husband, who was a carpenter, had, by industry and economy, with her assistance, acquired their little home, and surrounded the yard with flowers and creeping vines, which Mrs. Strong had carefully arranged with her own labor, for her husband employed his time working at his trade. Mr. Strong was a finished workman, and a master builder, residing in the flourishing village of Utica. He had commenced the world with nothing, and marrying in early life, he and family removed to Utica in 1813, then a village containing a population of 1700 souls. Mrs. Strong, the reader may imagine, was an heir of poverty. On the contrary, she was the only daughter of wealthy parents, living in one of our eastern cities, highly accomplished and educated. She was the idol of her parents, and no pains had been spared to place her on the pinnacle of fashionable society. Mr. Strong was employed to do some work for her father, where she first became acquainted with him, when they became ardently attached to each other. When her father discovered the attachment, he paid Mr. Strong for services rendered, and discharged him. But Mr. Strong was not to be defeated. Watching his opportunity he secretly corresponded with her, and an hour was appointed for him to meet her in a solitary place, and she eloped with him to the above village.

Western New York then was comparatively new, and there was no conveyance west except by stages, for then there was no canal or railroad to convey travelers west. Many years after Mr. Strong settled in Utica, the Erie Canal was completed through the State from Albany to Buffalo, a distance of three hundred and sixty miles, which opened a way for the transportation of the products of western New York. Prior to that there was no other way to transport the farmers' produce but by large covered wagons holding sixty or seventy bushels of wheat and drawn by four horses, and occupying several days before reaching Albany. But the completion of the Erie Canal tapped those rich agricultural counties west of Cayuga Lake, and transported the grain to Albany by canal and the Hudson river to the sea board. This caused the forests to fall before the ax of the sturdy pioneer, and the plough of civilization was soon tossing up the bones of the aborigines. Where the Indian had so long dwelt in his wigwam, and roved through the fertile valleys of the Genesee country, where for years he had held undisputed sway, was now fast becoming the habitation of civilized man. Cities and villages sprung up like magic, and the village of Utica increased so rapidly in population that in February, 1832, it was incorporated a city.

When Mr. Strong first emigrated to Utica he soon found employment, and business increased so fast that only two years had elapsed when he owned the home alluded to in the commencement of this story. Mrs. Strong was happy during those two years. She had married contrary to the wishes of her parents, but the only objection they had to Mr. Strong was that he was a poor mechanic, and as she was the daughter of wealthy parents they would not consent. She was informed that her parents knew where she lived, but she had never received a letter from them. Mrs. Strong was perfectly happy in the first year of her marriage. But now a great change had taken place. Her husband used to spend his evenings at home, but becoming fond of the intoxicating bowl, he associated with dissolute company at the ale house; and would come home late at night intoxicated.

Mrs. Strong looked out of the window, watching the passers-by till darkness set in, then lighted the candle, seating herself by her babe, and commenced sewing. The storm had increased and she heard the wind whistling and the rain falling. She thought to herself how happy she would be if her husband would spend his evenings at home. As the evening advanced her anxiety increased, for the storm was raging with great violence. Presently the noise of footsteps was heard, and then a loud knock at the door. But oh, what was her surprise when she saw her husband borne home by two of his old companions, less intoxicated than himself. They quietly shut the door, leaving Mr. Strong lying on the floor, his clothes dripping wet, for they had missed their way and had been exposed to the cold storm for some time. Mrs. Strong had seen her husband intoxicated before, but she had not till then seen him perfectly helpless. She had hoped till then that he would reform, but now the hope had forsaken her, and she began to experience a drunkard's home. Her husband now spent most of his earnings at the ale house, and she thought to herself as she saw him lying intoxicated before her, "Must we lose our home—must we contend with poverty?"

Intoxicating drinks then were sold in every place throughout the country. In every borough, hamlet, inn, store and grocery, could be seen decanters filled with liquors, and intemperance prevailed among all classes. The mechanic used it in his workshop, the farmer in his field, the merchant in his counting-room, the professional man in his study, and the laborer at his work. Temperance societies then had not been introduced, and could we wonder that Mr. Strong did not reform. Gradually did the habit steal upon him, and he would come home and abuse that same wife that he had sworn at the marriage altar to cherish, to protect, and to love. Mrs. Strong's future prospects were gloomy, for she had incurred the displeasure of her parents in marrying contrary to their wishes, and probably the doors of her father's house would forever be closed against her. Every comfort that she had enjoyed she was gradually being deprived of, for her husband would spend everything he could get to purchase rum, and at last mortgaged his home to the rumseller. How scarred and dead and callous must be the heart of man that will deal out the fatal poison to his fellow men. The rumseller's darling object is money, and it matters not to him how he gets it. Does he ever think of the widows and orphans that he has made, that a day of reckoning will come, and that he will surely meet divine retribution.

Mrs. Strong was sitting one evening in her little room, in the month of May, with her three small children around her, and her countenance was care-worn. She had sustained the hardships of emigration, and the privations of poverty, the burdens of increasing toil and unrequitted care, without murmuring. She had seen him whom her heart's affection had garnered up, become a prey to vice. She had left the home of her birth, and she had written to her parents informing them of her situation and the utter destitution, the squalid penury, and the heart-rending agony of mind she was now suffering. The letter would have melted a heart of stone, but it was in vain that she looked for an answer, for her parents spurned her entreaties with indignation. Sometimes I think there is so little love and charity existing between man and man, that the whole world before me appears a barren waste. Pardon me, ye dear spirits of benevolence, for making this assertion, for your benign smiles and cheerful giving hand have strewed sweet flowers on many a thorny path which my fate has forced me to pass. Think not that in thus condemning I forget the spring whence flow all the blessings I have enjoyed from you. Oh no, I look up to you as bright constellations gathering new splendors from the surrounding darkness. But ah, while I adore those benignant rays that cheer and illuminate, I mourn to think that your influence does not extend to all the sons and daughters of affliction.

Mrs. Strong put her three children to sleep, and waited with unceasing anxiety for her husband. Midnight was fast approaching, and occasionally she would hear the noise of footsteps, but they gradually died away. Her husband had never remained away from home so late before. The clock told the hour of midnight and he had not arrived. With a heart crushed with grief she retired to rest. Oh what a night that was to her, for she thought that she would never see him again alive. Sleep had fled from her eyes. She thought of home, the image of her parents was before her, that mother that had watched over her from her earliest recollection to the day that she left the parental roof. For her welfare she had been never weary, and the arms of her love were continually around her. Would they refuse their Mary, thought she, if she was obliged to go home, merely for marrying a poor mechanic, and send her and her three children out in a cold and unfeeling world. Such thoughts as these filled her soul with intense agony, and her tears fell like rain drops. But the dreary night passed away and the morning came with no tidings of her absent husband. News soon spread through the village that Mr. Strong was missing. A search was immediately made and at the close of the following day he was found in the canal. He had been drowned, as it was supposed, during the darkness of the night, when returning from the ale house. Venturing too near the brink of the canal while intoxicated, he probably lost his balance and fell in. Late in the afternoon Mrs. Strong's attention was arrested by a group coming slowly through the main street. A terrible foreboding came over her. She thought they bore a corpse. It was indeed the corpse of her husband. Utter prostration of spirit came over the desolate mourner.

With heaviness of heart was the victim of intemperance borne from the house and laid in a drunkard's grave, and there we leave him. It may be asked, "Did the rumseller shed tears of contrition." No, his heart was adamant, and but a few months elapsed when he foreclosed the mortgage he held against Mr. Strong, and purchased the property and sent Mrs. Strong and her three little ones to get a living on the cold charities of the world. Mrs. Strong's situation was now painful in the extreme, for her cup of sorrow was filled to the brim, and she was compelled to drink from the very bottom of that cup the bitter dregs of trouble. But yet there was a ray of hope.

Her husband in the year 1817 purchased a small tract of new land in Erie county, near where the city of Buffalo is now located, and she resolved on trying to get a living there. Having saved a little money from the proceeds of her house in Utica, which the rumseller purchased under foreclosure, she took the stage for Buffalo in May, 1822. Buffalo then contained only two hundred and fifty dwellings and a population of some two thousand inhabitants. Mrs. Strong's lands lay but a few miles from the village, and on arriving there she found a log house which had been built by a squatter who had abandoned it. Mrs. Strong and her three children took possession of their new home. Her eldest son Charles was now old enough to assist her in the labor of enclosing a yard around her dwelling. Having purchased a few farming implements from Buffalo, Mrs. Strong commenced cultivating the soil. A kind neighbor gratuitously broke up several acres of ground for her with his ox team, and she and her son Charles planted it with corn. With the products of her garden and a little assistance from a kind neighbor, and what few productions she gathered from the woods, for the farm was mostly covered with forest, she managed to get along very comfortably. She did not get her corn planted till the last week in May, but the fall being favorable the crop matured, and she had a plentiful corn harvest. Little Charles and herself gathered the crop and secured the stalks, and with the proceeds of the corn crop she purchased an ox team for the coming spring. But the next year the Erie canal was completed, and it greatly developed the resources of Buffalo, and in 1832, only ten years after Mrs. Strong settled there, it became a city containing a population of 18,000 souls. The completion of the Erie canal greatly enhanced the value of land, and Mrs. Strong's farm lying near the village of Buffalo and the Erie canal, soon quadrupled in value. As her children grew up they became very useful to her. Her sons Charles and Jacob soon leveled the forest, and converted it into meadows and wheat fields, and after a lapse of years they erected a splendid dwelling and substantial outbuildings. Mrs. Strong lived there in the decline of life surrounded with everything that luxury could desire, with three interesting children around her. She never visited her native place after she married. She had written several pathetic letters to her parents when she was in reduced circumstances, stating her misfortunes and trials, but she received no answer to those letters, and now her parents were no more. They had gone to that bourne from whence no traveler returns, and she did not inherit any of her parent's property. But a kind providence had provided for her. Thirty years more had passed away and the city of Buffalo contained 29,773 inhabitants, and Mrs. Strong was still living at an advanced age, and her farm within rifle shot of the city, the great commercial emporium of Western New York. Seventeen years more Buffalo contained nearly 90,000 inhabitants, and the farm that Mrs. Strong owned was within the suburbs of the city. But the Mechanic's Wife is no more. She lived to a good old age, and went down to the grave like a shock ripe for the harvest.

FARMERS THRIFTY AND UNTHRIFTY.

It was the beginning of April and the warm sun had dissolved the snow, and the verdure had again commenced clothing the trees and fields. The spring birds were warbling in the groves and hedges, and farmer Unthrifty was getting his ploughs and plough harness in order so as to be ready to commence turning up the earth as soon as the frost was out and the soil was sufficiently warm. The winter had been cold and dreary, for the snow had fallen early and deep, and farmer Unthrifty was fearful that his provender would not last till his grass in the fields was sufficient to supply his cattle and horses with food. He had wintered a large amount of stock, and now he had commenced stinting them in their food so that they were meagre. The horses and oxen with which he intended to break up his corn ground had not sufficient strength to work through the day, and if he should increase their feed, so as to enable them to gain sufficient strength to perform the labor easy, he would be obliged to purchase hay and grain before the foddering season was over. This farmer Unthrifty did not wish to do, for he was in debt, and the first of May he had interest money to pay, and he must try and get along as economical as possible. Farmer Unthrifty was one of those farmers that always overstocked their farms. His pasture fields were always fed close in summer, and in the winter his cattle and horses were fed on short allowance, and in the spring his working teams were too feeble to perform much labor. His crops were scanty and his dairy yielded him poor returns, so that he was always pinched for money. His farm contained two hundred acres of land and was mortgaged for only $2,000. He was oftentimes unable to pay his interest when due. Farmer Unthrifty was a man of good habits, industrious and economical, and his family thought he was frugal in the management of his business, and they had toiled hard for years on his farm without making one cent to pay the principal. Their neighbor, farmer Thrifty, had a farm now free of incumbrance, and ten years ago he paid more interest money than Unthrifty, and himself and family toiled no harder, nor economised no more. This farmer Unthrifty did not understand, for Thrifty's farm was not so large as his, and when his interest came due he paid it promptly, and two or more hundred dollars on the principal, and now he owed no man.

Farmer Thrifty's farm naturally was no better than Unthrifty's, but it was the manner in which he cultivated his farm which made him so much more successful. He did not keep as much stock as farmer Unthrifty, but his horses and cattle were well fed and housed in winter, and had abundant pasture in summer. In the spring every farming utensil that farmer Thrifty had was in order; his ploughs, his harrows, his plough harness were seen to, the horses and oxen with which he intended to break up his corn ground were well provided with hay and provender, so that when he commenced ploughing in the spring his team would perform double the labor of Unthrifty's team. Farmer Unthrifty had to pay the same wages for workmen as his neighbor Thrifty, and his horses and oxen were scarcely able to drag the plough. His workmen were always behind, and it was so late before he finished planting his corn that often the Autumnal frosts destroyed the crop before it was sufficiently matured. His farm was so poorly fenced that his cattle often broke through their inclosures and destroyed his grain, and in the spring of the year he was obliged to let them rove over his mowing grounds in order to lengthen out his hay. This caused his hay crop to be poor and scanty. His dwelling house and outbuildings were in a dilapidated state, and he had not the means to repair them. But on the contrary, farmer Thrifty's farm was in a high state of cultivation. His crops were abundant and his fences were sufficient to protect his crops, and his cattle were so well provided with good pasture, that they were not taught to be unruly. He seeded heavily with clover and timothy, and sowed his grass lands with plaster. This, with what manure he could make, and sometimes leaves from his forest, and muck from his low grounds, his farm was enhanced in value every year. The two farmers had commenced the world in straitened circumstances. One was now wealthy, the other no better off than when he first commenced business for himself. Farmer Unthrifty was sitting one day, in the month of July, under the shade of a large forest tree. The sun darted its fiercest rays over the earth, and his workmen made slow progress, as the weather was intensely hot. He was thinking how unsuccessful he had been in farming. He was in no better circumstances than when he commenced life. He had often deprived himself and family of comforts, and this to him was very painful. His neighbor Thrifty's family dressed better, and had everything for their comfort and happiness. His farm, his buildings and fences were in order, and with all the outlays on his farm he was free of debt and now had money at interest, and ten years ago his situation was no better than his. Seated as he was, his face buried in his hands, he heard the noise of approaching footsteps, and looking up saw neighbor Thrifty near by. Farmer Thrifty accosted him at the same time, remarking that he felt careworn and thought that he must feel unwell. "No," said Unthrifty, "I was thinking how we commenced life. Our circumstances were much the same, and my farm, I thought, was naturally as good as yours. We purchased our farms the same year, and we commenced farming then, and I have been industrious and more economical than you. I have denied myself and family many comforts which yourself and family have, which has caused me many hours of sorrow, and I am informed that you cancelled the mortgage on your farm last May, and now have become a money loaner. Your family has been larger than mine, your farm and buildings are in good repair, and mine are going to decay, and the mortgage on my farm now is the same as when we commenced to be farmers." Farmer Thrifty listened very attentively as Unthrifty related his story, and he felt grieved to hear him relate his ill success in farming. He saw years ago that he lacked judgment, and he thought if he did not exercise more skill in the management of his farm he would never live to see the time when he would be free from debt. Farmer Thrifty was one of those men that never interfered with his neighbor's business, and could often times have given his neighbor Unthrifty advice, but he thought that he might receive it unkindly. But now he had opened the way for him to give him some friendly advice. He informed Unthrifty that for years he had seen his bad management; that the process he had practised for years impoverished his farm; that he kept too many cattle and horses; he seeded so sparingly that he had little or no pasture in summer; his hay crop was so light that his stock was stinted in their food through the winter, and he lost more or less cattle in the spring from starvation, and those cattle that survived the winter it required the whole summer to get in a thriving condition. By constant tillage and the exhausting of crops, his farm was impoverished. Half the stock on his farm well wintered and summered would afford him double the profit. And ploughing half the number of acres with good teams, thoroughly cultivated and well manured, he would raise twice the number of bushels of grain with half the labor. He would have more grain and more butter to sell. With double the quantity of seed and plaster, and taking pains to collect manure, his farm would soon enhance in value and he would have means sufficient to repair his buildings and fences and pay his interest when due, and a hundred or more dollars on the principal. Farmer Unthrifty had never thought till now that he erred in judgment. His neighbor Thrifty had enlightened him, and the information that he had just received he thought that he would profit by. He thanked him for imparting that knowledge to him, and when they separated he promised his neighbor Thrifty that he would lend him a helping hand if he would assist him in the management of his farm, so at the commencement of another year he would be able to reduce the mortgage on his farm.

It was again spring, and another long winter had passed, and farmer Unthrifty was again making preparations to resume his spring ploughing. The balmy days of April had come and the warm zephyrs were wafting their soft breezes over the face of nature. Everything indicated an early spring. The bilberry was in full blossom, the tulip tree had unfolded its buds, and the purple willow was shooting forth its tender branches. Farmer Unthrifty had commenced turning up the earth and preparing his corn ground to receive the seed. His horses and oxen that were performing the labor were in a thriving condition, for Unthrifty had turned over a new leaf in farming. He had reduced his stock to half the original number, and now he had a sufficient quantity of hay and provender to feed his cattle and horses without stinting them, so that he was not obliged to turn them on his mowing grounds or feed off his pasture fields so early that he would have no feed for his cows in summer and autumn. Farmer Unthrifty had given his corn ground a thorough top dressing of manure, which he had taken great pains to collect, and he had surrounded it with a fence sufficient to protect the crop from being destroyed by unruly cattle, which had always more or less injured his grain ever since he had commenced farming. His grounds which were to receive his spring crops were prepared with great care, and his corn was planted in season. The instructions which he had received from his neighbor, farmer Thrifty, now began to be a source of profit to him, for his dairy yielded him large returns. His cows had been well wintered and now they had pasture abundant, and farmer Unthrifty had cultivated his garden and his farm with the greatest care. Farmer Unthrifty's courage began to revive as he looked over his farm, for he saw his fields of grain waving to the breeze, and he waited with patience for the coming harvest, and with what joy did he hail the time when his harvest was ripe and ready for the work and he was gathering his sheaves in his garners. His corn, too, of which he formerly lost more or less by the early frost, had now thoroughly matured, and the stalks were well secured from the autumnal rains. Farmer Unthrifty had cut a larger hay crop, cau   by keeping his cattle off his mowing grounds in the   , and the profits which he realized from the proceeds of his beef cattle and dairy were double that of any former year.

The first of May was again approaching, for the winter had passed, but farmer Unthrifty had different feelings than formerly. He had his interest ready and a payment to make on the principal. When the first of May arrived, it was to farmer Unthrifty a happy season, for he paid his interest and two hundred and fifty dollars on the principal, the first payment he had made since he purchased his farm. It so revived his drooping spirits that he redoubled his energies and he informed his neighbor Thrifty of his success.

Farmer Thrifty was not disappointed, for he saw the decided improvement that Unthrifty had made in farming the past year. His farm was enhancing in value, for he was building fences, clearing his farm of bushes that he had suffered to grow and encroach upon his grass and plough lands for years. He had reclaimed his swamps and converted many acres into fruitful fields, and he was now repairing his dwelling houses and outbuildings. He had seeded his farm heavily with clover and timothy, and sowed his grass land with plaster. Farmer Unthrifty had taken great pains in the cultivation of his crops and in the improvement of his dairy, thus enabling him to have a large surplus of corn and wheat and butter, which he sold at a fair price, and with the money he made those improvements and paid his interest promptly and reduced the mortgage on his farm, which for ten years had made himself and family labor hard, while he could only pay the interest. Farmer Unthrifty continued to improve in the management of his farm, and he at length became so thoroughly master of farming that he canceled the mortgage upon his farm in less number of years than Farmer Thrifty, after he had made the first payment on the principal, and now he was in affluent circumstances. The two farmers in the decline of life were wealthy, and were living on substantial farms at their ease, for their children had taken their places, and had relieved them of the cares and business of life, and their latter days were the most prosperous and happy.

Who can describe the happiness that reigns around the home of a thrifty farmer. It has been well said that agriculture is the most useful and noblest occupation of man, for it is the cultivation of the soil that distinguishes the civilized man from the savage. Without it, Daniel Webster says, man must have lived on a scanty supply of roots and berries, and yet how many of the rising generation who have been rural born have left their homes and farms and rushed to the great metropolis for the glittering chances of mercantile life. Hard chances, too, many have found them. Some have been driven to the docks and even beyond; a plunge into the dark roaring waters has been their refuge and oblivion. If the youth of our country who have been reared on farms handed down to them by their fathers, would be contented in following their honorable calling, and become masters of their business, as the two farmers in this story, they would occupy a higher position in society, and probably in the decline of life be in more affluent circumstances than if they had studied for the learned professions, or had engaged in mercantile life. Before the Norman conquest, famines were frequent in Britain, in consequence of the neglect of agriculture, but after the conquest of England by William of Normandy, the agriculture of the country was improved. The Normans introduced instruments of husbandry, such as carts, harrows, ploughs and sickles. This soon improved the condition of the Briton, and enabled him to take his place among the great nations of the earth, and now the sun never sets on his dominions. Agriculture, then, is the bulwark of every nation. Neglect it and commerce will become annihilated, large cities dwindle into insignificance, and man will recede into barbarism.

THE OLD FARM HOUSE.

Just after the close of the Revolution, the inhabitants of the thirteen states were poor, and the cities they contained were small. The population of the largest did not exceed thirty thousand, and, like the villages, were few in number. Ohio and Michigan were then a wilderness. Illinois, Wisconsin and Iowa were immense prairies, inhabited by savages and beasts of prey, and even New York, west of the Mohawk Flats, was a dense forest, the habitation of the Six Nations of Indians. The counties located on the Hudson river furnished the city of New York with her supply of grain and provisions, and those counties contained but a few villages. Large landholders occupied the soil and most of them were the owners of slaves. Some Dutch farmers owned a score. Their houses, many of them, were built of stone, and were only one story in height, with steep roofs, and large fire places taking in wood cord length. But few of their houses were painted, and their floors were without carpets. They had no carriages or one horse wagons—only heavy lumber wagons, and many farmers had but one, with no seats but sitting chairs taken from the house. The lines and traces of their harness were of rope, and with such wagons and harness they would go to church.

Their clothing was mostly of their own manufacture. Such was the condition of the inhabitants of Dutchess county before the year 1800. But the reader must not imagine that they were destitute of the solid comforts of life. They had everything that the soil produced in the greatest profusion. Wheat, corn, vegetables, poultry and fruit in abundance. As luxury had not then been introduced amongst them, they needed but little money, and the Dutch farmers were then in more comfortable circumstances in that respect than many nabobs of the fast living age of the present day. They often visited each other, and as neighbors were kind and obliging, and during the long and severe winters the young people would meet together and spend the evenings in cultivating friendship. They would dance and sing, and have various amusements, and thus the winters would pass pleasantly away.

In a certain section in Dutchess county, formerly stood a Dutch farm house. The owner of it had a large farm, containing several hundred acres of land, and owned a number of slaves. His dwelling house and barn were built in ancient Dutch style, with very steep roof, and his house was only one story in height. The kitchen was located lower than the house, and it required two or more steps to ascend to reach the large room wherein the family lived. This kitchen was occupied by negro slaves. Richard Snadaker— for that was his name—lived in the simple style of Dutch farmers of the latter part of the eighteenth century. He had married in early life and had a large family; and with his slave labor his farm was well cultivated. It produced him abundance of grain, cattle and fruit, and supplied most of his wants, for himself, family and slaves never eat the bread of idleness. Richard Snadaker was a christian, and every clear Sabbath morning he would get up his large wagon and take his family and slaves to church. Churches then were few and far between, and Richard Snadaker lived several miles from New Hackensack church, the place where he attended and worshiped.

The nearest neighbor to Richard Snadaker was Petres Vosburgh, and they were both born and reared on their farms. Petres had an only son, whose name was Hendrick, and he endeavored to give him a good education in the useful branches, such as writing, reading, spelling and mathematics, for then there were no district schools in Dutchess county. The inhabitants then hired a teacher, who charged for a scholar a certain sum of money per quarter, fuel and other incidental expenses included. As Richard Snadaker had several sons and daughters to send to school, himself, Vosburgh, and several of their neighbors, hired a teacher for the winter season, for we must remember that our Dutch forefathers paid great attention to the education of their children, and none more so than Petres Vosburgh and Richard Snadaker. The winters then in Dutchess county were generally severe, and the snow would often fall early and deep, and the wind would whirl it in eddies, and pile it up in drifts across the highways and often render them impassible, and it would be difficult for the scholars to get to the schoolhouse. But no weather hindered Hendrick Vosburgh. He would mount the snowdrift, and brave the cold winter to get to school, for he loved education and he was an apt scholar. Often would he go to Richard Snadaker's and persuade the children to go to school when they thought the weather too cold and stormy, and often would he break the path and help the girls over snowdrifts, when going to school, and after the school was dismissed he would assist them in getting home. Hendrick Vosburgh was of a kind disposition and often would he visit Richard Snadaker's, and many an evening would he spend there pleasantly with his family.

Years had now rolled away and Susan Snadaker was the girl that Hendrick had so often assisted through the snowdrifts to get to school, and she had now grown up to rosy womanhood, and he had become ardently attached to her. On one cold winter day, Richard Snadaker and family had returned from church and the remainder of the Sabbath he sat in his large room reading his Dutch Bible, and Susan had a fire built in the parlor, and the floor had been cleaned and sanded. The large fireplace was piled full with hickory wood, and the smoke was curling up the chimney and she sat there alone, occasionally looking out of the window, as if expecting some one. The wind was whistling over the snow, and twilight was fast disappearing from the vision, when in the distance a horseman was seen approaching. Susan watched with intense interest as he drew near, and she was not disappointed. It was Hendrick Vosburgh. He dismounted, and Pompey, the negro slave, soon had his horse safe in the stable, and Hendrick was soon comfortably seated in the parlor. The large hickory fire was blazing upon the hearth, and Susan ordered Pompey to fetch in more hickory wood to supply the fire. Darkness had now spread over the landscape, and the family had retired for the night, and nothing was heard but the wind howling through the locust trees that stood around the farm house. Susan often replenished the fire, for the cold without was intense. The Sabbath had passed, and strange to say, Hendrick had not made the attempt to leave. As often as he had visited Richard Snadaker's he had never prolonged his visits, and now, as if unconscious of time, the hours passed by unheeded. He sat in the large jamb in the fireplace, for the hickory wood was all consumed, and the large fire which blazed so freely in the evening, now exhibited nothing but a few embers and a heap of ashes. The candle had burnt down to the socket in its stick, and the conversation had partially subsided. A cooler atmosphere began to pervade the room, and he did not make known his business to Susan until the gray dawn of the morning was breaking up the dark clouds in the east. The negro slaves were already up; some were building fires in the large room and kitchen, and Pompey and Sanco were out to the barn feeding the horses and cattle. When Pompey opened the door of the stable, he burst into a hearty laugh and said to Sanco:

"Massa Hendrick's horse here yet?"

"Yes," says Sanco, "don't you see de light in de parlor."

Hendrick had now left the house, and hurriedly throwing on his overcoat, he ordered Pompey to place the saddle on his horse. He mounted, and pushing him to the top of his speed, he soon reached home, and throwing himself on his bed he soon fell asleep. When he awoke it was noon, but a happier man than Hendrick Vosburgh never lived.

Hendrick had yet to get the consent of Richard Snadaker, and he dreaded to ask it. But he inquired of himself why. Had he not always been received by him kindly, and how many pleasant hours he had spent there, and how often he had invited him to his house, and how pleasant he made it when there. Indulging in such thoughts, the burden was partially removed. It was a cold, stormy evening in the winter. Richard Snadaker sat in his large room with his family around a large fire. He had just taken his iron tongs, and picked up the brands that lay scattered on the hearth, and placed them in the center of the fire, when a rap was heard at the door. It was soon opened, and the person who entered was none other than Hendrick Vosburgh. Snadaker politely invited him in the room, and he was soon comfortably seated near the fire. Mrs. Snadaker ordered Fillis to fetch from the cellar a bowl of apples and a mug cider, and place them before the fire, and after they were sufficiently warmed the family and Hendrick partook freely of the contents. His visit that evening was of special interest, for he had an important question to ask, and it was to him a momentous occasion, and yet he delayed. It was getting late and the family had all retired but Mr. and Mrs. Snadaker and Susan, and he thought that he could postpone his business no longer. In the presence of Susan, Hendrick asked her parents' consent for their daughter in marriage. In doing this he betrayed considerable emotion, and Snadaker perceived it. He then plainly informed him how much he thought of him, and he reminded him of former days when he was but a boy, how often he visited his house, and the interest he took in his family and what exertions he made in stormy weather to get the children to school, how he opened the path through the snowdrifts for them, and for promoting their happiness and welfare he was never weary, and the arms of his love was continually around them. Before Snadaker had finished talking, Hendrick burst into tears, for the language he used was entirely unexpected. He knew that Snadaker had always treated him kindly, but he did not know till then that he cherished that affection towards him. His tears were not tears of sorrow, but of joy. Pale and trembling, young Vosburgh stood before him, in the bloom and freshness of early manhood, and full six feet in height. His straight manly form, and tasseled locks hanging over his forehead, and pallid cheeks was moistened with his tears, when Snadaker gave his consent and said nothing would add more to his happiness than to see them united. Susan said nothing, for she had not even the power to speak, for she had listened with intense interest to her father when he informed Hendrick of the affection that he manifested towards him, and the happiness it would afford him in seeing them united, and the language that he used, and the manner in which he expressed himself, thrilled the very fibers of her soul, for she had given Hendrick the warm gushings of her heart, and her affections had for years clung unreservedly to him, and now to deprive her of him would deprive her of life.

Who can tell the happiness experienced where two beings are united, and that, too, in the bloom of life?

With hearts pure and uncontaminated, and souls congenial, awaking to the realities of religion, what can be more heaven-like or angelic? When their love becomes so riveted that nothing but death can break it asunder. That love crushes every difficulty that lies in its way; it breaks up the fallow ground of the heart, and makes it tender and soft. That love is stronger than any passion that exists under the canopy of heaven. It is paramount to all. The love of a father, of a mother, of a brother, may be blest, but that love is founded on a different relationship, it is predicated on another basis. It is of the same genus, but of a different species. It is sweeter than the incense of Persia, yea, more delicious than odors from a field of Arabian spices, wafted by pleasant gales.

It was late when Hendrick left Snadaker's, and the snow was falling fast and the wind was blowing and drifting it in heaps in the highways and rendering them impassible, and he was fearful that he could not get home. But he had a powerful horse, which had been standing in an out-shed the whole evening, and he soon placed himself in the saddle, and the noble animal was soon braving the storm, as if knowing the anxiety of his rider, he plunged through the snow and passing every drift with ease, he soon reached home in safety.

But the winter soon passed away, and spring returned, and the warm sun had dissolved the snow, and the verdure had again covered the fields, and the leaves on the locust tree that stood around the old farm house began to put forth. The lilac had long unfolded its bud, for then the locust tree and the lilac were the only ornamental trees that graced the farmer's dooryards in Dutchess county, and Richard Snadaker had his share of them. The pear trees and apple orchards were covered with blossoms, and the bobolink and blackbird were singing merrily in the trees. Pompey and Sanco were cleaning the dooryard, and the old farm house never appeared more beautiful. The low ceiling and uncovered timbers were thoroughly scoured in the parlor, and the floor was cleaned and sanded. The large fire place was filled with evergreens gathered from the forest, which added a zest to the room, and the exterior of the building was neatly whitewashed, for Mr. Snadaker was making great preparations for the wedding. It was a beautiful day in the month of June, the loveliest of the year, and all was bustle around the old farm house. Fillis and Juda was dressing the poultry which had been killed for the occasion, and soon friends and neighbors were fast collecting, and the large lumber wagons were filling the yards. The ceremony was performed in the presence of a large assemblage; the negro slaves occupying the rear. Susan and Hendrick were happily united, and after a sumptuous repast the affair was ended. What a contrast does such an occasion present to those of the present day, for then there were no expensive tours to Niagara, Newport and the White Mountains. No large sums of money expended for presents to the bride, nor costly gewgaws, as at the present day.

Mr. and Mrs. Snadaker, Hendrick and Susan, have long since slept with their fathers, but it may be asked, Where was the old farm house? I said in a previous part of my story that it formerly was located in a certain section in Dutchess county. A portion of it still exists. In one of the southern towns it can be seen standing and another story has been added to it. What tender recollections cluster around it, and how many happy hours have been spent in it. No fashion and luxury was there then to corrupt the people, no fashionable religion to contaminate them. Oh, return, return, those happy days of my ancestors. Would that I had lived in that happy golden age, and how often do I recall to mind the names of Mr. and Mrs. Snadaker, Susan and Hendrick, and the old Farm House.

THE UNGRATEFUL FATHER.

In the southern part of the County of Dutchess, there once lived a wealthy farmer, whose name was George Cushman. The farm that he occupied had been handed down from father to son for several generations. It was admired by the traveler as he passed by it, for its high state of cultivation, and the beauty of its arrangement. The dwelling was tastefully located on a rising knoll surrounded with ornamental trees, beautiful lawns, and pleasant walks.

Deacon Cushman, as he was called, had lived nearly to the age of three score years, without seeing much trouble. His hair, which in earlier years had been of a raven blackness, was now slightly silvered, his eye of bright blue, beamed with the expression of benevolence and good will, and for more than a quarter of a century he had been an ornament to society and to the church of which he was a member. He had married in early life, and had but two children, a son Henry and a daughter Emma, she being the youngest, who had now arrived at the age of eighteen years, was the pride of her doting parents, and no pains had been spared in educating her, and giving her the best advantages.

Mrs. Cushman was a descendant of one of the aristocratic families of the county of Dutchess, and with inherited wealth and occupying a high station in society, she looked forward to the marriage of her daughter to a lofty connection in life. She was her only daughter, and her whole happiness was centered in her.

Near the residence of Mr. Cushman was a little village, in which lived a cabinet maker who was very poor; and having a large family to support, he was obliged to work diligently. From early morn till late at night, he had toiled for years, and as he was something of a politician, his friends had secured to him the postoffice, so that he managed to live comfortably. As he could not give his children any property, he made every exertion to give them an education. His eldest son, Isaac, being thus qualified for it, attended to the business of the office. Often would Deacon Cushman come to the postoffice with his letters, and he observed the ready dispatch with which Isaac mailed them, and as readily perceived that he was well qualified for business generally.

The poor cabinet maker finding it necessary to have his children earn their living, one day asked Deacon Cushman, as he was sitting in his shop, if he could not employ his eldest son Isaac, he being now old enough to support himself, as the younger one could readily supply his place. Mr. Cushman replied favorably, and they soon agreed as to what Isaac should receive, and the following week he engaged in his service.

Isaac was now about nineteen years of age, and as he had been instructed by pious parents, he was dutiful and obedient. He was of a kind disposition and ardent temperament, and being social and agreeable in his manners, his society was courted by many. Mrs. Cushman often employed him in the garden, and he sometimes drove the carriage for her and Emma when they wished to make a call, and he was ever ready and willing to comply.

Mr. Cushman's son was now from home studying for a profession, so that the services that Isaac thus rendered proved valuable, and an extension of his engagement was found to be desirable to the Cushman family, which was acceded to.

On account of the high standing of the Cushman family, Emma was not permitted to associate with any of the young ladies in the village, though she visited some of the most noted families in the county, while a portion of her time was spent in the city. She did not inherit that high headed, aristocratic feeling of her parents; she regarded character as the test of merit in selecting her companions in society. Her distinguishing trait was meekness, with a modest shrinking delicacy, which seemed to unfit her for the rude intercourse of the world. Her nature seemed moulded, indeed, by the secluded spot in which she had been matured, amid the shady stillness of the locust grove in which their residence was situated, and to be in harmony with the delightful spot, and on many a pleasant evening would she and Isaac sit in that grove for hours, without the knowledge of her parents.

She soon became ardently attached to him, though she did not let him know of the affection she cherished for him; she knew that her parents would not consent for her to marry the son of a poor mechanic, while at the same time they could have no other objection. He had now lived with them for nearly two years, and had performed the various duties assigned him with perfect satisfaction.

He, too, loved Emma fondly, though he entertained no idea of securing her, as he knew that she was an only daughter of wealthy parents, and he smothered his attachment, without daring to make it known to her. He regarded her favorable notice of him as nothing more than friendship.

On one pleasant evening in September, Emma and Isaac were seated in the grove, when Emma plainly expressed her views and feelings, and declared that wealth and station had no charms for her, like the possession of intelligence and character. At these words Isaac was agitated; he looked up in her face and burst into tears, as he inquired of her if she could look with favor upon a poor young man of humble birth. To this she answered favorably, and declared her preference for him over those of higher pretensions, who moved in fashionable life. He told her that he was nothing but the son of a poor mechanic, and could not expect one like herself could love such as himself, to which she replied that she could readily share with him all the privations that they would be liable to meet with in this world, and that poverty was nothing of a dread to her. She added that her parents no doubt would object to their union, but she would seek to ascertain their feelings on the subject, as best she could, as she felt that she could be happy with no other. Isaac made no reply, and as the evening was advancing they separated.

Isaac passed a sleepless night, and thought of the

high station that Emma occupied in society, her noble birth and wealthy parents; he knew that they would be violently opposed to his marrying their only daughter, and he trembled to think of the decision of her parents.

Deacon Cushman often sent Isaac to the postoffice of an evening for letters, and sometimes he would remain at home with his parents until morning, particularly when there was nothing to carry back. But a few evenings had elapsed when he was thus despatched to the postoffice, and if there should not be any letters he could remain home till morning.

Emma while seated near her mother, as her father was busily engaged in reading, ventured to speak feelingly of Isaac, and as she betrayed considerable emotion, her mother perceived it and began to question her, when she revealed the secret at once, greatly to the astonishment of both her parents.

Deacon Cushman dropped his book, and raising his spectacles, listened to Emma as she related to her parents the intimacy that had so long existed between her and Isaac, and the ardent attachment they cherished for each other. Cushman's hair appeared to stand on end, and his countenance denote anger, as he declared to Emma, that if she accepted that poor mechanic's son, she must leave his house forever, reminding her what pains he had taken to educate her, of the high station she occupied in society, her noble birth and ancestry, and that now to think of marrying that poor mechanic's son was too much to endure. Her parents then endeavored to persuade her to think and determine otherwise, but all was unavailing, and the father threatened to disinherit her, as a last resort.

Isaac, while at home with his parents that night, could find no sleep; he thought of Emma, and he dreaded to return again the next morning. At an early hour he went to his work in the garden, and he was not called in to breakfast with the family as formerly, but was obliged to eat with the domestics, and Mr. Cushman was cold towards him. He, moreover, went to the village and informed the cabinet maker that he should need Isaac's services no longer. The poor man was much surprised, as he supposed his son had done something wrong, though he could not think that Isaac had taken anything wrongfully, or proved himself distrustful, yet there was something that was not right and he was desirous at once of seeing him. Isaac soon returned and informed his father of the only difficulty that existed, and his father said that as he was of age he must take his own course in the matter.

To prevent their further intercourse, Emma was sent to the city, and after she had been there a few days, she wrote to Isaac and informed him where she was, and it was not long before he joined her there, and the marriage ceremony was performed. Emma then wrote to her parents, informing them of this, and that she would soon leave with her husband, for a distant place.

As Deacon Cushman read the letter to his wife she burst into tears, and her agony of mind was indescribable. Her only daughter had now left her, perhaps forever. She thought they had proved themselves ungrateful to her Emma, who had devotedly loved Isaac, and all the objection that could be brought against him was his being the son of a poor mechanic. She regretted that they had thus opposed their union, as they had wealth abundant and Isaac was capable of managing the affairs of Mr. Cushman in the absence of his son Henry, who probably would remain from home for some length of time. Often would she sit alone and weep for her absent Emma, and deplore her departure, but her husband said nothing, and not a murmur escaped his lips, not a tear moistened his eye. He was stern and haughty, and though he felt the infirmities of age, the same unbending will yet existed, and the same determination to disinherit his daughter as when she first made known her intention. Emma and Isaac proceeded to one of the Southern States and stopped at a flourishing village where was a large manufacturing establishment, and upon taking up a paper, Isaac saw an advertisement for a clerk wanted in the same, and he recognized also the name of the advertiser as a firm well-known to him in his own county some time before. He quickly applied and was not disappointed. Mr. J. had been engaged in the manufacturing business in the county of Dutchess, and having failed, left for the South, where he was now doing a profitable business. Isaac made known to him his situation and he was readily employed. He soon rented a small house and as their funds were small, and his salary was moderate, they were obliged to live economically. After the first year his services were deemed indispensable, and his employers advanced his salary so as to enable him to live quite comfortably, and they found themselves pleasantly situated as to a home, and if her parents would but overlook her disobedience, Emma now felt that she would be quite happy. After having lived thus for about two years, Emma determined to write to her parents, though she was fearful that it might make matters worse, and while pondering it in her mind, Isaac came home one evening from his daily task and complained of being unwell, and although Emma paid every possible attention, and did all in her power to afford relief, he continued to grow worse and soon found himself unable to sit up.

A physician was called in, who quickly perceived that he was very ill, and as he saw the anxiety of Emma, he withheld from her any intimation of the dangerous situation in which he found her husband. He had a violent fever, which proved of the typhus character. Soon his case was evidently hopeless, and his wife's feelings can be better imagined than described, as she sat by the bedside of her dying husband. He was mostly in a stupor, and his mind was so affected that he could only converse rationally at intervals; he would sometimes point significantly to his little boy, Georgie, sitting on his mother's lap, as if he would undertake to tell her something, but it was quite unintelligible, and soon he closed his eyes in death.

Mr. J. and Emma were the only persons in the room when Isaac breathed his last. Emma was inconsolable, and her cries were truly heartrending. Mr. J. endeavored to console her, but she would not be comforted, and for weeks after his death she was continually weeping. Mr. J. advised her to return home to her parents, assuring her that she would be received with kindness.

The death of Isaac was now making rapid inroads on Emma's constitution, from excessive grief, which Mr. J. perceived, and as Isaac had something coming to him, he persuaded her not to delay so doing, for she and her little boy needed kind protection; she consented, and he secured a passage for her to the city, where having arrived weak and exhausted, she took the first train for her early home. A friend assisted her from the cars and helped her to the mail stage, which soon brought her to her own little village, when she was so feeble that she was obliged to be carried. It was in the evening when the stage arrived, and having informed the cabinet maker of the death of his son Isaac, he accompanied her to her parents' home. It was a cold bleak night in November, and the wind whistled through the tops of the tall locusts that stood around the stately mansion. Mrs. Cushman had retired for the night, and Deacon Cushman and his son Henry were sitting in the room alone, when the door bell rang. Upon learning that his daughter was thus at his door, Mr. Cushman haughtily ordered it closed against her, though he did not inform his son nor Mrs. Cushman of Emma's arrival. He had a restless night, and in the morning a messenger informed him that his daughter was lying dangerously ill at the house of the poor cabinet maker.

Mrs. Cushman and Henry repaired hastily to the village, and as they entered the little room where Emma lay, they were horror struck to find her on a poor bed without hangings, and she cast an imploring look upwards and said "Mother," and pointed to her little darling boy sitting on the cabinet maker's lap. She uttered a few unintelligible words and her lips ceased to move; she was dead. Mrs. Cushman fainted and fell senseless on the floor.

Her remains were conveyed to the paternal mansion, and had a decent burial, though during the mournful funeral obsequies the unfeeling father was not seen to shed a tear. Mrs. Cushman survived her daughter Emma but a few short months, and Deacon Cushman, who lived for some years after, was known as the Ungrateful Father. After his death his son Henry disposed of the estate and went to reside in some distant part, and the name became extinct in the southern part of the County of Dutchess, where it had been kept up so long with pride.

THE TAILOR AND THE BACHELOR.

In the south part of the county of Dutchess, is some of the best land in the State of New York. That portion lying in the valleys in East Fishkill is very productive, and under thorough cultivation it returns a rich reward to the husbandman. Dotted with beautiful country seats and stately farm houses, it presents to the eye of the traveler a fine appearance. Situated in the central part of one of these valleys is a little village comprising about a hundred inhabitants. Like most Eastern villages its growth is slow. The dwellings of the wealthy are not extravagantly built, most of them being in the style of those that were put up about the beginning of the present century, intended rather for comfort and convenience than elegance and display. In this village lived a bachelor who was quite wealthy. He had inherited more than one-third of his property; he was a man of good habits, and the love of gain was his predominant passion. He cared for none but himself; unsociable and arbitrary, he exercised tyranny over his tenants, which rendered him unpopular. He had rented one of his shops to a tailor who was very poor. The tailor had to work hard to support his family. He had met with a misfortune in having lost the use of one of his hands, which had incapacitated him for his business for more than three months, which was one cause of his getting behindhand. His rent would soon be due, and he knew the bachelor would expect him to pay it promptly. The bachelor was unacquainted with the expenses of a family, and probably had never given it a thought, while the poor tailor had to exert all his energies to secure a living. Provisions were dear, and the tailor's last loaf was on the table. He went to his supper thinking how he should pay his rent, as what little money he had he wanted to get necessaries for his family to subsist on. It was the early part of April, and the weather was cold, the Spring being uncommonly backward, and vegetation had scarcely commenced. Occasionally a snowbank was seen on the north side of the buildings, and in some obscure corner where the rays of the sun could not reach. The past winter had been one of extreme severity, and the snow had fallen early and deep, while the wind had whirled it in eddies and piled it up in huge masses along the streets, and around the dwellings of the villagers. The tailor had experienced the severity of the winter, and during the intense cold weather he had to use a great deal of fuel to keep his family comfortable. Sitting at the table, his wife noticed a change in his countenance; he ate but little, and soon took a seat by the fire, buried his face in his hands, and seemed to be deeply agitated. His wife observing this, asked him the cause of his sorrow. "My dear," said he, "our rent is due next week, and Mr. P. will expect us to pay it." He could say no more, his voice failed him, he covered his face with his hands, and the gushing tears moistened his cheek. His wife saw with pain the upheavings of his bosom, for she well knew the bachelor's miserly disposition, and expected that he would show them no mercy. The sun was fast sinking in the west and its rays shone through the windows and shot its bright beams across the rag carpet in the little room where they sat. The tailor's wife was waiting on the little ones around the scanty table, the youngest lying in the cradle by the fire. It presently commenced crying, and the tailor made no effort to pacify it. He arose from his seat, seized his hat, left the room and went to his shop. The April wind was sweeping through the village, and whistled around the shop of the tailor. He had just commenced his work, when the bachelor landlord entered. The tailor saw at once that he had a downcast look and he commenced walking the floor with a hurried step. He had promised a certain amount of money and he was fearful that he could not fulfill his engagements. He asked the tailor if he could pay his rent the following week, and he plainly told him that he could not. The severe winter, sickness and expensive living had used all his means, and now he had not sufficient to buy bread for his family. The landlord said he "could not afford to build houses and shops and have people occupy them for nothing. Materials and labor were high, and to receive no rent for his buildings was something he would not submit to. You must pay me the rent next week, if not I will send an officer that will drive you from the premises." The tailor made no reply, but thought of his wife and little ones. Although it was not necessary for mechanics to work at night at this season of the year, yet the tailor plied his needle earnestly and worked later than usual, his eye fixed intently on his work. The bachelor seated himself in a large arm chair by the stove, biting his finger nails, and appearing in deep meditation. A deathlike silence pervaded the room for some time, when the bachelor told him the rent must be paid the next Tuesday or the premises must be vacated, and he then left the shop. The tailor worked until ten o'clock, and then went to his home. The moon was now at its full, and shone brightly in the windows. As he entered he saw his wife engaged in patching an old garment by a small light in one corner of the room. The tailor opened his Bible and read the twenty-third Psalm, which reminded him of his own situation, when David saith, "He maketh me to lie down in green pastures, He leadeth me beside the still waters." He prayed that like the psalmist of old, he might be made to lie down in green pastures, and be led beside the still waters; that the bachelor's heart might be softened, that what he had said might sink deep in his soul, and that he might shed penitential tears over his past doings. He hoped that the gospel balm might so renovate his heart that his name would at last be found in the records of eternal mercy. The next day a friend kindly offered him a part of his house, and bade him not communicate the fact to any one. He had no interview with the bachelor again until the first of May, who was disappointed when he saw the tailor busily engaged in moving what little goods he had to Mr. A.'s. He said nothing, but appeared to regret what he had said. What few friends he once had in the village had now forsaken him, though he was very fond of company, and to live without friends, to have no one in time of trouble to come near him to wipe away the trickling tear that rolled down his cheek, no one to pour the oil and wine of consolation in his bosom, was something that filled him with despair. Under circumstances like these his situation was peculiarly afflicting. To manifest any contrition for past deeds was something his proud spirit could not brook. He went from store to shop, but he could find no friends there. His other tenants, too, talked of leaving him, and upon reflection he resolved to sell his village property. He advertised it for sale at auction. It was sold at a reduced price and the bachelor left for one of the Western States, and there we leave him for the present. The tailor again rented the same shop of the new owner. By diligence in business he was enabled to pay the rent and have something left. In a few years he was able to buy the shop, which he enlarged, opened a large clothing establishment, and business increased so rapidly that in a few years he purchased the homestead of the bachelor, also tore down the old edifice, built a splendid mansion in the place of it, and as he accumulated wealth, he beautified the grounds, set out ornamental trees, fenced it with iron railing, and surrounded it with everything that luxury could desire. The tailor, after some years, beginning to get old, thought of retiring from business, and as property had doubled in value since he had been in business, he sold his store for a large advance, and lived the remainder of his days on the homestead of the bachelor, enjoying all the comforts that this life affords. The villagers all loved the tailor.

and he often invited them to his hospitable mansion to partake of the rich dainties, and to enjoy themselves in his parks and pleasure grounds.

Reader, would you like to know what has become of the lone bachelor? He lived yet in a Western village, where he never let it be known who he was or where he came from. He purchased a tract of land, held possession of it a few years, when a claim came against it, and after a year's litigation the claim was proved to be a good one. Mortified and chagrined at the loss of his property, he strove to regain it, but in this he failed. The bachelor in despair lived alone in a small hut in the suburbs of the village, supporting himself in doing a little business for some of the villagers, and by a small office they gave him out of charity. Years had now rolled away, and his native place had not heard from him while his name was almost forgotten. The tailor often thought of him and desired to see him before he died, but the bachelor had made up his mind never to return. Often would he shut himself up in his hut and think of his native home and give vent to his tears. He had now arrived at the age of fourscore years and his desire to return thither increased. He thought if he could see it once again he would be willing to die. But would he find any friends there? Would he be likely to be known there after a lapse of so many years? Such thoughts as these filled his soul with intense agony, but to die there he must. He took a confidential friend to his hut and told him all his misfortunes, how he was nursed in the lap of wealth, how unpopular he became, how he sold his property at a reduced price, came here and bought and lost his all, and he was now on the verge of the grave. He hoped that he had atoned for his past offences and had made his peace with Heaven, and now he wished to go home, as he termed it, and there to die. This friend exerted himself and raised money enough to take the bachelor to his native place. The bachelor took his departure as soon as circumstances would permit, and with tottering steps he got in the car, and in a short time was in the County of Dutchess. The stage soon rolled him to his native village. He refused to be taken to any particular place, and was let out on the sidewalk. It was now in the month of September, and the heat was oppressive. His eye scanned the village, and he saw the old homestead in the distance, but instead of the old wooden building he now saw a splendid mansion reared in its stead, and as he drew near with faltering step he ventured to approach it; a thrill of horror penetrated his soul. The tailor had just taken his dinner, and was smoking a cigar in his woodbine alcove. The bachelor opened the iron gate, walked up on the porch and pulled the bell for admission. A servant came and he asked who lived there. He was told it was a Mr. ——, the tailor, upon which he fell insensible on the porch. The tailor hearing an unusual noise, hastened to the spot and ordered the old man taken in and laid upon a sofa in the hall. He sent the servant to bring a glass of wine and water, and with little difficulty the bachelor revived. He asked the tailor if he knew him, who said no. He told him he was his former landlord. So surprised was he that both burst into a flood of tears, and for some minutes not a word was spoken. After recovering a little, the bachelor was so overcome that he desired to lie down for a while, and he was soon supplied with refreshments. The tailor anticipated much pleasure the next day in the society of his guest. It was late next morning, however, before he would allow him to be disturbed, when he sent to his room to tell him that breakfast was awaiting him. No answer was had, and on going once again with noiseless step, the tailor approached the bed, but the bachelor was no more; he was sleeping the sleep which knows no waking.

A TALE OF THE EARLY SETTLERS.

FOUNDED ON FACT.

About the beginning of the eighteenth century, what are now known as the towns of Fishkill and East Fishkill, were a vast wilderness. The tract of land purchased by Francis Rombout of the great Indian Sachem Ninham, included the original town of Fishkill, extending from the Hudson River east sixteen miles, or four hours walk of an Indian. Rombout had an only daughter who married a person of the name of Brett, and settled on the patent on the banks of the noble Hudson. At the death of her father she became sole heir to the patent. The great Sachem and his tribe were allowed by her to occupy that portion of it now called Fishkill Hook. This tribe at one time numbered more than a thousand warriors, but from the encroachments of the white man on their territory, and mingling with the tribe, thus introducing intoxicating drinks and various contagious diseases hitherto unknown among them, they were soon reduced to about half that number.

A squatter of the name of Langdon located about this time on the patent, and but a little distance from the Indian village. He had a son of the name of Jacobus, who had emigrated with him from Long Island, and they together commenced the work of leveling the forest and cultivating the soil for a livelihood. Young Langdon was a mere youth of fifteen years, and had come with his father to share the privations and hardships of the wilderness. He assisted in felling the mighty oak and lofty pine that had braved the storms and winds of centuries, and after finishing their log cabin and effecting a clearing sufficient to supply them with food, and securing an enclosure for their cattle to protect them from beasts of prey, Jacobus and his father would occasionally take their guns and go into the forest in quest of game. The sharp crack of their rifles would often stop the bounding deer, and start the prowling wolf that infested their plantation.

The Herald of the Cross had not yet been on his errand of mercy above the Highlands, except perhaps at Albany, where there was then a missionary station, supplied by a minister of the Reformed Dutch Church, whose name was Megapolensis, and who was the first minister that sailed up the Hudson river. Langdon had been brought up and educated in this church, and when he resided on Long Island, as often as the blessed Sabbath returned, the sound of the bell would summon him to listen to the preaching of the Gospel.

Now, however, living here in the rude wilderness, where no ambassador of Christ had yet ever been, his Sabbaths brought him little or no true enjoyment. The nearest church to him was some miles below the village of Peekskill, and he resolved to go there and worship as often as circumstances would in any way permit.

On one Saturday afternoon, after giving his son Jacobus instructions with regard to the proper care of the sheep and cattle, and enjoining him to drive them early into the enclosure for fear of the wild beasts, he mounted his horse, shouldered his rifle, struck an Indian trail, and soon disappeared in the depths of the forest. Jacobus went early to look for the cattle, and in doing so he penetrated the woods nearly to the Indian village. As he was standing under the thick branches of a large pine, he suddenly saw a beautiful Indian girl paddling her little canoe on the Wiccapee, a stream of water but a little distance from the settlement. She was the daughter of the Sachem, and had come thus to amuse herself in her little vessel, built of birchen bark, with a net which her father had given her to fish in its limpid waters. Thus would she pass hours, as well as in angling in the shade, upon its verdant banks, and dream away her life in pleasant solitude, for being a woman of high birth, with the Indian maidens of the tribe she had little or no congeniality. Her occupation and pursuits were in a measure like theirs, yet her mind was above them, and although like them she could clamber the steep sides of the mountain, or swim like a mermaid in the waters; though she even excelled them in the curing of venison, and could prepare the evening meal of corn bread and fish with more than ordinary skill, yet there her common interest ended. In her rambles through the forest she was ever found alone, for thus she held more sweet communion with nature, and her free thoughts were echoed back by the woods and streams with which she thus held converse.

Jacobus eyed the Indian girl as she plied the paddle and sped her canoe along the water. Her waist was encircled with a crimson scarf, and over her back hung a quiver of arrows and a bow, while a moose skin of the finest texture lay gracefully over her shoulders.

It was the first time he had seen the Indian maiden Mantaseo. He had been with his father to the Indian village, but he had never entered the wigwam of the Sachem. He now cautiously approached the banks of the stream, and Mantaseo saw him as he advanced, and pushed her canoe ashore. She kindly asked him in broken English whither he was going, when he told her he was looking for the sheep and cattle to drive them early to the enclosure, as his father had gone to church below the mountains. Jacobus then stepped into the canoe and Mantaseo carried him across the water. She admired the pale face as the breezes of the Wiccapee were sifting through the clustering curls that hung over his forehead. The sun was getting low in the west, and the tall trees threw their long shadows over the water, when Jacobus said he must leave and complete his errand, as the howling of the wolves was distinctly heard through the forest. Mantaseo retraced her steps homeward, and as she left she cast a wistful look at the pale hunter, as she called him, for he had already made an indelible impression on her heart. One low whisper from him now would be as nectar to her, and far more pleasant than the soft murmurs of the Wiccapee.

She preferred to hearken to his words rather than to sit dreamily listening to the ripple of its currents, or to slumber on its banks listening to the music of its lullaby, and now how intensely full of interest became her life; henceforth to watch for his footsteps, to ramble with him over the mountain path and through the leafy forest, to sit beside him under the spreading shade of some broad armed tree, and drink in even as the flowers drink the dew, the tender accents so musically low, to catch his burning glances, calling the crimson tide from her heart, and to feel his warm breath on her cheek, as his lips met hers, was now the glorious dream of her being.

Jacobus tarried longer than he intended with the Indian girl, and found that it was getting late. His mother was alone, and he knew she would be alarmed for his safety. He hurried through the woods to find the sheep and cattle. The tinkling of the bell soon guided him to where they were grazing, and he soon got them safe in the enclosure. The country at that time was but sparsely settled, and there were but few white families on the patent, and they were mostly squatters. To get to Long Island, through the interior, was difficult and dangerous, as there were tribes of hostile Indians roving through the country, and to go by way of the river was tedious and uncertain, as there were no vessels that regularly stopped between New York and Albany. The only way for the traveler when he espied a sail was to hoist a signal on the shore, and this was the only means of travel.

This difficulty caused Jacobus' visits to his birthplace to be few and far between, and a trip to Long Island then was like going to the unsettled West now. He spent most of his time with his parents, working hard to clear the ground of heavy timber, and what leisure hours he had, he would hunt in the forest, or fish in the Wiccapee. While engaged in such employments he would meet the Indian girl Mantaseo, and she delighted in assisting in taking the trout and winfish that abounded in the waters. At other times she would amuse him in showing her skill with the bow, in shooting the arrow at a mark. Months and years passed away and Jacobus never let his parents know his intimacy with the Indian girl. At an appointed time he had promised to meet her in the forest, where she declared the attachment she had for him since she first saw him, and that if he cherished the same for her, desired to know if he would be willing to marry her. Jacobus at once assented, provided she would renounce her Pagan superstition and live a civilized and a Christian life, and to this she readily consented.

After Jacobus parted with Mantaseo he thought what his parents would say when they should hear that he was engaged to an Indian girl. But could they have any objection when she had promised to leave savage life and embrace the true religion. But she was of a different race. He recollected reading in the Scripture that all descended from one common parent, and were aiming for one Heaven. And then, too, she was a daughter of the Sachem. Such thoughts as these occupied his mind as he returned home. His father was a descendant of the Hollanders, but his mother was an English woman. What education he had received was mostly from her. She had taught him to pray, and to him nothing was so deep as a mother's love.

Indulging in such thoughts as these his tears fell

like raindrops, and he knelt beside a large tree and prayed to the Giver of all good to comfort and sustain him.

The country had now considerably improved. Emigrants were coming in, and Madam Brett had succeeded in opening a road from her residence east to the foot of the mountain, and there was a missionary station on the patent, where Fishkill Village is now located, supplied by a Reformed Dutch minister of the name of Van Schie, and he was the first minister that preached in Fishkill. He was located at what is now Poughkeepsie city, and once a fortnight he would preach at his station on the patent. Langdon esteemed it a great privilege to have the gospel thus preached so near him, and when the appointed time arrived for service, he and his wife would always be found there. The manner of traveling through the country at that time was upon a pillion. Wheel carriages were not in use. By this mode the horse could be guided so as to avoid fallen trees and sunken holes.

On one fine Sabbath morning, when the appointed time had arrived for the Dominie to preach, Langdon had gone to church, leaving Jacobus at home to look after the plantation, and on their return they were greeted by a stranger in their cabin. It was the Indian girl Mantasco, who was now dressed in civilized costume, while her long dark hair flowed gracefully over her shoulders. She was sitting by the window with the Bible in her hand, endeavoring to read it, when Langdon entered. Jacobus introduced her as the Sachem's daughter, whom he had brought here while they were absent, because he felt a deep interest in her welfare, and he intended also to take her as his companion for life. He then related to his parents the intimacy that had existed between them for years gone by, the many happy hours they had spent alone, hunting in the forest and fishing in the Wiccapee, and assured them of the ardent attachment they cherished for each other, and that now she had promised to leave the wigwam of her parents to unite herself with him and live a Christian life, and desired to know if they could have any objection to such a union. His mother said not a word as she sat in a corner of the cabin, resting her head upon her hands, while the tears were trickling down her cheeks. His father delighted in the happiness of his son, and as she was the daughter of the Sachem, and had promised to live a Christian life, he readily consented.

It was a fine afternoon in the month of October, when Jacobus and his parents were sitting in their cabin, anxiously awaiting the arrival of a certain personage. All was calm without, and not a cloud obscured the horizon; the sun was just disappearing behind the western mountains, and its rays tinged the the top of the forest and reflected brightly o'er their scarlet leaves, when a horseman was seen approaching. He wore a large cocked hat and with a heavy coat wrapped around him, he rode up to the cabin and dismounted. It was no other than Dominie Van Schie. The marriage ceremony soon took place, in the presence of his parents, and of the Sachem Ninham. Jacobus soon after purchased a farm* of Madam

---

*The farm is the one now owned by Joseph Sherwood at Johnsville.

Brett, and with his wife became members of the Dutch Church at Fishkill Village as soon as it was organized. and lived the remainder of their days on the farm they had purchased, and died. as I trust, in the hope of a blessed immortality.

THE MYSTERIOUS PACK.

About forty years ago there lived in Greenwich street New York, a wealthy retired merchant who had accumulated property during the distracted state of our country with England, in the war of 1812. The financial crisis which then occurred, causing a general crash among the merchants, proved a source of profit to him, for at the close of the war merchandise depreciated nearly half its former price. He then purchased a large amount of goods, and realized large profits from the sales, which in a few years enabled him to retire from the business. Mr. Alger, for that was his name, had been born and reared in the city, and had now arrived at the age of three score years. He wished to spend the few remaining years of his life in the country.

Western New York then presented great attractions to the inhabitants in the eastern counties of the state. The sturdy pioneers had partially cleared the forest, and the description of the country given by the historian was very inviting, particularly the Genesee country. The richness of the soil, the salubrity of the climate, and the healthfulness of the country, all contributed to the increase of emigration. Mr. Alger having purchased a map of the country, and read a description given by a traveler passing through the country to Niagara Falls, he concluded to visit the country. Accordingly, in the Spring of 1823, Mr. Alger left the city of New York for the Genesee country, which then consumed more time to reach than it would now to go to Chicago, for the facilities for traveling west from Albany were only the stage coach and canal. Railroads then had not been introduced. Arriving in the Genesee country, Mr. Alger was highly pleased. The fertility of the soil, the balminess of the atmosphere, and the healthy climate, were a strong inducement for Mr. Alger to locate there. Accordingly he purchased a large tract of land there and returned to the city, and the following Autumn he removed his family on the farm he had purchased. Mr. Alger lived through the winter in an old log house which had been built by a pioneer when the country was entirely new. He managed to make it comfortable for himself and family during the winter. Early in the Spring Mr. Alger sent to New York for a number of mechanics, who promptly responded to his call, and the following summer he erected a splendid mansion and furnished it equal to any residence in Greenwich street, in the city of New York. When Mr. Alger left New York the wealth and fashion of the city was below the Park, and Greenwich street contained the residences of some of the most wealthy merchants in the city. Mr. Alger's house there was most elegantly furnished, and he concluded to furnish his new residence equal to, if not excelling it. This astonished the natives, for they had not been accustomed to see such splendor, for wealth and fashion had not then reached Western

New York. Mr. Alger's house contained a large amount of silver plate, which was very valuable, and splendid mirrors and paintings that were suspended on the side walls of his mansion, which he gave his neighbors permission occasionally to look at, little suspecting that a plot was secretly planning to rob and murder him. Mr. Alger employed many laborers to cultivate his large farm, and keep his premises in order.

The country yet was comparatively new, large forests were interspersed through the valleys, untouched by the woodman's axe. Trees standing so thick that no wheeled carriage could enter, and some of them reaching to the height of one hundred feet, making the forest dark and gloomy, affording a safe retreat to the robber. Mr. Alger did not apprehend any danger living there. He was quite remote from any neighbor, and he enjoyed himself in that seclusion very much, for the health of his family was much improved, and although accustomed to city life, his retirement from the din and bustle of the great metropolis, contributed more to his happiness than the luxury and fashion of Greenwich street. Having lived there more than two years, Mr. Alger and family concluded to pay a visit to the city, and making all necessary arrangements, he gave his servants strict orders not to keep any travelers over night. He assigned to them their portion of the work, and to secure the house and outbuildings. Every door of the premises was carefully guarded. After Mr. Alger had given his domestics their instructions as to taking care of the valuables in the house, having as he thought safely secured the silver plate, he and his family took the stage for

Albany. Mr. Alger's servants guarded his premises with the greatest care, and admitted no neighbor in the house. Mr. Alger had been absent about a week, when a traveler approached the house late in the day, with a large pack on his back, asking permission to stay all night. A female servant informed him that he could not, as the owner of the mansion had gone to New York on a visit with his family, and would not return in two weeks, and he gave strict orders to keep no one through the night. The traveler appeared to be weary, and said that he was very tired, that his pack was very heavy, and that his strength was not sufficient for him to walk with his pack to the nearest neighbor's to obtain a night's lodging. It was in the month of October, and the atmosphere was chilly and raw, and the traveler still persisted, but the domestic sternly refused. The traveler still tarried, and she sent for Richard, the foreman, and informed him of the traveler's wish to stay all night. Richard reiterated the same story, informing the traveler that he must leave immediately. The traveler lifted the pack with great difficulty, and succeeded in regaining the yard and deposited his burden, saying that he could proceed no farther, and at the same time asking permission to leave his pack, and he then could walk to the nearest neighbor and remain all night, and return in the morning for it. If they would consent to that proposition they might lock the pack in a room, as he had valuable goods in it, and then it would be perfectly safe. Richard seeing the weariness of the traveler, and thinking the pack could do no harm, consented to let the pack remain there all night.

It was now near sunset, and the traveler left. Richard carried the pack into an unoccupied room. The servants had done their accustomed work as directed by the foreman, and at supper he informed them of the traveler's pack he had consented to keep until morning. Their curiosity became excited to see it, which the foreman readily consented, and taking the key unlocked the door. The pack lay in the middle of the room on the floor. One of the servants remarked that it was shaped like a man. Another swore that he saw it move. This alarmed Richard, and all of the inmates of the house. Finally, after some moment's conversation, one of the workmen said that he would put a ball through it if Richard would only let him. Richard said yes, as quick as thought. Joe had a loaded rifle in his bedroom which he lost no time in getting, and taking deliberate aim he fired, the ball passing through the pack, and in a few moments it was crimsoned with blood.

Richard taking a knife ripped open the pack, and to his astonishment it contained a man. The ball had passed through his heart. Richard then examined the pack and found false keys. The dead man had a belt on stuck with pistols and cutlass, and the pack contained various other instruments of death. Richard and the whole household now were much alarmed, and what course to pursue he did not know. The day was spent, and darkness was fast approaching, but no time was to be lost. Richard and Joe, each mounting a horse, proceeded to alarm the neighbors. Taking different routes they succeeded in collecting about sixteen men and guns at the house by ten o'clock. A strict watch was kept through the night, but no robbers had made their appearance. Richard concluded that there was a deep plot laid to murder the inmates, and then rob the house. He was determined to defend the premises and sacrifice his life if necessary. Joe, too, was eager to get a clue to the traveler's pack. The man in the pack, thought Richard, was the one to commence the robbery. His false keys were intended to open the door of the room where the pack was deposited, and then his accomplices would be notified, and they would probably murder the inmates, rob the house, and set it on fire. Richard succeeded in getting his neighbors to hold guard over the premises the second night. Among other articles that Richard discovered in the pack was a whistle which he blew the second night about one o'clock. Presently the tramp of horses was heard at a distance and Richard summoned every man to be ready to fire. The night was dark and cloudy, and darkness reigned throughout the house, for Richard had taken the precaution to have no light burning. The robbers no doubt thought that they had succeeded in their attempt, for they came hurrying up to the door, supposing their friend in the pack had possession of the house. But how sadly they were disappointed. Richard gave the word to fire, and it had the desired effect, for they heard several fall from their horses. They beat a precipitate retreat, and all was still. Richard would not allow any one to open a door or leave the house, but with guns reloaded they remained there until morning. After daylight Richard cautiously unlocked the door and looking out he saw three men and two horses lying dead in the yard. Upon examining the dead bodies they proved to be strangers.

The three robbers and the two horses that were shot lay there during the day and the following night, when Richard blew the whistle again, but no robbers made their appearance, for Richard and his neighbors were well prepared to receive them. But what was their surprise when morning came to see that the robbers who were shot the night previous, had been carried off so noiselessly that none that watched through the night knew anything of it till morning.

Richard secured the services of these men to guard the house every night until Mr. Alger and family returned, and no further attempt was made to rob the house. When Mr. Alger returned and heard the story as related by Richard, and was shown the room where the robber was shot, the blood still visible on the floor, the place where they had buried him, the pack, the brace of pistols, the cutlass, the whistle and the false keys that the pack contained, he and his family were very much alarmed. He immediately organized a company to search the country, and they traversed the forest for miles in various directions, every thicket and secret nook was explored, but no clue could be obtained. It has always remained a mystery. The traveler and the robbers all escaped detection, and the stranger has often been shown the mansion which contained the mysterious pack. Mr. Alger handsomely rewarded his neighbors for their services in guarding his premises, and he gave Richard and Joe a sum sufficient to purchase new lands and to secure them a comfortable home for life.

TEN CENTS A DAY.

It was the commencement of Autumn, and farmer Brown had secured his summer crops of wheat and hay, and now he was preparing his fallow ground for sowing his winter grain. The season so far had been propitious, and farmer Brown was well rewarded for his labor. His family and workmen had toiled hard through the long hot days of summer, and they had filled his barns with grain and hay, and he anticipated an abundant crop of corn.

Farmer Brown had commenced life with nothing. He was the son of poor though honest parents, and he had earned his property by patient though stubborn industry. Marrying in early life, he had to contend with poverty, working as a laborer on a farm for twelve or fifteen dollars per month. He could save but little at the end of the year, but that little was carefully saved, for when he was quite a lad he was sitting in the store in his native village one evening, listening to three of the older men of the village. The conversation turned upon the accumulation of property. One man remarked that ten cents a day saved, with the interest added, would amount to the sum of ten thousand dollars in forty years. He thought to himself, "I am yet in my teens, and if I should live till I arrive at the age of sixty years, I can save ten thousand dollars. I use tobacco, and often smoke two or three cigars a day, and that uses up the ten cents," and he just threw away his pipe and tobacco and went to work, and every night laying aside his ten cents, and at the end of the year he had thirty-six dollars and fifty cents. Farmer Brown continued to save ten cents a day and safely investing the money, he purchased the farm alluded to in the commencement of this story, before he was forty years old. He was now sixty years old, and though his hair was silvered, his step was firm and elastic as ever. He had outstripped all of his associates in the accumulation of property, for he had saved his ten cents a day. That ten cents had laid the foundation of his wealth. "It is not," said he, "what a man earns, but what he saves, that is the true secret of making money."

Farmer Brown was now pleasantly situated on one of the most valuable farms in Western New York, with an interesting family around him, trained to habits of industry and economy. There he had resided twenty years, and had become rich in lands and flocks, and was steadily increasing in wealth. His children had now relieved him of the cares and business of life, for they had the supervision of his large estate.

Farmer Brown was sitting one day in the month of June in his dooryard, reading, and enjoying all the comforts that is allotted to man in this world, for it was the loveliest season of the year. He dropped his book and surveyed his premises. He had just built a stately mansion, and had surrounded it with beautiful ornamental trees, lawns and pleasant walks. His mind reverted to his native village, the time when he heard the story that ten cents saved a day with interest added, would amount to the sum of ten thousand dollars in forty years, and that ten cents a day had amassed him a fortune. He thought of his associates that resided there when he was a youth, wondering if they still lived there, when his attention was suddenly arrested by a stranger entering his gate, calling him by name as he approached him, and asking how he got along. Farmer Brown replied that he had the advantage of him, for he could not recognize him. The stranger said that his name was Mr. C., formerly living in the village of S. Mr. Brown then immediately knew him, for they were born in the same village, and after the customary salutations were passed, the conversation turned to passing events and the history of their journey through life from their boyhood to the present time, for they had not seen each other for more than thirty years. Mr. Brown then related the history of his life since leaving his native village, and how long he had resided there in Western New York; and the large tract of land he now owned, and now he owed no man a cent. Mr. C. surveyed the premises, his eye glanced over the fields of wheat stretching through the valley and up the hillside, his dark green corn waving to the breeze, his flocks of cattle and sheep, his mansion, his outbuildings, his lawns and ornamental trees, all attracted his attention. When Mr. Brown informed him that he was the owner of all that property, Mr. C. anxiously inquired how he came in possession of so much wealth. Mr. Brown replied, "By saving ten cents a day." Mr. C. could not comprehend his meaning. Mr. Brown then informed him of the story that he heard related when he was a boy in his native village, that ten cents a day saved, with the interest added, in forty years would amount to the sum of ten thousand dollars, and he thought to himself, "I am not yet twenty years old, and can I save ten cents a day, and if I should live till I get sixty years old, will it amount to ten thousand dollars? I use tobacco, and often I smoke two or more cigars a day, and that will cost me ten cents; and from that time until now I have not used tobacco nor drank a glass of liquor only for medicine. I commenced then saving ten cents a day, and with the proceeds of that money I purchased this farm before I arrived at the age of forty years, and now own all the land within sight through this valley." Mr. C. contrasted his situation with Mr. Brown's, for he was worth nothing. "I have used no tobacco," thought he to himself, "but then I have drank my glass three or four times a day for nearly half a century; that, with the interest added, would now have placed me beyond the reach of want, and if I had been industrious and economical as Mr. Brown, and saved my ten cents a day, I might now be the owner of a farm valuable as his." As he sat absorbed in deep thought he was much affected, and then he related to Mr. Brown the history of his life, how he commenced tippling before he was out of his teens, the money and time he had wasted, the bad habits he had formed in youth still clung to him in after life so strong that he could not eradicate them, and now he was incapacitated for labor, and nothing now remained for him in the world but poverty and remorse. By this time Mr. Brown's family had gathered round him, and they heard Mr. C. relate his story, and saw the tears roll down his cheeks. His person was dirty and meanly clad, and his baggage consisted of a bundle of old clothes, which he carried across his shoulder, resting on a stick. His poverty-stricken appearance, his haggard countenance, his long snowy locks and faltering step, caused Mr. Brown and his family to be deeply moved. Mr. C. was traveling through the country on foot, begging for subsistence. He had commenced life under more favorable circumstances than Mr. Brown, for he was a good mechanic, earning a dollar and a quarter a day, but forming bad habits in early life and increasing as he advanced in years, brought him to poverty and shame. Ceaseless dissipation requires large resources, and the young man that steps aside from the path of virtue and sobriety and is gradually drawn into the haunts of vice, in nine cases out of ten is irrevocably lost. If he gets in the gutter before he is twenty-one, seldom does he come out of the mire and corruption, for habits formed in our youth generally go with us through life. How necessary then it is for us to form good habits in youth. Oh, how my heart has yearned for that young man when I have seen him gradually yielding to temptation. Step by step has he been drawn into the vortex until he drags out a miserable existence and a terrible death. Happy the youth that have resisted those evils, and become useful members of society, a blessing to the country and a benefit to the world.

Mr. Brown kindly invited Mr. C. into his house, and himself and family endeavored to make him comfortable, but Mr. C. was suffering too much mental agony to be happy. The ten cents a day he could not dismiss from his mind, and to undertake to save it now was too late. He was present when the story was told in the village store as related by Mr. Brown, and recollected it well.

Mr. C. tarried all night with Mr. Brown, and he gave him a comfortable lodging, for Mr. C. had often been obliged to pass the night in barns and out-houses. The following morning Mr. Brown gave Mr. C. a decent suit of clothes and replenished his purse, and when he left Mr. Brown he could not refrain from weeping. But Mr. C.'s time here on earth was short, for he died the following winter a pauper.

The history of Mr. C. taught Mr. Brown's children a salutary lesson, to form habits of sobriety in youthful days, and save their ten cents a day. Mr. Brown, too, had early taught his children by his success in life, that industry and economy is the way to wealth, and he often related the story of ten cents a day saved to them, which if he had not heard when he was young he probably now would have been in limited circumstances, if not poor. How many of the rising generation are there at the present day that uselessly spend their ten cents a day, thought Mr. Brown one evening, as he was sitting in his room with his family around him, and how many, thought he, had been wrecked in the slippery paths of life, from the age of fifteen to twenty-five, and he exhorted his children to remember the story of ten cents a day, and to abstain from intemperance, impurity of language, and falsehood. In so doing they would save their reputation, preserve their credit, and by usefulness prevent the tear of anguish from flowing down the cheek of a loving father and mother, and the richest of heaven's gifts would descend and bless them.

Mr. Brown's advice to his children did not pass by unheeded, for he lived to see them all married and settled around him on farms which he gave them, prosperous and happy, occupying high positions in society. All of this, reader, was caused by hearing the story of Ten Cents a Day.

A TALE OF THE GREAT REBELLION.

It was the month of March, which in our latitude is one of the most disagreeable months in the year. A mixture of rain, snow and hail, had fallen during the day, and the evening in Farmer Brewer's house was as dreary as the weather was without, for he was in rather an unpleasant mood. He had purchased his farm before the outbreak of the great rebellion, for a moderate price, as he thought, and had made great exertions to liquidate the debt, but the expense of living and the increase of taxes during the four long years of the war was bearing so heavily upon him, that now he could hardly collect money enough to pay his interest, which would soon be due. His two sons, Elihu and Leonard, had enlisted in the war, and he was left alone to work his farm and get along the best he could. Where Farmer Brewer lived, laborers were very scarce and commanded exorbitant prices, which he was unable to pay. It was true that the products of his farm sold for large prices, but the scarcity of labor obliged him to cultivate but little, and oftentimes he had to trudge along alone.

It was the early part of March, and the snow yet covered the earth, for the winter had been one of uninterrupted sleighing, and the rays of the sun had not yet sufficient heat to melt the large bodies of snow which had fallen during the winter. Farmer Brewer sat with his family around his cooking stove. His farm having a limited supply of wood, he could not afford to purchase coal, which then sold at twelve dollars per ton, and one fire was all that he was able to support. This had to suffice for the warmth and comfort of his family, and to accommodate his neighbors who came to see him during the long winter evenings. His neighbors, who were in affluent circumstances, had an extra fire when they received company, and when Farmer Brewer paid them a visit, and saw the pains and expense they had taken to accommodate himself and family, he would go home unhappy.

He was sitting around his cooking stove with his family, consisting of his wife and two interesting daughters, with his face buried in his hands, absorbed in deep thought. The March wind whistled around his dwelling, and the hail and storm were pelting against the windows. Nothing was heard within but the hissing of the old tea-kettle on the cooking stove, and the chirp of the cricket in the jambs of the old fireplace. Farmer Brewer was now thinking of his two sons, who were in General Grant's army and had followed him from the Rapidan to Richmond, through all the bloody battles, without being even wounded. They had seen the brave Generals Sedgwick and Wadsworth fall, and had seen their comrades shot down side by side in the battles of the Wilderness, and had followed the retreating rebels to the strongholds of Richmond.

Farmer Brewer was thinking that evening whether his sons would live to see the end of the war and return in safety. This had been a great source of trouble to him, for he now needed the assistance of his sons. He was far advanced in life, and was getting infirm, and would soon be unable to endure the labors of farming.

The first of May was approaching, and Farmer Brewer had his interest to pay, and he was fearful that he would not have wherewith to meet it. The little he had raised off of his farm he was obliged to consume in his family and to pay his taxes with. If he had employed a laborer through the past summer, he might have raised extra produce enough to pay for the labor and have something to sell to pay his interest, but the draft had taken the working class and even his two sons for the war, so he was obliged to work his farm alone. Farmer Brewer now was in trouble, yet he was thankful his two sons had not fallen in the great struggle, and if he had means sufficient to meet his first of May engagements he would be happy. Under circumstances like these Farmer Brewer was discouraged, and truth compels me to say that he was unpleasant to his family. Before the war he was an affectionate husband, a kind father, indulgent to his children; now he was morose and cross, with little conversation evenings as he sat with his family around the old cooking stove.

Another month had passed away and April had come. A series of battles was going on between Generals Grant and Lee, and Farmer Brewer read the news with more than ordinary interest, of the advantages gained by our armies over Lee. The strongholds which the rebel General had held with such determined resistance, were now forced to succumb to our arms, and eventually the rebel army of Northern Virginia was forced to leave their capital and beat a precipitate retreat in the night, and was hotly pursued the next day by Grant. This was the second of April. Lee was trying to force a junction with Johnston, which then would enable him to keep the enemy at bay, and probably make his escape with his grand army across the Rio Grande, and take up his abode in Texas. If unsuccessful, then he could retreat into Mexico, and there prolong the war for some time. But headed off by Sherman, he was compelled to surrender on the ninth of April.

When Farmer Brewer read of the surrender of Lee and the grand army of Northern Virginia, and saw the rejoicings throughout the North, the flags and banners waving to the breeze, the orators and statesmen proclaiming the end of the war, he could hardly realize it. General Lee, whose fame had already reached the whole civilized world, was now Grant's prisoner, and when he received a letter from his sons that they had escaped unhurt, Farmer Brewer's feelings could better be imagined than described. If, thought he to himself, I could pay my interest the first of May, I would be happy, for the war is probably ended, and Elihu and Leonard are safe. They will soon be mustered out of service and return home again, and then they will assist me in working the farm, and thus will enable me to get along better. With the help of my two sons I may yet be able to keep my farm and cancel the mortgage. If I could find some way to pay my interest the first of May, thought Farmer Brewer to himself, it would be all that I would ask.

Little did Farmer Brewer think that his sons Elihu and Leonard thought of his situation. They knew that their father had interest to pay, and they were fearful that he had not money sufficient. A few days before the first of May Farmer Brewer was in trouble, being all alone in his barn where no eye could see him but the inscrutable eye of Him who sees every one. He walked the floor with a hurried step, thinking what excuse he could render to his creditors. He thought when his two sons would return home from the war and help him on his farm, he could by another year be able to meet the two years interest. But, thought he, would this satisfy Mr. S.? Such thoughts occupied his mind, when he was suddenly interrupted by one of his daughters entering the barn, saying that mother had just received a letter from Elihu, and wishing him to come to the house and read it. Farmer Brewer obeyed the summons immediately. Receiving the letter from his wife, he read the following:

"DEAR FATHER:—Knowing that you had some interest to pay the first of May, and thinking that you would want a little money then, we send you —— dollars which we have saved out of our earnings. This we present you that you may appropriate to your own use. All well. P. S.—Remember us to mother and sisters. Your sons, ELIHU AND LEONARD."

Nothing could have been more opportune to Farmer Brewer, for the first of May was close to hand. Now the problem was solved, and when the first of May morning arrived, Farmer Brewer was ready.

Farmer Brewer had contracted a few debts with the merchants and mechanics, which now he was ready to discharge, and having performed this duty it inspired him with the hope to commence the year anew. He had just received the news that Johnston had surrendered with his entire army on the same terms as General Lee, and he rejoiced in the anticipation that the war was at an end, and soon his two sons would get an honorable discharge and return home, and that peace would once more smile upon our beloved country, which for four long years had been deluged with blood, and bedewed with the tears of widows and orphans.

Farmer Brewer, as I have said, had for the past year been unpleasant in his family, but it was his pecuniary embarrassments that made him so. He was prosperous in early life, but meeting with reverses, and the draft taking his two sons from him, made him feel unhappy. But now a bright day was dawning. They would soon return, and he felt confident that he would see better days.

A beautiful May evening Farmer Brewer was sitting again with his family in the same kitchen around the old cooking stove, but he did not exhibit the same disposition. His former cheerfulness had returned, and there with his family he was enjoying a happy hour. The spring was further advanced than usual at that season of the year. Already the fruit trees were in blossom, and the valley and fields were clothed in a verdure of green. Nature appeared to Farmer Brewer more than ordinarily beautiful, at a season when she decks herself in her most brilliant garments. The air without was balmy, and the old cooking stove did not need to be replenished with fuel. Farmer Brewer is again the same affectionate husband, a kind and indulgent father, and we trust he will ever remain so. His two sons were once more in the bosom of his family. God grant that he be spared many years, and when his days on earth are numbered may he die in the hope of a blessed immortality.

Historical Sketches.

Local Historical Sketches.

EARLY HISTORY OF DUTCHESS COUNTY.

Dutchess county was formed Nov. 1st, 1683. It was provisionally annexed to Ulster, and was first represented separately in the General Assembly in 1713. Livingston Manor was taken off and annexed to Albany county in 1717, and Putnam was taken off in 1812. It is on the east bank of the Hudson, about midway between New York and Albany, and ranks among the first in the state, containing a large class of wealthy farmers located on substantial farms, well cultivated and improved. This county has been the habitation of the white man for nearly two centuries. It was settled mostly by the Dutch and French Huguenots, an industrious people, who cleared the forests, reclaimed the swamps, and erected stately farm houses. The county was originally purchased of the aborigines by patentees. Francis Rombout and others were the first purchasers. Their patent bears date October 17, 1686. The number of acres it contained is not definitely known, but it included the original town of Fishkill, now divided into Fishkill, East Fishkill, and a part of LaGrange. The second purchase was the Great or Lower Nine Partners, by Caleb Heathcote and others. The patent bears date May 27, 1697. The Nine Partners purchased nine water lots extending from the Hudson River east to the Connecticut line, including the county north of Beekman's patent. The third purchaser was Henry Beekman, June 5th, 1703. That purchase included the central part of the county. The fourth purchase was Little or Upper Nine Partners, by Sampson, Boughton, and others, April 10, 1706. This purchase included the towns of Milan, Pine Plains, and North East.

The Amenia Times recently published an interesting account of the "Great Nine Partners," most of the facts being obtained from Mr. Newton Reed, of South Amenia, and from which we make the following extracts:

"There are two tracts of land in this county named the 'Nine Partners'—the lower or 'Great Nine Partners,' and the upper or 'Little Nine Partners.' The name was formerly used and applied to several different localities wide apart, even after the incorporation of the several towns included in these tracts. Our Dutch ancestors, who settled in Fishkill in the year 1690, had evidently an eye upon the finely located lands in this section, for in the year 1697 they obtained a Royal Patent from the crown of England, and the corporate name of the 'Nine Partners.' This tract of land was about twelve by sixteen miles in extent, and embraced about thirty thousand acres. The old Red

Meeting House was located on this tract, as was also the Friends' school, in Washington, known as the 'Nine Partners' Boarding School.'

"The lower or Great Nine Partners covered the territory nearly included in the towns of Clinton, Pleasant Valley, Washington, Stanford, and all the old town of Amenia, except what is termed the Oblong. Nine residents of the county obtained this patent, to-wit: Caleb Heathcote, a descendant of a noble English family; James Emmot, the ancestor of our distinguished countryman, now of New York city, and Judge of the Supreme Court; William Creed, David Johnstone, Jarvis Mitchell, Henry Ten Eyck, Henry Filkin, after whom the old town of Filkintown was named, (now in the neighborhood of Mabbetsville;) John Aarston, and Augustus Graham, the latter of Scotch descent—and this tract was divided into thirty-six principal lots of nearly an equal number of acres. There were four tiers running north and south, and each one of the aforesaid proprietors had a lot in each tier—the eastern was embraced in the town of Amenia, and the town lot, number twenty-eight, was owned by Augustus Graham. The lots next in order north belonged to John Aarston, Henry Filkin, Caleb Heathcote, James Emmot, William Creed, David Johnstone, Jarvis Mitchell, and Henry Ten Eyck. Besides these thirty-six large lots there were nine long narrow lots, one to each partner, running from near the southwest corner across the town of Hyde Park to the Hudson river, and these were called water lots. The lot lines, as shown on the larger maps of Dutchess county, are not in every instance correct.

"The upper or 'Little Nine Partners' covered the territory now nearly included in the present towns of Milan, Pine Plains, and that part of North East (except the Oblong) which was formerly a part of Amenia.

"The town of Amenia, until the year 1823, embraced that part of North East which lies south of a line running through the north part of the village of Millerton.

"This tract or patent for lands was granted by the Crown in the year 1706 to nine men also, to-wit: Sampson Boughton, George Clark, Rip Van Dam,— whose father was an alderman of New York city in 1695—James Graham, R. Lurting, F. Franconier, Thomas Wenham, Richard Mompesson, and Richard Sackett, who was the first white settler in Amenia, and who subsequently purchased large quantities of land from the Indians located in and about Sharon. This tract of land was divided into sixty-three lots of different areas and various localities. The Nine Partners' grants were of much earlier date than the ceding of the Oblong to this state—and east of which was then the Connecticut line—the Oblong west line runs near the residence of Mr. Allen Wiley, about half a mile east of Amenia station.

"It is related of the proprietor of a celebrated hosterlie many years ago in the city of New York, that when he saw the name of a guest from Dutchess county on his register, he would ask the question, 'Were you born in Dutchess?' If the reply was in the affirmative, he would remark, 'I never lost a cent by a Dutchess county man—they are all gentlemen!'"

The first civilized man that visited Dutchess county

was Hendrick Hudson, an Englishman by birth. In 1607 a London company fitted out a ship under his command for the purpose of discovering a northwestern passage to the East Indies. This voyage and another the following year for the same purpose both proving unsuccessful, the company suspended their patronage. Hudson then went to Holland and entered the service of the celebrated Dutch East India Company. This company fitted out a small ship named the *Half Moon*, under the command of Hudson, with a crew of twenty men, Dutch and English. Hudson left Amsterdam on the 4th, the Texel on the 6th of April, and arrived on the American coast on the 18th of July, 1609, near Portland, Me. Turning his course southward, Hudson came to Cape Cod, where he landed about the 3d of August. After this he sailed southward and westward for twenty-one days, until he came to the entrance of Chesapeake Bay, about the 24th of August. From this point he returned northward along the coast, and on the 28th discovered Delaware Bay. During the six following days he pursued his northerly course, and on the 3d of September, 1609, he anchored within Sandy Hook. Here he remained several days for the purpose of exploring the country. A boat was sent ashore every day and the natives manifested a friendly disposition toward them, and showed a strong desire to barter the products of their country for articles the ship contained, such as knives, beads and cloths. On the 6th of September he sent a boat manned with five hands to explore what appeared to be the mouth of a river at a distance of about five leagues from the ship. Here a good depth of water was found. In exploring the bay and adjacent waters the boat's crew spent the whole day. On their way returning to the ship towards night they were attacked by the natives in two canoes, one carrying fourteen and the other twelve men. A skirmish ensued in which one of Hudson's men, named John Colman, was killed by an arrow which struck him in the throat, and two were wounded. The next day the remains of Colman were interred on a point of land not far from the ship, which from that circumstance received the name of Colman's Point, and which was probably the same that is now called Sandy Hook. On the 11th of September Hudson sailed through the Narrows, and on the 12th he first entered the river which bears his name. From the 12th to the 22d of September Hudson was employed in ascending the river. The natives were not friendly until he had passed the Highlands, and when he had ascended the river as far as Dutchess county, Hudson says they found a very loving people and very old men, and they were well used. Hudson went ashore a few miles north of Poughkeepsie and a sachem took him to his wigwam and made him good cheer. At that place the savages flocked on board the ship in large numbers, bringing with them corn, tobacco, pumpkins and grapes.

Tobacco, which is now consumed in such quantities under various forms, was first introduced into England from Spanish America, by Sir Francis Drake and Sir Walter Raleigh, in the year 1586, and met with an early and violent opposition. The clergy and physicians were bitterly opposed to its use, and

King James the First wrote a book against it, entitled the "Counter Blast to Tobacco." It appears that it was universally used by the aborigines of America. Hudson found it here with the natives of Dutchess county. But Hudson introduced a deadly poison among the natives more destructive than the fabled Upas. He was the first white man that gave the Indians of Dutchess county ardent spirits, and it was the first in this part of the American continent. Several of the natives he designed to make drunk, and as the nature of the savage was naturally inclined to intemperance, Hudson found little difficulty in making several of their principal men drunk. Some soon became perfectly helpless. These the sober Indians thought would die, for they knew nothing of the nature of ardent spirits, but on becoming sober they expressed themselves in better health than before, and were eager again to partake of strong water. Hudson sailed up the river a little above where the city of Hudson now stands, and beyond that point he himself never ascended. He sent a boat with five hands, including the mate, who had the command of the expedition. The boat proceeded beyond where the ship lay at anchor eight or nine leagues, but finding the river more shallow, and the depth in some places not more than seven feet, it was judged unadvisable to attempt any further progress. It is supposed that the boat went as far as where the city of Albany now stands. Hudson traded with the natives until he began to descend the river, which was the 23d of September, some of them fetching beaver and other skins, which they exchanged for hatchets, knives, beads, and other trifles. The river abounded with fish, among which were great quantities of salmon, now unknown in its waters. When these fish made their last visit to the waters of the Hudson is not known; it must have been shortly after its discovery. Hudson makes no mention of animals in his voyage. That the buffalo existed in Dutchess county there is not the least shadow of doubt.

Hudson, in trading with the natives, penetrated but a few miles into the country, and probably saw no buffaloes. As the animals generally herd in large numbers, he might not come in contact with any, as he was but ten days exploring the river. Animals have existed here in our river counties which became extinct before they were settled by civilized man. Ogilvie, in his description of Autumn, speaking of these parts, makes mention of lions which abounded in the mountains. He says, on the borders of Canada there is sometimes seen a kind of beast which hath some resemblance to a horse, having cloven feet, shaggy mane, one horn, just on the forehead, a tail like that of a wild hog, and a deer's neck. He furthermore gives a picture of this strange beast, which resembles exceedingly a unicorn. The mastodon, an animal that has never been seen alive by civilized man, once probably existed in Dutchess county. Several skeletons have been found in Orange county, mostly in the town of Montgomery and vicinity. One of these was exhibited many years in Peale's Museum, Philadelphia. One found in 1844, by Nathaniel Brewster, twenty feet below the surface, was thirty feet long. The whole number of bones was two hundred and twenty, and the aggregate weight nearly 1,995 pounds. The mastodon may not have been extinct when this continent was discovered by Columbus, and even as late as when Henry Hudson sailed up the river that bears his name, there may have been some living mastodon found in our river counties. The progress of civilization was extremely slow. From the time when Columbus discovered America to the first permanent settlement of the United States, was a period of one hundred and fifteen years, and from the time that Dutchess county was discovered to its first permanent settlement was three-quarters of a century. The mastodon probably became extinct in this country just before it was occupied by the Europeans, for according to the opinion of learned men those skeletons that were found in Orange county could not have lain there more than five centuries. The weight of those animals when alive must have been enormous, when we consider that the bones weighed nearly two tons.

The mastodon has existed in Orange county, and although there have been no skeletons found in this county, several large ones have been found across the river. Dutchess county was not so favorable a location for the mastodon as Orange county. Dutchess county contains more low, wet and swampy ground, and the mastodon being a large animal, could not venture on these grounds on account of his weight, and consequently he sought a more favorable location. The mastodon was probably a carniverous animal, and lived on other animals, which might be one cause of his becoming extinct. If he lived on herbage, as some historians say, he could not have subsisted here all through our long winters, as he could not obtain sufficient food when the ground was covered with snow, and would have died of starvation. The different tribes of Indians probably united together and destroyed him in order to save the game for their own wants.

As I have already remarked, Hudson began to ascend the river the 23d of September from where he lay at anchor to where the city of Hudson is now located. On his way down his men went frequently ashore, and had several friendly interviews with the natives, who expressed a desire that they would reside amongst them, and a sachem of Dutchess county made Hudson and his crew an offer of lands for that purpose, which was declined. When the ship came below the Highlands the savages appeared to be of a different character, and were extremely troublesome, especially those who inhabited the western side of the river. They tried to rob the ship, and frequently shot at the crew with bows and arrows. Hudson's men discharged several muskets at them and killed ten or twelve of them. In these conflicts, which were frequently renewed during the first and second days of October, none of the ship's crew appear to have been injured. On the fourth day of October, just one month from the day on which he landed within Sandy Hook, Hudson came out of the river, and without anchoring in the bay immediately stood out to sea. He headed directly for Europe, and on the 9th day of November following he arrived in England. Hudson never revisited Dutchess county, but he made another voyage to this country in 1610, and discovered the great northern bay which bears his name. There he was compelled to pass a distressing and dangerous winter. In the spring he found a spirit of dissatisfaction and mutiny growing among his men, and at length manifesting itself in open violence. A majority of his crew arose, took command of the ship, put Hudson and seven others in a boat, turned them adrift on the ocean, and abandoned them to their fate. They were never heard of more.

After Hudson discovered Dutchess county, there were no permanent settlers in it for nearly three-quarters of a century. Most of the river counties were settled prior to Dutchess. Ulster county was the first between New York and Albany. It commenced upon the present site of Rondout in 1614. This early settlement was broken up by Indian hostilities, and a new one was commenced between 1630 and 1640. This was again attacked by the Indians, and in 1665 was abandoned. Before 1660 settlers had again located at Kingston and vicinity, which was again attacked by the Indians. A destructive war ensued, in which the Ulster county Indians were nearly exterminated. From this we date the permanent settlement of Ulster.

In 1614 the Dutch built a trading house at the southern extremity of Manhattan island, (now New York island,) called New Amsterdam, and another at Albany called Fort Orange, and in the meantime they carried on trade with the Indians in Dutchess county, stopping at Fishkill Landing and Poughkeepsie. When Westchester, Orange, and Ulster counties were settling, Dutchess county contained no inhabitants. A delegation numbering ten or more persons was sent across the river from Ulster to view the country. On their return they reported the land worthless and not fit for the habitation of man. Could we wonder that Dutchess county settled so extremely slow, when a historian says, that in 1693, Dutchess having very few inhabitants, was committed to the care of Ulster. The first settlers were obliged to go to Esopus to attend court. But eventually some pioneers ventured into Dutchess county and began to clear the forests, and as they gradually opened the woods, giving the sun's rays a chance to warm the earth, the waters in the marshy grounds retreated and became absorbed in the atmosphere. Those stagnant pools which were so unhealthy to the early settlers dried up, and the ground was converted into natural meadows. But emigration was so slow that it was not till 1720 that the county wore the aspect of civilization. Then emigration was rapid.

Fishkill and Rhinebeck were the first towns settled. The Amies, Brinckerhoffs, Alyurks, Hays, Pincels, Depuysters, Linderbecks, and Swartouts were among the first settlers in Fishkill. The first settler in Rhinebeck was H. Beekman, before 1700. Poughkeepsie was next. Balties Van Kleeck built the first house within the present limits of the city, in 1702. Amenia was the next town settled. Richard Sackett bought large tracts of land of the Indians, and in 1711 settled in this town. Beekman was next settled. A colony located in 1716 and kept an inn at an early day. The remaining towns in the county were settled somewhere between 1720 and 1750. The only villages in the county before the Revolution were Poughkeepsie and Fishkill. Fishkill then was the most wealthy and populous. It could boast of an academy while Poughkeepsie had none. The celebrated divine, the Rev. John H. Livingston, of the Reformed Dutch Church, was born at Poughkeepsie in 1746, and when old enough to attend school, there being no academy in his native place, he was sent to Fishkill, and put under the care of the Rev. Chauncey Graham. It would appear from this that Poughkeepsie had only a common school in the village before the Revolution. There was a school house located in Main street east of the City Bank, the precise spot not now known, which stood there till after the Revolution. That school house contained pupils that afterwards became distinguished men in Poughkeepsie. The Hon. Judge Emmot, deceased, received the rudiments of his education there. After the Revolution, Poughkeepsie being the shire town of Dutchess county, it arose phœnix like, for where the Morgan House is located was nothing but an extensive field, containing a race course and a few old dilapidated dwellings. Splendid buildings were soon erected, and in 1798 the Rutzer Hotel was built, which was then the finest hotel between New York and Albany, as the historian said when finished, "it is elegant and spacious." While the first settlers of Ulster, Orange, and Westchester counties were constantly annoyed by the Indians, and their histories are recorded with bloody battles, nothing of the kind occurred between the first settlers of Dutchess and the Indians. The different tribes that occupied the county were remarkably peaceful. There is no record that a battle was ever fought, or that the people even found it necessary to fortify against their attacks.

The oldest deed on record in the county bears date

January 28th, 1698, in the reign of William the Third, for lands stated to have been patented on the 7th of May, 1697. It is signed by John Rodsnan and Mary his wife, William Kuddleston and Sarah his wife, of the city of New York, to Thomas Rathburn. The next oldest deed is dated July 20th, 1702, given by Myndart Hermanse and Robert Sanders to Myndart Van Kleeck, for property in Pockepsung. As I have remarked, the first settlers were obliged to go to Esopus to attend court, then called Wiltwyck, and it wasn't till 1717 that the colonial legislature authorized the building of a Court House and Jail at Poughkeepsie. It was not till 1721 that the Court of Common Pleas was established. The following is a copy of the first Court of General Sessions held in Dutchess county:

"At a Court of General Sessions of the Peace held at Poughkeepsie, the third Tuesday in October, being the Seventeenth day of the same month, in the eighth year of the Reign of our Sovereign Lord George, by the Grace of God of Great Britain, France and Ireland, King, Defender of the Faith, &c. Ano Domino 1721: Present Leonard Lewis, Jacob Kipp, Barent Van Kleeck, Court opened. The Commission being read, the Grand Jury being called and sworn, Court adjourned till four o'clock in the afternoon. The Grand Jury the next morning brought in a presentment against the defendent John DeGrass for suspision of felony."

THE FIRST CHURCHES IN DUTCHESS

COUNTY.

The first preaching in Dutchess county was probably by the Reformed Dutch Missionaries, unless it was, as some historians assert, by Missionaries of the Moravian Church to the Indians in Pine Plains, or Chicomico, as it was then called. The Reformed Dutch Church in the county was organized at Poughkeepsie in the year 1716, by the Rev. Peter Vas, of Kingston, and the same year he organized the Reformed Dutch Church of Fishkill. Probably they were the first churches organized in Dutchess county. The church at Poughkeepsie was erected several years before the church at Fishkill, for according to the records of the county the deed was given by Captain Jacobus Vanderbogart, Mr. Peter Velie, and Mr. Johannas Van Kleeck, conveying to them a lot of land in Poughkeepsie, on which to erect a Dutch Meeting House, in connection with the church in the Netherlands. The deed bears date December 26, 1718, and was acknowledged before Leonard Lewis, and probably the church at Pockepsing, as it was then called, was soon after built. It stood in the center of what is now known as Market street. The burying ground extended along Main street eastward for several rods and west of the church to the lot adjoining, covered by the Court House. Rev. A. M. Mann, in an historical sermon of said church, in 1858, says that the Reformed Dutch Church of Poughkeepsie was organized, as nearly as can be ascertained, about the year 1700, but by what classis or minister is not definitely known. He says that around the first thirty years of its existence there has gathered a profound and impenetrable darkness. Again, he says: "What was its style of architecture, or the material of which it was built, we have no means of ascertaining." We disagree with the reverend historian. It is a fixed fact that the Dutch Church of Poughkeepsie and Fishkill was organized in 1716, and that around the first thirty years of its existence there is no profound and impenetrable darkness. As I have said, the deed was recorded in the county records, December 26, 1718, and about two years after the church at Poughkeepsie was organized, and soon after the church edifice was erected. The material of which the church was built was stone, with a hipped roof, and a moderate tower in front. The tower extended above the peak of the roof a short distance, and there the bell was suspended, and over the same was a small tapering spire, and surmounting that was the rooster. There was but one entrance, and that was in the tower, which fronted Main street. That church existed till the close of the Revolution, when it was demolished and a new one erected some seventy feet from Main street, and on a lot known as the old burying ground, a short distance northeast of the Poughkeepsie Hotel, where a portion of the foundation may still be traced.

The Reformed Dutch Church of Fishkill was not erected till the year 1731. A petition that year, of the elders and deacons of the Reformed Dutch Protestant Church of Fish Creek, Dutchess County, in the Province of New York, in behalf of themselves and the rest of the members of said church, addressed to his excellency, John Montgomerie, Esq., recorded in the Historical Documents, Vol. 3, humbly sheweth: That the members of the said congregation being in daily expectation of a minister from Holland, to preach the Gospel amongst them, according to the canons, rule and discipline of the Reformed Protestant Churches of the United Netherlands, and therefore have agreed amongst themselves to erect and build a convenient church to the public worship of God, nigh the said Fish Creek, in the county aforesaid; but finding that the said building would be very chargable, and therefore, as in like cases has been practiced and is usual in His Providence, they would desire the aid, help, and assistance of all charitable and well-disposed christians within this Province for the completion of the said building. They therefore most humbly pray for your Excellency's license to be granted, to collect, gather and receive the benevolence and free gifts of all such inhabitants of this Province as shall be willing to contribute, &c.

The first church was built where the present one is now located. The dimensions every way were the same, and the material used was stone. It had a barrack roof with a small cupola in the center, which supported a bell, and a rooster surmounted the same. The upper story had port holes in the walls, to enable the inhabitants to defend themselves as in a fort, in case of an attack by the Indians, to which they were subject when the country was first settled. The only entrance was on Main street, and in front of the church was a large oak tree that was necessarily taken down when the present edifice was erected. The celebrated spy, Enoch Crosby, who figured in Cooper's writings as Harry Burch, made his escape when confined in the same church, by leaping from the upper window to a limb of the same tree. Four years after the close of the Revolution the old church was demolished and the present edifice erected, though it was not, for the want of funds, entirely completed until the year 1800.

After the Reformed Dutch Churches of Poughkeepsie and Fishkill were organized, there was no settled minister over either of these churches for several years, but they enjoyed the occasional services of the Rev. Peter Vas, of Kingston, Rev. Gualterus Dubois, of New York, Rev. Vincentius Antonides, of Kings County, Long Island, and the Rev. Mr. Van Deusen, of Albany. These men in their visitations were in the habit, it seems, of administering the ordinance of baptism and the Lord's Supper. Probably these men were the first that preached in Dutchess county, but the editor of the Poughkeepsie Eagle, in his paper of May 15, 1858, says: "Probably the first preaching the people of Poughkeepsie, Fishkill, and Rhinebeck ever heard, unless it was from the Moravian Missionaries to the Indians, in Pine Plains, or Chicomico, as it was then called, was by Dominie Backerus, of New York, about 1645, when he began to visit the settlements." Dominie Backerus left New York for Holland in 1648, and never returned, and at that time there were no permanent settlers in Dutchess county. He could not have preached in Dutchess county then, as there were no inhabitants to preach to, and as late as 1714 Dutchess county contained only 445 inhabitants. There is no authentic authority that Dominie Backerus was ever in Dutchess county.

The first minister regularly called and settled over the churches of Poughkeepsie and Fishkill, was the Rev. Cornelius Van Schie, who was sent by the classis of Amsterdam, in Holland, in the year 1731, just fifteen years after the churches were first organized. The call was signed by the Rev. Vincentius Antonides, of Long Island, and by the following persons, who constituted the first consistories of the above churches: Of the church of Poughkeepsie, the elders were Peter Palmatier, Johannis Van Kleeck; deacons, Laurens Van Kleeck and Myndert Vanderbogart. Of the church of Fishkill, the elders were Peter DuBuys, Abram DuBuys; deacons, Abram Brinckerhoff and Hendrick Phillips.

These churches continued to be united for a number of years, probably to the close of the Revolution. In 1772 it still subsisted. In the minutes of the Consistory, May, 1789, we find in the record, that the members of the corporation of the First Reformed Protestant Dutch Church of Fishkill Town, met for the first time after their incorporation, and September, 1789, the Consistory appointed a committee of two to visit Poughkeepsie and inquire into the state of the glebe belonging to the churches of Poughkeepsie and Fishkill. From these records it would seem the union had been but recently dissolved. Accompanying the above call, which these churches sent to the classis at Amsterdam, was a sum of money sufficient to defray the expenses of the minister and his family to this country. The amount of which, the record states, was 502 guilders. On the 4th of October, 1731, the Rev. Cornelius Van Schie, the first pastor of the united churches, was installed over them by the Rev. Gualterus Dubois, of the city of New York. Of Mr. Van Schie we have no further knowledge than that he continued to serve these churches in the gospel till about the year 1738, when he was released from his pastoral charge and removed to the city of Albany, where he died in 1744. The second pastor was the Rev. Benjamin Meinema, whose call bears date 1745. But the first account of him on the consistorial records is in 1749. He remained pastor of these churches till the year 1758. The next in order was the Rev. Jacobus Van Nist. His call, from the elders and deacons of the Reformed Dutch Churches of Poughkeepsie and Fishkill, designates him as a candidate for the ministry. It bears date 1758, and was moderated by the Rev. Mr. Vanderburg, of Raritan, New Jersey. Mr. Van Nist's ministry was short, for he died in early life. He was buried in the church yard at Fishkill, near the highway, now known as Main street. The tombstone had entirely disappeared. It was accidentally discovered when digging a grave where he was interred, and the following inscription in Dutch was on the stone, originally placed there: "Jacobus Van Niest, Preacher of the Holy Gospel at Poughkeepsie and Vis Kill, Died 10th of April, 1761, in his 27th year." The stone is now placed against the rear of the church.

From what we can learn of the history of the above churches, there was but one pastor who had the sole charge of them, even so late as the year 1761. The glebe or parsonage was located at Poughkeepsie, and the minister resided there, and probably divided his time equally between Poughkeepsie and Fishkill. He might have had some other missionary station in the county. What salary he received we have no means of ascertaining. The churches being some sixteen miles apart, the country new, and the roads being sometimes almost impassable, rendered it difficult for the pastor to be punctual to his appointments. The Dutch Church at that period was the most numerous of any sect in the State of New York. She was the first to follow the footsteps of Hudson, and her ministers were the first to proclaim the glad tidings of salvation to the dark benighted savages of the new world. At that period of her history the inhabitants would come from Rhinebeck, Beekman, and LaGrange, to Poughkeepsie and Fishkill, to have their faithful pastors break to them the bread of life. How different it is now. At the present time churches in the town of Fishkill are within rifle shot of a population of ten thousand inhabitants.

The decease of Mr. Van Nist occurred about the mid period of the difficulties occasioned by the unhappy strife between the Coetus and Conferentia parties. It was at that time that these associated churches became so agitated and distracted on the subject, that the congregations were divided. In 1763 the Conferentia party of Poughkeepsie, Fishkill, Hopewell, and Rhinebeck, united in sending a call to the classis of Amsterdam, to be disposed of according to their wisdom. This call was placed by classis in the hands of the Rev. Isaac Rysdyck, who having signified his acceptance of the same, was regularly installed as the pastor of these churches.

On the 11th of December, 1769, the Coetus party presented a call to Henricus Schoonmaker, a candidate for the ministry, which call was accepted. So vehement was the opposition of the Conferentia party to Mr. Schoonmaker and the Coetus party, that at the time of his installation at Poughkeepsie, they forcibly closed the church door against him, and the services took place under an old apple tree not far distant from the present site of the First Church. This state of things continued until the year 1771, when a reconciliation took place between the contending parties, brought about chiefly through the influence of the late Dr. John H. Livingston. In point of numerical strength the parties were about equal to each other; in other respects there was a marked difference between them. The former excelling in practical preaching, zeal and industry; the latter having the greatest share of learning. The two parties now completely organized and prepared for war, took their stand against each other with evidences of resolution and feeling which forebode a long, obstinate and dreadful conflict, and so it proved. The peace of the churches was destroyed. Not only neighboring ministers and congregations were at variance, but in many places the same congregation was divided, and in those instances in which the numbers, or the influential characters on different sides were equal, the consequences became very deplorable. The church at Fishkill was locked up by one part of the congregation against the other. Tumults on the Lord's day at the door of the church were frequent. Quarrels respecting the services and the contending claims of different ministers of the two bodies often took place. The ministers were sometimes assaulted in the pulpit, and public worship was either disturbed or terminated by violence; and on one occasion a minister of the Coetus party was forcibly taken out of the pulpit by one of the members of the opposite party, whose name is familiar at the present day.

Peace being again restored, Isaac Rysdyck relinquished his charge of the church in Poughkeepsie, and confined himself mainly to the care of the churches of New Hackensack, Hopewell, and Fishkill, until his death, which took place November 2d, 1790. He died on Sabbath morning, very sudden, from paralysis. The congregation of New Hackensack, Hopewell, and Fishkill, had assembled that morning for service, when a messenger arrived and informed them that Rysdyck was dead. So sudden and unexpected was the message to them that many of the congregation wept. They had heard their pastor's last sermon; he had delivered his last message; he had left home and friends and came here to spend his life in his Master's service, and he died at his post. He was found dead alone in his room, his sermon in manuscript lying before him. The faithful ambassador of Christ knows no fear like the soldier. Flushed with the expectation of victory, he girds on his armor and enlists in his Master's service, and is ready and willing to spend his life for his guilty fellow men, whenever and wherever the lot may be opened to him. So it was with Rysdyck. He had spent his life in preaching the Holy Gospel.

His funeral took place the following Tuesday at New Hackensack. There was no funeral sermon preached, as it was not customary in those days. The elders and deacons were the pall bearers, and his remains were placed beneath the floor in front of the pulpit, (an ancient Dutch custom,) in the church at New Hackensack, which stood from 1766 to 1835. His remains lay there undisturbed until the old edifice was taken down, in 1834, when they were removed and buried in the graveyard. In the yard is the following inscription: "The remains of the Rev. Isaac Rysdyck, the first Pastor of this church, lie in the southeast corner of this plot."

He was settled over the churches of Poughkeepsie, Fishkill, New Hackensack, and Hopewell, in the year 1765, and continued his ministery in the three latter churches until his death.

POUGHKEEPSIE.

Poughkeepsie is the shire town of the wealthy and flourishing county of Dutchess, situated on the banks of the noble Hudson, equidistant between New York and Albany, containing a population of twenty-two thousand inhabitants. The original name of Poughkeepsie was Apokeepsing, an Indian word signifying "Pleasant Harbor." The first permanent settler in Poughkeepsie was Baltus Van Kleeck, who built the first house within the present limits of the city in the year 1702, on land now owned by Matthew Vassar, which was demolished in 1835. It was incorporated as a village, March 27th, 1729, and as a city, March 28th, 1854. Dutchess county was organized by the first Legislature in 1683. It derived its name from Duchess, the wife of a Duke. The first Court House in Poughkeepsie was built in the year 1717. An Act was passed that year by the Colonial Assembly to authorize Dutchess county to build a Court House and Prison, the notice of which, addressed to the county authorities, bears date, June 11th, 1717. Pursuant to the provisions of that act, the freeholders of the county were commanded to meet at the house of Leonard Lewis, on the 22d of June, 1717, and appoint by a plurality of voices two persons, being freeholders, to superintend the construction of the building. Leonard Lewis, Baltus Van Kleeck, and Johannas Terbots, signed an order addressed to Cornelius Van Der Bogart, constable, commanding him to summon the freeholders to attend the meeting. At this meeting Capt. Baltus Van Kleeck and Jacobus Van Der Bogart, supervisors, were chosen to build the Court House and Jail. In the order from the Provincial Secretary it is said the meeting shall be held in Pockepsink. The certificate of the result is signed by Leonard Lewis, Judge, Capt. Baltus Van Kleeck, and Michael Palmateer, Justices. But notwithstanding that the colonial legislature authorized the building of a Court House and Jail as early as 1717, a Court of Common Pleas was not established until 1721. The following is a copy of the order for the establishment of such court, issued July 6th, 1721, by his excellency, William Burnett, Esq., Captain General and Governor-in-Chief of the Provinces of New York, New Jersey, and Territories depending thereon in America, and Vice Admiral of the same, etc.:

"In Council, An Ordinance For establishing a Court of Common Pleas and a Court of General Sessions of the Peace in Dutchess County, in the Province of New York:

"Whereas in the Establishment of the Courts of Common Pleas and the General Sessions of the Peace, hitherto in the County of Dutchess, on the East side of the Hudson River, over against the County of Ulster, there has been no Courts of Common Pleas or General Sessions of the Peace Erected and Established to be holden and kept within the said County, but the inhabitants of the said County have sometime formerly been subjected to the Jurisdiction of the Justices of the aforesaid County of Ulster, For remedy whereof for the future I have thought fit by and with the Advise and Consent of his Majesties Council for the Province of New York, and by virtue of the power and authority unto me given and granted under the Great Seal of Great Britain, and do hereby Erect, Establish, and Ordain, That from hence forward there shall be held and kept at Poughkeepsie, near the center of said County, a General Sessions of the Peace on the third Tuesday in May, and the third Tuesday in October yearly, and every year forever; which General Sessions of the Peace in every Sessions shall not continue for longer than two days, but may finish the business of the Sessions possibly in one day, and that from hence forward, there shall be held and kept at Poghkepson, near the center of the said County, a Court of Common Pleas to begin the next day after the said Courts of General Sessions of the Peace terminates, and then only if business requires, hold and continue for two days next following and no longer, with the like power and jurisdiction as other Courts of Common Pleas in other Counties within the Province of New York have used and enjoyed, any former Ordinance, Practice or Usage to the contrary hereof in any wise notwithstanding.

"Given under my hand and seal at arms in Council, at Fort George, in New York, the Sixth day of July, in the Seventh year of the Reign of our Sovereign Lord George, by the Grace of God, King of Great

Britain, France, and Ireland, Defender of the Faith, &c. V. V. BURNET."

By order of his Excellency in Council, Robin D. M. Coun, the Court House was soon after erected, and was destroyed by fire in time of the Revolution, when a new one was built which was also burnt down in 1808, and the present structure was erected in 1809. The original cost was $29,000. Putnam County, which then belonged to Dutchess, raised $4000. The building was repaired and a new Jail built separate from the Court House, about 1860.

At a meeting of the Supervisors, held in January, 1721, among the items of expense allowed are the following: To Trynte Van Kleeck, widow, for victualling the assessors and supervisors, justices and clerks, sider, shuger, candles, 13.£ 9d. To Col. Leonard Lewis, for two gallons of rum for assessors and supervisors, 9s. To Jacobus Vander Bogart, Esq., for the assessors and for horse fodder, 3s.

In the list of expenses allowed at a session of supervisors and assessors in 1726, the following are among the items allowed: To Col. Leonard Lewis, for three gallons of rum for assessors and supervisors, at two meetings, at 5s per gallon, 15s. To Widow Vander Bogart, for victualling assessors and supervisors, and clerk, and sider furnished, £1 7s. To Hendrick Bass, for destroying a wolf, allowed in the act, 6s. To Harmanus Reynders, for tending and waiting on the justices and assessors and supervisors, clerk, is allowed for a year's service, £2. To Cornelius Van Der Bogart, Collected for two people that ran away out of his tax list the last year, which he did not receive, their taxes in all three shillings, 10s.

For nearly a century and a half Poughkeepsie has been the shire town of the wealthy county of Dutchess, but her early history is written in tears of blood. We look back with horror in English history, in the bigoted and bloody reign of Queen Mary, when man was burnt at the stake for his religious zeal. But in the early history of Poughkeepsie we find that scenes took place almost as cruel and revolting as in the bloody reign of Mary Tudor.

The burning of a white man and negro for incendiarism about a century ago, took place in Market street, and was witnessed by a great concourse, and the horrors were indescribable. It seemed as if the sufferers never would die, but continued their screams of agony longer than it was thought possible they could live. After the wood was nearly all consumed, and their bodies charred and half consumed had fallen among the coals and ashes, the negro's jaws continued to open and shut, as if yawning, for some minutes, as the people crowded around to witness the end. But there was another scene of horror which took place in Poughkeepsie in the early part of the Revolution, which exceeds, if possible, the burning above alluded to. Two boys from Fishkill, only about sixteen years of age, were arrested as spies. Being without friends, they were undefended, tried and condemned to be hung, and actually were hung on what afterwards was called Forbus Hill. But the trial and execution of a poor man from Beekman, whose name was Brock, which took place about the year 1770, is too melancholy to dwell upon. He was poor and friendless, and was arrested for passing a counterfeit hard dollar, which was proved to have been given him. On the trial he had no defence, being unable to employ an attorney, and he was found guilty and sentenced to be hung, and have his body delivered to the surgeons for dissection, all of which was done at Poughkeepsie. But a brighter day has dawned, those laws which then took the life of a fellow being for so trivial crimes, have long since been obliterated. They have been erased from our statute books, for the diffusion of knowledge has so enlightened man that it has enabled him to frame laws founded upon equity and justice, and at the present day, when a criminal is tried for a crime, he has justice done him; and in all cases, when necessary, mercy is exercised.

Poughkeepsie has kept pace with the age, and has always had her share of learned men. That venerable Court House has its history. It was the nursery of the genius and eloquence of Edmonds, Jourdan, Talmadge, Williams, Cleveland, and others who have filled distinguished positions in American politics. At the bar, one of the most interesting cases which ever occurred in Poughkeepsie, was the Collins will case, which had been in litigation for years. The closing scene took place in the winter of 1861, and the summing up occupied a week. It called out the talent of the prominent members of the bar, and the learned counsel on either side displayed the finest specimens of forensic eloquence.

Poughkeepsie is truly a city of churches. There are twenty-two churches. The first church in the county, Dutch Reformed, organized in 1717, was erected there. It also abounds in schools, many of which are of the highest order of excellence. The Collegiate School (of late years turned into a hotel for summer boarders) was located on the summit of a hill about a mile from the Hudson, and nearly half a mile from the business part of the city. This strucure is modelled after the ancient Parthenon at Athens. It commands an extensive view of the surrounding country. From the colonnade, which entirely surrounds it, the eye of the spectator can encompass a circuit of fifty miles. In company with a friend on one pleasant day in winter we ascended College Hill, and the scene was imposing. On the west and north, where in the summer the Hudson rolls on with pride and beauty, the river was covered with a bridge of ice, and the rays of the sun glistened over the snow clad hills, sparkling like diamonds. Far ahead in the distance could be seen the azure summits of the Catskills reared to the clouds, and stretching beyond the vision's utmost limit. The far famed Mountain House is distinctly seen, at an elevation of nearly three thousand feet above the river. At our feet, like a beautiful panorama, lay the city of Poughkeepsie, with its church spires looming upward, wrapped in snow and ice, and glittering in the rays of a winter's sun. Far away eastward, clothed in winter's garments, reposed the fertile fields of Dutchess, bounded by the rugged snowy hills of Connecticut. On the south the Highlands terminate the view, and the country is dotted with beautiful country seats, mansions, and thriving villages.

THE EARLY HISTORY OF THE

TOWN OF FISHKILL.

What a contrast do the towns of Fishkill and East Fishkill present now with their appearance a century and a half ago. Then they were a vast wilderness, inhabited only by savages and beasts of prey. The traveler in passing through the towns then could witness nothing but the Indian singing his war dance or kindling the blazing faggot around some expiring captive whom he had taken in battle, while his ear was greeted with the howling of wolves and the yell of panthers. What a change hath been wrought in that time! Now we can witness smiling villages, beautiful country seats, stately farm houses, and Christian temples for the worship of the true God. The philanthropist may rejoice to think that a savage race which so long held sway has been exterminated; and that a Christian people now occupy the land; and the historian can find ample scope for his mind in gleaning over the pages of history in search of knowledge, from the first settlement to the present time.

The first settlement of the original town of Fishkill dates back as far as sixteen hundred and eighty-two.

EARLY HISTORY OF FISHKILL. 315

Prior to that the original town of Fishkill was purchased by Francis Rombout, a distinguished merchant of New York city, and Gulyne Ver Planke, for the following articles, the schedule of which is copied from the original Indian deed of sale, in the Book of Patents of this State:

One hun^d Royalls, One hun^d Pound Powder, Two hun^d fathom of White Wampum, one hund Barrs of Lead, One hundred fathom of black Wampum, thirty tobacco boxes, ten holl adges, thirty Gunns, twenty Blankets, forty fathom of Duffills, twenty fathom of stroudwater Cloth, thirty Kittles, forty Hatchets, forty Hornes, forty Shirts, forty p stockins, twelve coates of R. B. & b. C., ten Drawing Knives, forty earthen Juggs, forty Bottles, forty Knives, fouer ankers rum, ten halfe, fatts Beere, two hund^d tobacco Pipes, &c., Eighty Pound Tobacco.

This purchase was made of the Wappingers Indians, through Claes, an Indian interpreter.

Rombout's only daughter, Catharine, married a man whose name was Roger Brett, and after the death of her father, she became sole heir of the patent. She, with her husband, in the year 1710, located on the patent, where the Teller mansion now stands, and they gave her the title of Madam Brett.

As I have said, the first settlement dates back as far as sixteen hundred and eighty-two. The name of the first settler was Nicholas Eighmie. He came over with an army from Holland, commanded by Prince Rupert, the gallant relation of Charles the First, to assist that unfortunate monarch in his warfare against Hamden, Cromwell and others. He remained in Britain when his Prince returned, settled in Scotland, and was among those who came to America about 1672 with Robert Livingston, the first lord of the manor of Columbia county. On ship board he became acquainted with and married a handsome Dutch girl from Holstein. Unwilling to be a mere retainer of Livingston, young Eighmie soon left the manor and went to Fort Orange (now Albany) with his wife. They first intended to settle upon and cultivate an island in the Hudson, just below Fort Orange, within Van Rensselaer's manor, but the free spirit of Eighmie could not succumb to feudal tenor, and in 1682, having saved a little money, he started boldly for the then nearly unbroken wilderness of Dutchess county. He settled himself at the mouth of Fishkill Creek, purchased a tract of land of the Indians extending from that creek to Poughkeepsie, and eastward to the Connecticut line, the termination of New Netherlands in that direction. He soon found that the Beekman patent, from Charles the Second, already covered that territory, and that it belonged to another. He purchased a large tract in the Clove, in Beekman town, from the charter proprietors, and some of it is in possession of his descendents, the Eighmies, at the present time.

While at Fishkill, young Eighmie's wife gave birth to a daughter, the first white child born within the precincts of Dutchess county. About the year 1700 a young man from Holstein, whose father and Eighmie's had been acquainted in the fader-land, found his way to Dutchess county. His name was Peter Lasinck. The little Fishkill maiden had grown up to rosy womanhood, and young Lasinck and Katrina Eighmie wedded and settled within the present domain of East Fishkill, and successfully cultivated the soil. They had four sons and four daughters, and when the oldest child died, the other seven were still living, the youngest seventy-five years old. One of the three sons, William Lasinck, according to the records of the county, was the King's collector of taxes in Fishkill precinct, in 1726. He was the first born of Peter and Katrina.

An incident is related which illustrates the necessary hardihood and perseverance of the Dutch pioneers. Until about the year 1712 there was no blacksmith within the present domain of Dutchess county. The nearest one to the Fishkill settlers was at Esopus, then called Wiltwyck. One of Peter's boys was sent thither on horseback with a ploughshare to be sharpened, lashed to the saddle. Having traveled an Indian trail homeward for a dozen miles, the fastenings gave way, and the ploughshare fell to the ground; the point was broken, and the lad was compelled to turn back to the Esopus blacksmith and have his work done over again. Altogether he traveled nearly a hundred miles to have a ploughshare prepared for spring use. Our young farmers now, with all their new implements and facilities, have easy times when compared with the difficulties of their great-grandfathers.

The next permanent settler was at Fishkill Landing. His name was Peche Dewall, and he located there in the spring of 1688. He cleared about three acres of land and planted his corn as well as he could between the stumps of the trees that he had felled. Not having a team, his wife assisted him in tilling his corn and clearing the forest. In the fall he had a tolerable crop of corn, and the following winter he built him a handsled and went to New York and bought a half bushel of salt and a side of sole leather, and drew it home. The road from there to New York was most of the way nothing but an Indian trail. In the spring he bought him a horse for three pounds sterling, which was considered fair value for a horse in those days.

From that time till 1700, Eighmie and Dewall were almost the only settlers on the patent. There were a few squatters on the patent that would put up a small shanty, and stay a year or more, and then abandon it.

Dutchess county was not settled as early as Westchester, Orange, or Ulster counties. As late as 1714 Dutchess county, including Putnam, contained only 445 inhabitants, and at a census taken in 1731, Westchester county contained 6,033 inhabitants, Orange county contained 1,969, Ulster county, 3,728, while Dutchess, including Putnam, contained only 1,727 inhabitants. Dutchess county in its natural state was covered with heavy timber, and the land in many places was wet and swampy. The early settlers thought it unhealthy. None but the Dutch would venture on those grounds. An Englishman was loth to settle on the low grounds of Fishkill, but the Dutch were from a low country, Holland, a name derived from the low situation of the country, hollow land, and in many places lower than the sea, and the water but a few feet below the surface and the ocean is backed at a prodigious expense by dykes and dams. For the draining of its waters innumerable ditches are cut, and the waters so drained are carried off by the action of windmills and conveyed into canals, whence they are conducted by the means of sluices into the rivers. Our Dutch ancestors were not afraid of the low grounds of Fishkill, and most of the original town was settled by them. Hence they called it Vis Kill— in English Fish Creek, and the creek where Fishkill Village is now located was the great fishing ground of the Indians. Consequently when a Dutchman was going to emigrate from Long Island, if he was asked where he was going, he would reply, to Vis Kill, in Dutchess county. And at this day, epitaphs on the old Dutch tombstones in the burying ground at Fishkill Village can be seen with the name of Vis Kill upon them.

As I have said, Eighmie and Dewall were almost the only permanent settlers on the patent till the year 1700. Their situation was by no means enviable. Remote from any settlement, they were mostly alone. Occasionally Dewall would see a vessel sail up the river, and sometimes the Captain and crew would come ashore and tarry a few hours with him and entertain him with the news from New York, and when they left all was solitary again. The privations and hardships they had to endure, the fear of being murdered by the savages, and their cattle and sheep destroyed by beasts of prey, and oftentimes during the long, severe winter, provisions scarce, heightened their troubles. But with iron wills and patient and stubborn industry they persevered, and how it gladdened their hearts when the pioneer began to arrive on the patent, and the sound of his axe awoke the silence of the forest.

From 1700 till 1715 settlements progressed very

slowly, mostly along the river. The Indians were quite numerous. Their head-quarters were at Fishkill Hook. Their Chief, Ninham, had a fort for their defence, on a hill known as Fort Hill to this day. It is located on the farm of William Anning, deceased, and some of the ruins may yet be seen.

Fishkill Hook was the favorable location of the Indians. Game was more plenty and the country produced more food. They had set out apple orchards, and a few of the apple trees still exist on the farm of William Waldo. They had also a little clearing on the farm of Theodore Van Wyck and Johnson, where they raised a little Indian corn, a grain wholly unknown in Europe, and which has been the means of saving this country and Europe from famine several times since it became known to the Europeans. But it cannot be raised in England, the climate being too cold and wet. It can only be successfully cultivated in the hot Summers of our country.

Theodoris Van Wyck was one of the first settlers in Fishkill Hook, and one of his boys, a lad of twelve years old, used to go to the Indian village, occasionally, and the squaws would give him something to eat. He happened to go there one day, and they were all absent, old as well as young. Their dinner vessel was swung over the fire, and he ventured to look in and see the contents, and to his surprise he saw a piece of an old horse with hair on it, seasoned with some beans, and from that time he ate no more with the Indians. The reason they were all absent was, they had got track of a bear, and they were pushed with hunger, and they left their homes and went in pursuit of him.

But more about Theodoris Van Wyck hereafter. As I have said, as late as 1714, Dutchess county, including Putnam, had only 445 inhabitants, of whom only eleven men and one woman were over the age of 60 years. Here is a list of all the freeholders or heads of families, put down on the census of 1714:

Jacob Hip, Jacob Plough, Matieis Sleyt, Evert Van Wagenen, William Ostrander, Lowrens Ostrout, Peter Palmater, Maylvell Pullmatier, William Tetsort, Hendrick Pells, Peter Vely, John Kip, John De Grave, Leonard Lewis, Elena Van De Bogart, Bartholomus Hogenboom, Baltus Van Kleck, Frans Le Roy, Barent Van Kleeck, John Ostrom, Hamen Rinders, Mindert Van Der Bogart, Johanes Van Kleck, Lenar Le Roy, Swart Van Wagenen, Henry Van Der Burgh, Elias Van Bunchoten, Thomas Sanders, Catrine Lasinck, Wedo, Peter Lasinck, ——ey Scouten, Mellen Springstun, Johnes Terbets, John Beuys, Garatt Van Vleit, Abram Beuys, William Outen, Andreis Daivedes, Frans De Langen, Aret Masten, James Husey, Roger Brett, Peter De Boyes, Isaac Hendricks, John Breines, Jeurey Sprinstan, Peek De Wit, Adaam Van Alssed, Cellitie Kool, Harmen Knickerbocker, Johanis Dyckman, Sienjar, Jacob Hoghtslingh, Dirck Wesselse, Willem Schott, Jacob Vosburgh, Tunis Pieterse, Hendrick Bretsiert, Roelif Duytser, Johannis Spoor, Junjoor, Abraham Vosburgh, Abraham Van Dusen, Willem Wijt, Lauwerens Knickerbocker, Hendrick Sissum, Aenderis Gerdener, Gysbert Oosterheut, Johannis Dyckerman, Junjor. It is not probable that this census was near complete, as the people were much scattered and difficult to find. The total population in 1723 was 1,082, and in 1731 it was 1,727, and in 1737 it had increased to 3,086.

Where Johnsville is now located was originally a dense forest, and the small streams that run through the village were obstructed with fallen trees, so that the water collected in stagnant pools and rendered it very unhealthy. These pools were the habitation of venomous serpents and various amphibious animals, such as otter, beaver and muskrat. The early settlers would hardly venture out after dark for fear of being bit by some poisonous snake which might be lurking near their dwelling. They were obliged to drive their cattle and sheep in enclosures every night for fear of beasts of prey, and often would the wolves and panthers break through the enclosures and carry away some of their cattle and sheep to their dens in the mountains near by.

The first settler nearest Johnsville was Rodolphus Swartout. His dwelling was located a few rods north of the present residence of James B. Montross, and existed as late as 1809. That year it was demolished. It was a small building, only one story, built of stone. Rodolphus had a son whose name was Tomus, and a negro slave of the name of Sanco. Tomus and Sanco were employed most of the time in leveling the forest and opening roads, in order to get out to the river to get a supply of provisions, which would come from New York to destitute settlers. One day, as they were at work fencing in a small lot near the house, they saw a collection of Indians near the present highway. They hastened to the spot, and to their surprise they saw a dead Indian, and the others were rejoicing over him. Tomus asked them who killed that Indian. They all cried out in broken English, "I, I, I." It appeared from the information he could gather, the Indian belonged to a tribe below the mountains, and they were at war with that tribe, and had overtaken him there and stoned him to death, and all claimed the honor of killing him. His scalp was soon taken off and given to their chief, Ninham, as a trophy, which he rewarded them for.

Swartout was a native of Long Island. His parents were descendants of the Hollanders and could speak the Dutch language only. But Rodolphus had mingled more with the English, and could speak the Dutch and English fluently, and could impart information to the settlers, whether Dutch or English. Two Englishmen whose names were Ogden called on him one day to get information with regard to where they would locate. They were viewing Madam Brett's patent. Swartout showed them through the woods and proceeded to where is now the residence of General Abram Van Wyck. Ogden thought it rather low and wet, and the labor of clearing and draining the land too great an undertaking. As far as the eye could reach presented an unbroken forest, and he thought that they would proceed farther. They went on through the woods an easterly direction until they arrived at the top of the mountain not far from where Farmer's Mills is now located, and settled, and the land is owned by their descendants (the Ogdens) at the present time. The tract of land that Swartout wanted the Ogdens to purchase is now owned by General Abram Van Wyck, and was purchased by Theodoris Van Wyck in the year 1736. It is now one of the finest tracts of land in Dutchess county, and it has been in the possession of his descendants till the present time. Swartwout's farm contained 400 acres. The heirs sold 200 acres, for £1,000, to Joseph Burroughs in 1792, and in 1793 they sold the remainder of the farm to Adam Montross, who came from Westchester county, for £1,200, and his descendants still retain it. The Montross farm then included all of Johnsville on the north side of the road.

East of Swartout settled an Englishman whose name was John Wood. He was a carpenter by trade, and the house he built existed as late as 1816. It was located on the precise spot where C. Delevan now lives. That year it was taken down and the present stately edifice was erected by Nathan Sherwood, who then owned the farm. Wood kept a tavern there till his death, which took place in the year 1791. He was buried in the Presbyterian church yard near Brinckerhoffville, and the following epitaph is on the tombstone erected at the head of his grave:

"This monument is erected to the memory of John Wood, late of Fishkill; he died January 31st, 1791, aged 59 years, 8 months and 15 days. He possessed a fine, clear estate, which he acquired by his prudence and industry. His beginning was no other than his naked hands, and his will to work withal.

"Farewell, vain world, I've had enough of thee,
And now am careless what thou sayest of me,
Thy smiles I court not, nor thy frowns I fear,
My cares are past, my head lies quiet here,
What faults you saw in me take care to shun,
And look at home—enough is to be done."

After leaving a handsome dower to his widow he bequeathed the remainder to his nephews, nieces, and charitable uses.

South of Swartout, in Fishkill Hook, settled Francis Way. He came from Long Island with several others. Among them were the Brinckerhoffs, Depuysters, Algarks, Woods, and others. Way was by trade a mason, and he built his own house mostly himself. It was located near the foot of the hill known as the Way hill to this day. Where the house stood is now the property of General A. Van Wyck. Way purchased his farm, then a wilderness, of Madam Brett, and lived there the remainder of his life on the premises. He had several sons. One by the name of Ouise settled on a corner of the farm now owned by Charles L. Du Bois. Way's widow survived him a few years, and after her death the farm was sold. The purchaser was Benjamin Burroughs, who lived adjoining Way. Burroughs died in the year 1812, and his heirs sold the whole tract, including the Way and the Burrough farm. The house which Way built was taken down by Benjamin Burroughs, and a new one erected on the north side of the hill just spoken of. The Ways were very fond of the chase, and spent much time in hunting.

The first settler east of Burroughs was John Bedell, who leased a farm of Madam Brett. He was Captain of a militia company in Rombout Precinct in the Revolution. This farm contained 200 acres of land. Bedell kept a tavern and company trainings were held there. After Madam Brett's decease, this farm was sold by the heirs to Robert Benson, of the city of New York. Benson sold it to Simon Schouten in 1795, for

371 pounds. Schouten kept tavern there, too. The old house stood a little west of the present one; it was painted red and was destroyed by fire in 1843. In those days it was not necessary for a tavern to be located on the main road to do business; in fact there were no thoroughfares and a tavern located on cross roads would do its share of business, and Schouten's tavern was a rendezvous for the surrounding country. There the inhabitants would congregate. Horse racing, raffling, and shooting matches took place there, especially on training and holidays, and when the horses were ready and mounted, the road fence along the highway that leads to Johnsville was lined with men and boys; and women, too, would sometimes turn out to see the race. Turkeys, geese, and fowls of all descriptions, were set up at a certain distance as a mark for the sharp shooters, who would venture a few pence for a chance to try their luck, and the best marksman took the bird. This was a favorite sport on Christmas and New Years. The poorest shooter treated all around. Schouten let one of Bedell's sons have a field to cultivate, who put in a crop of wheat, and when he harvested it he put it in shocks, and then they undertook to divide the crop. There was an odd number of shocks. That shock they both claimed. Finally it led to an angry discussion. At the same time a thunder shower was rising in the west, and the roar of the thunder and the flashes of lightning were incessant, but they heeded not the fury of the elements, when suddenly a flash of lightning struck the shock of wheat they were contending about, and set it on fire, and in a few minutes it was consumed. This ended the dispute, and there was

no further difficulty in dividing the crop. In 1802 Schouten sold this farm to Garret Du Bois for $4,200. His descendants still hold it.

The next farm south was a lease farm of Madam Brett to one Brown. After her decease this lease was extinguished, and Robert R. Brett, son of the Madam, sold the farm, containing 115¾ acres, to Henry Char lock, for £255. A wood lot on the mountain was included in the sale. Charlock built a new house and erected a grist mill on the Wiccopee, a creek which runs close to the house. He dressed in the ancient English costume. He wore a cue and small clothes. He often officiated as a Baptist clergyman, preaching in private houses and schoolhouses, as churches then were few and far between. The old mill was taken down many years ago. Charlock came from New England.

The farm south of Charlock was in possession of Samuel Cure, at an early day. Cure sold this farm in the early part of the present century to Jacob Ladue, and removed to western New York.

The next farm south of Cure's was a lease farm, too. After Madam Brett's decease it was held by her heirs for some years, and finally it was sold to William Besley, April 27th, 1796, for one thousand seven hundred and fifteen pounds. It contained 309 acres. Besley was a native of Westchester county. This farm extended south to the great Highland Patent. The Indian tribe who sold this tract of land to Rombout remained in Fishkill Hook long after Rombout bought their lands. They claimed this farm as a reservation, until finally they removed and united with other tribes west. This was the last one given up by them. Their villages and apple orchards were located on this and the farm now owned by Charles Emans. Many Indians lingered in Fishkill until after the French and Indian wars, and then they all left Fishkill. Some of the Ninham tribe came back at different times, and pretended to claim this farm, as they had never signed away their right and title. Sometimes they would remain a month or more, camping in the woods, begging provisions of the neighbors, and shooting what game they could find in the woods to subsist on, and then return to their homes in the west.

We will now return to the place from whence we started, and take the west Hook. South of Bedell was a lease farm of Madam Brett. The lessee's name was John Way. After her decease this farm, by heirship, came in possession of Robert Brett, grandson of Madam, who made this farm his home and died there in 1831, in the 80th year of his age. After his death his son James inherited the farm and still retains it. This farm has always remained in the Brett family, and the present owner, Mr. James Brett, is now 82 years of age, and retains the full possession of his faculties, and is the nearest heir of Madam Brett now living, being her great-grand son. He married his wife in Westchester county, 53 years ago. She is yet enjoying good health. Mr. Brett erected a new house on this farm in 1842. The writer obtained from him valuable information.

The next farm or farms south was also lease land, and the heirs of Madam Brett sold a large tract to Nathaniel and William Ladue. The Ladues were of

French descent. Stephen was the first that located in the town. His wife was the first who was interred in the Presbyterian burying ground at Brinckerhoffville. This was on the 27th of September, 1747. It appears that the Ladues occupied lease or tenant farms until after the Revolution, when they bought these lands as stated above. The old Ladue house stood nearly on the site of the one where James Ladue now resides. It was built pioneer fashion, painted red, and was demolished about the year 1851.

West of the Ladue purchase settled John Bloomer and Bram Wood. Joseph Carey settled south of Wood. His farm extended to the great Highland patent. His grandson, Thomas, now resides on the farm and has built a large double house in place of the old one. Hans Dubois settled north of Bloomer, on the farm now owned by Isaac Carey, who demolished the old Dubois house some 23 years ago, and built the present noble structure.

South of the Ladues settled John Jewell. The Jewells sold this farm after the war of 1812. It is now owned by Mrs. Merritt. John Van Tassel settled west of the Jewells at an early day. South of Van Tassel was one Clark Stone, who built a little house on the mountain. Reuben Wood and wife have lived on this place 57 years. Wood bought the place when first married.

South of Wood settled Michael Shaw. The old log house stood opposite the present residence of John Smith. His son Michael inherited this farm after his death in 1817. Michael demolished the log house and built the house where Smith now lives. This farm extended to the great Highland patent.

We are now through with Fishkill Hook, and will commence near the Cure farm, mentioned above, and follow the road leading to Shenandoah. The first one we shall mention is Edward Perry. Of him little is known. A. Scofield and then William Anning lived on this farm. It is now owned by John Merritt.

The next farm was a lease farm. Marvin Rowland was about the first occupant. It does not appear that he remained there long. He came from Long Island, and was a wheelright by trade. In the Revolution he lived on a corner of the farm now owned by Charles L. Dubois, known in this history as the Way farm. The house that he lived in was built by Francis Way for his son Ouise. This house was demolished about 1804. Rowland set up his business in Johnsville in 1799. In 1807 he removed to the Highlands, where he lived the remainder of his life. Daniel Lane lived on this farm in the Revolution. It is now owned by H. D. B. Sherwood.

East of this farm was a farm in possession of Stockholm, and in 1794 it was sold to Benjamin Hutchins. Hutchins was a blacksmith by trade and was a thriving man, adding farm to farm. After his death his son Israel came in possession of it. It is now owned by the Shenandoah Mining Company.

The next farm was owned at an early day Harmy Hilliker. It contained six hundred acres, and extended to Shenandoah on the south, and included what is now known as the Jaycox farm, the Griffin farm, the Warren farm, and the Phillips farm. The old house that Hilliker lived in, stood in a field west of the residence of John Jaycox. It long since disappeared. Hilliker owned one of the best farms in that vicinity, but he was not a thrifty man, and on this large farm he grew poorer every year. He hired a man whose name was Griffin, by the year, and when the year came around, Harmy was short. He had no money and Griffin took his note for services rendered; but Griffin was very economical, he used very little money, and Harmy's note he thought would answer, and then he would hire to him for another year, and when another year elapsed, Harmy was in the same condition that he was the preceding year, when Griffin would take his note again, and so it continued from year to year. Finally Griffin, to get his pay, bought a farm of Harmy, who commenced selling off his poorest land first, and his six hundred acres lasted not much longer than he lasted, and what little there was left after his death was soon spent.

The first settler in Shenandoah was Peter Rickey. He built the first house. It stood south of the present residence of Seymour Baxter, near where is a cluster of old pear trees. It was an ancient structure, with a long stoop, and was never painted. Rickey had several sons. He built a house for one of them. It stood just south of the Baptist Church. The Rickeys kept the first tavern and store in Shenandoah. When the first shows or menageries traveled through the country, an elephant would create almost as much excitement as Barnum's great show does at the present day. A show came to Shenandoah and stopped at Rickey's. The people had notice of its coming some days previous, by one of the company, who represented that they had recently imported from Africa an animal that heretofore was unknown in natural history, called a Dodo. This show drew out a large crowd, but the Dodo proved to be nothing what it was represented to be, some spurious animal which they had picked up to make money. The Shenandoahians seeing that they were sold, tore down the tent and carried the Dodo and a Shetland pony into Rickey's tavern. They then informed the showman that he must refund their money, if not, they would not deliver up his Dodo nor pony. The showman was in a dilemma, and did not know which way to proceed. Finally he offered to compromise with them by treating the crowd. This was at once agreed to, and then the showman got his animals and beat a hasty retreat, glad to get off so. Daniel Quick bought this farm in 1807, of Samuel Halsey. In 1812 he sold it to John Finch, who kept a tavern there. After his death Isaac Knapp bought the farm and lived there. He built a new house and died in 1859, in the ninety-fifth year of his age The two Rickey houses have long since disappeared.

The first settler south of Rickey's was David Gildersleeve. The house stood north of the present residence of Nathaniel Sprague. It was built of logs and not a vestige of it remains.

The Knapps came into Shenandoah just at the close of the Revolution. The first one, whose name was Mier, came from East Chester, Connecticut, and bought a large farm at the base of the Shenandoah mountain, for £3 per acre, with only a log house on the farm. The country south of Knapp's was then mostly a wilderness. Mier Knapp had two sons, Isaac and

Enos. They were thrifty men. Isaac brought up a large family and he lived to see his children and grandchildren settled around him. He came in possession of all the Rickey property, and as I have said, died on the Rickey farm at the advanced age of ninety-five years. Enos, his brother, died on the farm his father purchased. The farm is still owned by their descendants.

The next settler or squatter up the mountain was John Miller, who came from Westchester county. His farm extended to the Great Highland Patent. Some of his descendants live there at the present time.

Starting again from the forks of the road where Abram Knapp lives, the next house was a log one. It stood nearly opposite the residence of Daniel Gilbert. Grace Picket lived there in the Revolution. No trace of this house now exists.

David Taylor was the next settler. He erected a grist mill on a small stream, where he built his house. David Horton lived there many years and carried on the milling business. The property is now owned by his descendants. The mill has been torn down.

Henry Dingee was the next settler. The Hortons came in possession of the farm at an early day. James was the first who came from the Eastern States.

We again reach the Highland Patent. Now we will start from Shenandoah and proceed north to Gayhead. The first house north of Harmy Hilliker's was what is now known as the Strang farm. Caleb Rider lived there at an early day. Daniel Strang, who came from Westchester county, purchased this farm at the close of the war of 1812. It is now owned by Mr. Higelston.

The next farm is known as the Fosgate place. He manufactured brick at an early day. The farm is now owned by John Tompkins.

The Algarks came next. They came direct from Holland, and settled on the farm now owned by Oliver Barns. They erected a stone house, which stood just south of Mr. Barn's barn. The Algarks were very industrious and were the main supporters of the Hopewell Church when it was first organized. It does not appear that they left families, for the name was extinct at the beginning of the present century. One of them left a farm to Hopewell Church. Benjamin Hutchins came in possession of the farm in the early part of the present century. It is now owned by his descendants.

The first settler at Gayhead was Aaron Van Vlack, who came direct from Holland and purchased 600 acres of land of Madam Brett when the country was a wilderness. He built a log house just south of the residence of Abram Van Vlack, who is one of the lineal descendants, a great grandson. Aaron had several sons, one, whose name was Aaron, remained on the homestead. Tunis settled at the village of Gayhead. Marinus settled on the Hasbrouck farm. This farm has recently been purchased again by Abram Van Vlack. Another son, whose name was Abram, settled on the place now the residence of James O. Swartwout, and another settled on the farm owned by Bartow, formerly known as the Flagler farm. Tunis built the first grist mill at Gayhead. The tavern and store is an ancient structure. By whom and when they were built is vague and uncertain. It is said that Raynor and Hasbrouck kept a store there after the Revolution. The father of the writer carried on the mercantile business in the old building with a partner whose name was Coert Horton, in 1804. Then Horton owned the property. The partnership lasted three years. When my father went to New York to purchase goods, he took his bed and provisions with him, and on his return from the city, when the sloop arrived at Fishkill Landing, if his team was not there he would have to walk to Gayhead, a distance of twelve miles. There was no conveyance then to take people to and from the Landing, because there were so few passengers that it would not pay. The population was too sparse. My father often tried to find some one to take him to Gayhead, but could not get any one. The sloop, too, in those days, arrived at Fishkill Landing at no definite time. It depended upon the wind and weather.

Then there was no church in the town below Fishkill Village. The Rev. Dr. Cornelius D. Westbrook was installed pastor of the Reformed Dutch Church in 1808. He used to lecture at Fishkill Landing in a small schoolhouse which then stood on the old Fishkill road, about half way between Fishkill Landing and Matteawan, once a fortnight, perhaps oftener. That was all of the preaching there was then below Fishkill Village, except occasionally a Methodist circuit rider, as they were then called, would ride through the country on horseback and preach in schoolhouses, barns, and private houses, as then there was no Methodist Church in the town, and only one in the county.

The Hortons, two brothers, Joseph and Coert, came from Murderers Creek, Orange county, at the close of the Revolution. They purchased the Van Vlack farm and mill, store and tavern. Their descendants own the property, except the store and tavern, which has been recently sold. Aaron Van Vlack, the first settler mentioned above, was interred in a burying ground on his farm, east of the log house that he built. This was the first burying ground in East Fishkill. Hopewell Church was not built until 1764, and until that time the pioneers, with the exception of those who had vaults, all buried their dead there. This yard has all been buried over, and with but few exceptions only, a rough stone taken from the fields marks the spot where the early settlers lie.

Aaron Van Vlack, son of the first settler, and grandfather of Abram, who now owns the farm, was one of the men who contributed largely when the first church of Hopewell was erected. This church was built of wood. An oaken frame of hewn timber was taken from the forests near where the church stood. The church had a gambril roof, with a tower in front; surmounting the tower was a tapering spire; at its apex was a ball, and a rooster crowned the summit. Every Dutch church in those days had a rooster on top of the steeple. There is but one church now in the county that is crowned with a rooster, and that is the Reformed Church at Fishkill. Hopewell Church stood seventy years, when it was taken down, not on account of its decay, but because it was not up with the times. When the present structure was erected, forty years ago, and finished, it was thought to eclipse anything of the kind in the country. There was then a poet in the congregation, whose name was Heton, who composed some verses on the occasion. The writer only recollects a few lines, which are as follows:

> "The deuce knows what all,
> New Hopewell Church, and that does top all,
> O yes, 'tis true, I say,
> Something new starts every day."

This church has had an addition added to it, a rear entrance and modern pulpit, since it was built, and has been most splendidly frescoed.

The first church of New Hackensack was built two years after the first church in Hopewell. It was built similar to Hopewell Church, and after standing seventy years, it was demolished and the present beautiful structure was erected. This church has recently had modern pews put in place of the old ones, and otherwise materially altered.

The next settler north of Aaron Van Vlack's was Schouten and John Luyster, who came from Long Island about 1740. Luyster's descendants now own the farm. Lock and Peter Bush were the first settlers where now is the residence of Daniel Bull. The next settler north of Luyster was John Brinckerhoff. Dr. Dennis Workman owned and resided on this farm the latter part of his life and died there. It is now owned by Cornelius R. Van Wyck.

The next settler was Cornelius Swartout, known at the present day as the Rapalyee farm. This farm reaches to the Hopewell road. One of the first settlers in lower Hopewell was Richard Van Wyck, a descendant of Cornelius Van Wyck, of Fishkill. He located where now is the residence of Lawrence Rapalyee. When this county was first settled, it was thought that these lands were worthless. The pioneers went around them, and when Van Wyck located there a great deal of that country laid out to the commons, and was covered with shrub oaks, and it was thought that Van Wyck would starve, notwithstanding that he owned several hundred acres of land, but the shrub oaks soon disappeared under skillful cultivation. Richard had two sons, Theodoris R., who was elected to the Legislature in 1803 and '4, and afterwards elected Judge, and Cornelius, who built the house west of Rapalyee. The farm is now owned by his descendants.

New Hackensack was settled by emigrants from Hackensack, New Jersey. The Van Benschotens, Snadikers, and Vanderbilts, were among the first settlers. It was named after Hackensack, New Jersey. The Monforts were the first settlers on Fishkill Plains. They came from Flatlands, Long Island, about 1740. There were two or three Peters. One settled along Sprout creek; he went by the name of Sprout Peter.

The first settler east of Gayhead was William Schutt, who purchased a farm of Madam Brett, October 29th, 1732, one hundred and fifty acres, for £125. This farm was purchased of Schutt by James Emans, who came from Long Island about 1760. His descendants still own it.

The next settler was Benjamin Hasbrouck, who built a stone house, still standing. He died in 1760, and was buried in the Van Vlack burying ground.

East of Cortlandville, on the road leading to Farmers Mills, Ostrander and Wiltsie were the first settlers. Honers Hill took its name from the first settler, who located on its top, and the Ogdens, whom we have mentioned, and Tompkins, who settled near the Black pond, again reaches the great Highland patent.

In giving an outline of the early history of the original town, it appears that after Madam Brett's death there were many lease farms in the east portion of her patent, in Fishkill Hook, extending east towards Shenandoah. After her death the heirs extinguished those leases and divided the property, as directed by her will, and then sold to actual settlers.

The first settler of the village of Johnsville, the ancient name of which was Wiccopee, was Johannas Swartwout. He having no money, leased the farm of Madam Brett for three fat fowls a year, the farm being covered with a dense forest. He soon cleared a small spot and erected a log house near an excellent spring of water, and in the year 1750 he set out an apple orchard; many of the apple trees still exist, one taken down some twelve years ago was twelve feet around at its base, and fifty feet high. After Madam Brett's death this farm by heirship came in possession of Rombout Brett, a grandson of hers, who located on it in the year 1770. He sold six acres off to a blacksmith, whose name was William Cushman. The deed was given in October, 1783. He was the first mechanic in Johnsville. The American army encamped near Fishkill Village in the time of the Revolution, and their barracks then standing were given to the inhabitants. Cushman, with the help of his neighbors, went to the barracks with teams, and hauled up the timber for his house and blacksmith shop, and built them that year. The house did not front the street as it does now, but fronted the south, and the roof was very steep and only one story. The house was painted Spanish brown. A small portion of it is still standing, the other was taken down in 1844 and rebuilt by the father of the writer. In 1807 the father of the writer purchased this house and lot of Thomas Youngs, for $1500, and the writer, who was born there in December, 1813, sold the premises to Jeremiah Concklin in 1866. Rombout Brett sold this farm to Peter Monfort in the year 1787, who came from Long Island and settled on Fishkill Plains. He gave the farm to his son Adrian, who came there in the spring of 1787, and lived there till his death, which took place in the year 1849, at the advanced age of ninety-four years. The farm is now owned by Floyd Quick.

The next settler in Johnsville was Joseph Wood. His house was located on the precise spot where Mrs. Wood now lives. Like most of the dwellings of the first settlers, it was built only one story, with a long stoop in front. The roof of the house extended over sufficient to form the roof of the stoop. The house had very small windows, as window glass was very dear, which made the rooms very dark. There was no wall overhead, and the large timbers were uncovered, and the fire places were large enough to take in wood cord lengths. The upper part was finished barn fashion, with the shutters made in the gable ends to open so as to admit the light. The house was covered with cypress and white wood, and never was painted. The floors were laid with white oak. Wood, being located near the mountain, was very much annoyed by beasts of prey, and he drove his sheep and cattle in enclosures nights, and often they would attempt to break through. His cattle yard was so situated that from his window he could shoot in the direction of the wolves and panthers when they attempted to molest them, and often the noise of those beasts woke him in the night. He would shoot from his garret window, and often would do good execution, for in the morning he would find a wolf or panther that he had shot. This dwelling house was taken down in the year 1830, and the present dwelling was erected by Cornelius Ostrander, who then owned the farm. They were the only dwellings there as late as 1807.

The next settler west on the road leading to Fishkill Village, was Francis DeLangdon. The house that he built was taken down in the year 1844, and the present dwelling built by John Secord. It is now owned by Joseph Sherwood. Near the house stands a large pine tree, and in the Revolution a cow-boy was hung on this tree. The cow-boys were a set of outlaws that would form themselves in a banditti and rob and plunder for a living, having no fixed habitation. They figured more conspicuously in the county of Westchester, near the American and British lines. Sometimes they would rob their nearest neighbors, inflicting cruel punishment to extort from them where their money was secreted, hanging them sometimes a certain length of time with their heads downwards, and committing depredations regardless of party. Whenever one of these cow-boys was taken he was hung without judge or jury. One was captured near Johnsville; he was immediately taken to this tree and hung. The rope was fastened to a large limb that shoots out over the highway. Langdon's farm extended along the highway to what now is known as the white bridge. The road then did not cross there. It continued along Fishkill Creek and intersected the road in the Highlands that leads to Fishkill Village.

The next settler was Cornelius Van Wyck, who purchased a large tract of land of Madam Brett in the year 1733, extending along the valley south of Fishkill Village to the top of the mountain, containing nine hundred and fifty-nine acres, one rood, exactly, for the sum of seven hundred and four pounds eighteen shillings, current money of the Province of New York. He came from Hempstead, Queens county, Long Island. This tract of land is now owned by the heirs of Cornelius Burroughs, Mrs. Cotheal, and the Van Wyck family. He built his house where Sidney Van Wyck now resides.

Crossing the white bridge, the first settlers where the Brinckerhoff's. They purchased a large tract of land of Madam Brett, in 1721, about 1700 acres, extending from Brinckerhoffville north to Swartwoutville, and west to the residence of H. D. B. Sherwood. One whose name was Abram, kept a store in Brinckerhoffville during the Revolution. The old building was demolished a few years ago by Matthew Brinckerhoff, who still owns a part of the tract of land. Abram Brinckerhoff built the mills now known as Dudley's Mills. They were destroyed by fire in the time of the Revolution, and the American army encamping near Fishkill, General Washington gratuitously offered a sufficient number of men to rebuild at once the mills thus destroyed. Accordingly a large number of soldiers were immediately set to work, some in hauling timber, some as carpenters, hewing and framing, and in a short time the present mills were ready to commence operations.

In the time of the Revolution tea was very scarce, and Brinckerhoff having a quantity on hand, he charged an exorbitant price, so that it was beyond the reach of the inhabitants. The women of Fishkill and Beekman could not afford to purchase the article, which exasperated them very much. Accordingly they mustered an army of one hundred, commanded by one Mrs. Catharine Schutt, and marching in military order in front of his store, demanded him to sell his tea at the lawful price of six shillings per pound. Brinckerhoff still hesitated, but Mrs. Catharine Schutt mounting her charger, said if he did not accommodate them with tea from his store at that price, they would proceed to throw his tea and merchandise out of doors. Brinckerhoff, seeing it was useless to desist, accommodated them with tea at the price demanded, and the women quietly dispersed.

Abram Brinckerhoff was a great patriot in the time of the Revolution. General Washington, Lafayette, and staff, coming through from Hartford to West Point in the time of Arnold's treason, tarried one night with him, and they left the day that Arnold received news from Andre that he was captured, and the whole plot was discovered, and advising him to make his escape as soon as possible. Arnold was at breakfast at the Robinson House, in Putnam county, situated on the east bank of the Hudson, about two miles below West Point, near the base of Sugar Loaf, one of the lofty peaks of the Highlands. Arnold was in the act of breaking an egg, when a messenger arrived in great haste, and handed him a letter which he read with deep and evident emotion. The self control of the soldier enabled Arnold to suppress the agony which he endured after reading the letter. He arose hastily from the table, told his aid that his immediate presence was required at West Point, and desired them to inform General Washington when he arrived. Having first ordered a horse to be ready, he hastened to Mrs. Arnold's chamber, and there with a bursting heart disclosed to her his dreadful position, and that they must part perhaps forever. Struck with horror at the painful intelligence, his fond and devoted wife swooned away and fell senseless at his feet. In that state he left her, hurried down stairs and mounting his horse, rode with all possible speed to the river. In doing so Arnold did not keep the main road, but passed down the mountain, pursuing a by-path through the woods, which is now called Arnold's path.

The Presbyterian church at Brinckerhoffville was the first Presbyterian church in the town. The society was organized in January, 1748, and the first church was built in 1750. The material used for the building was wood. In height it was two stories. The windows in the lower story had tight shutters, and one window shutter had a small aperture in it shaped like a crescent, so as to admit the light to guide the sexton right when opening the church. The center pews had very high backs, so when seated nothing could be seen of a person but his head. The side pews were square, with seats all around, surmounted with high railings, and seating twelve persons.

The pulpit was in the rear of the church, and was shaped like a wine glass, and over it was the sounding board fastened to the ceiling with iron rods. The stairs leading to the pulpit were on the left, and ascending three steps they turned, and three more led to the door of the pulpit. Along the edge of the stairs was a balustrade. The galleries were very high, supported by heavy columns, and the minister could not be seen from the rear seats in the gallery. The arch extended only to the front of the galleries, and under it were large timbers extending across the church to keep the building from swaying or leaning. Those timbers were planed and beaded and handsomely carved. This church suffered much damage during the Revolution.

While the American army was encamped south of Fishkill Village, the soldiers would get a permit to leave their encampment, and they would stroll about the country. They often came to Abram Brinckerhoff's store, and they stripped the siding from the Presbyterian church as high as they could reach, to boil their camp kettles. They destroyed most of the fence along the highway from Brinckerhoffville to Fishkill Village.

In the year 1830 this church was demolished and a noble structure erected, which was destroyed by fire on the 5th of March, 1866. The fire was discovered about two o'clock in the morning, when the flames had made such progress that it was impossible to save any of the interior. All of the church furniture was destroyed; the towering steeple fell with a tremendous crash about four o'clock. As the wind blew very strong from the north, other buildings were at one time in imminent danger of taking fire.

This church was two stories in height, built of limestone, and roofed with cedar shingles. The steeple went up in three sections: over the upper section was the lantern, surmounting that was a large ball, studded with arrows, and terminating with a forked prong at the top. In front of the church was a portico supported by heavy columns, with a floor of flagstones inlaid with brick. Over the portico, in front of the church, was a Venetian window, with a circular stone bearing date, 1830. A heavy belt of cornice crossed the church, both front and rear, over the upper story. The gallery extended all around the church, supported by heavy columns, and a moderate arch extended the whole width of the church. The first pulpit was in the front of the church, with a flight of stairs on either side, leading to it. All along the edge of the pulpit and the stairs was a balustrade of mahogany, trimmed with green damask of different shades. This pulpit was taken down some years ago, and a new one erected. The floor of the church was elevated so that those sitting in the rear seats could see the minister without difficulty. The extreme height of the steeple was one hundred and nine feet above the portico.

How the fire originated is a mystery. On Sunday was communion, and the services were longer than usual, and there was little or no fire in the church when the congregation left, as the sexton made no fire after the services commenced, and it was some fifteen hours after the services before the church took fire; and from where the stoves were located to the chimney was some sixty feet, and the latter was embedded in the wall of the church, which was thought perfectly secure from danger. The loss was over $8,000, on which there was no insurance. The congregation was small, but wealthy.

The first minister of this church was Rev. Chauncey Graham, and he divided his labors equally between Fishkill and Poughkeepsie precincts. The parsonage that belongs to the church was given by Madam Brett in the year 1750, containing ten acres of land. There was an Academy some rods east of the parsonage, built before the Revolution, but what year is not known. Graham had the supervision of it at that time. It was surmounted with a cupola and bell, and after the Revolution it was taken down and rebuilt at Poughkeepsie, and afterwards known as the Dutchess County Academy. Graham died in the year 1784, and was buried in the churchyard, and the following epitaph is on the tombstone placed at the head of his grave:

"In memory of the Rev. Chauncey Graham, who was born at Stafford, N. England, Sept. 8th, 1727, and departed this life March 30th, 1784, aged 56 years and 7 months."

The first settlers in Fishkill Village were Henry Terboss, and Rosekrance. Terboss' house was located near where Dr. Bartow White now lives. He was a very eccentric man. When the controversy arose in the Dutch church, he left and went to the Presbyterian church at Brinckerhoffville. On one Sabbath morning he ordered his negroes to harness his horses, and attach them to a large lumber wagon, and he took them with him to church, and marching to one of the square pews, opening the door ordered them seated, and seated himself among them. It caused a great excitement in the congregation. Some were greatly incensed, others were much amused. But some of the grave members waited on him after church, and informed him not to take his slaves in the pew with him again, as there was a portion of the gallery alloted to them. He never repeated it afterward.

Fishkill Village contains some Revolutionary classic ground. A portion of the American army was located half a mile south of the village, and the headquarters were at the house now occupied by Sidney Van Wyck, generally called the Wharton House. The soldiers' graveyard was situated near the base of the mountain. The small pox broke out in the army, and the Episcopal church was used as a hospital, and the old Dutch church as a prison. The Episcopal church was built about 1770, and was formerly surmounted with a towering steeple. After standing a half a century it was taken off, it being considered dangerous. The same church still exists.

The reason why the army encamped near Fishkill Village was, that Sir Henry Clinton had sent his fleet up the river to reinforce Burgoyne, who was getting hemmed in at Saratoga. They sailed up the river as far as Hudson, and hearing that Burgoyne had surrendered, returned. The Americans, supposing that they would effect a landing, collected this army near Fishkill Village to give them battle. The British army created great alarm when sailing up the Hudson, among the inhabitants in Fishkill. Many families fled to Beekman and Pawling, and some sought refuge even in Connecticut.

In the Revolution Fishkill Village contained two churches, the Reformed Dutch and the Episcopal, and one hotel kept by James Cooper. This hotel was destroyed by fire in December, 1873. It also contained some twelve or fourteen dwellings, two or three mechanics, and a school house. The school house was located on the south side of Main street, near John Beecher's blacksmith shop. It was built before the Revolution. On the south side of Main street, as late as the year 1800, there were but two dwellings, and the school house just spoken of.

The first settler west of Fishkill Village was John N. Bailey. The house he built was taken down a few years ago, and a splendid mansion has since been erected. Bailey left in the spring of 1778, and removed to Poughkeepsie. The next settler was Zebulon Southard, who purchased his farm of Madam Brett in the year 1760. The house which was built there is still standing, and the farm is in possession of his descendants at the present time. The next settler was Hendrick Kipp. The house he built is still standing. It is only one story. In front of the house in the walls is a stone bearing date, 1753, marked H. K. Of him little is known. Johannes Swart lived there in the Revolution, and owned all the land on the south side of the road to the Glenham Factory.

The first settler in Glenham was Simmerton. He kept a tavern there, and the first town meeting was held there. At a town meeting held at Simmerton's,

April 7th, 1724, the following business was transacted:

"At a meeting of Sundry Freeholders and Tenements of Dutchess County, assembled this, the first Tuesday in April, in the South Ward, at Dutchess County, the following persons were chosen by majority of votes to serve for the Ward, viz: Jacobus Swartwout, Supervisor; James Hussey, Francis De Langdon, Assessors; Hendrick Phillips, Constable and Collector; Isaac Lansing, Surveyor of the King's Highways; John Barry, do., road about the Fishkills; Daniel Bush, do., for the roads about Poughkeeacick; Peter DuBois, John Buys, Surveyors of fence. It is agreed in the South Ward on the day of Election by majority of votes, that all fences in that ward are to be in height from the ground upward to the uppermost part of the rail, or log, or rider, four feet four inches, English measure. It is also agreed that the hogs in the ward have privilege to run from the first day of October till the month of April; but if said hogs so running do any damage to any person or neighbor, then the owners of the said hogs that have done the damage shall yoke them, and if that will not hinder further damage to the person grieved, the owners shall keep in his own enclosures; which if he do not, he shall be obliged to pay all damages which have been so done by the hogs aforesaid. Further, that every inhabitor within the ward aforesaid shall be obliged to keep good fences around their corn burrows and stacks, which fence is to be close so that hogs nor shoats cannot get through the same where they run at large, which if neglected shall not recover damage."

Stormville was originally called Snarling Town, and

the Storms were among the first settlers. Three brothers, Isaac, Gorus, and Thomas, came from the south part of Westchester, about the year 1740, and purchased a large tract of land of Madam Brett, lying around Stormville. Most of it is still in possession of their descendants. The pioneers in the eastern part of the town used to cart their grain to Fishkill Landing. The wagons used in those days were clumsily built, and the roads were sometimes almost impassable through Johnsville and below Fishkill Village. They could take only twenty bushels of corn or wheat at a load, and that was drawn by three horses, a lad about fifteen years of age mounting the lead horse. They consumed the whole day going to and fro. The first stopping place was John Wood's. That is where Isaac Gildersleeve now lives. The second, Abram Brinckerhoff's, now known as Brinckerhoffville. The third stopping place was Simmerton's, at Glenham, and at the fourth start they drove through to Fishkill Landing. From this it would appear that there was no store nor hotel kept in Fishkill Village as late as the year 1750.

The first tailor in the town was named Clump. He came direct from Holland, and settled at Glenham. During busy seasons of the year he would keep his shop open most all night. Some of his apprentices used to get asleep, and for that offence he used to punish them by placing them on a three legged stool, and if he got asleep and fell off the stool he received a box on the ear. Clump owned some land attached to his place, which he cultivated, raising corn and potatoes. He had a horse which his apprentices had learned, when saying "Take care," to rear up on his hind feet. One day in the spring he set two of them ploughing a small lot to plant potatoes. Clump found fault that they did not do their work well, ordering one of his apprentices to dismount, and he himself mounted the horse. The apprentice that held the plough was named Pudney. The field had been lately cleared, and a scattering tree here and there was left standing. Pudney watching his opportunity, when the horses came directly under a large tree, halloed out, "Mr. Clump, take care." At that instant the horse reared up on his hind feet, throwing Clump up among the limbs. His stature was very diminutive, and his person uncommonly light, and as his horse came down, his clothes catching hold of the branches left him suspended several feet from the earth. Clump shouted at the top of his voice, "Help, dunder and blixum, help!" Mrs. Clump hearing an unusual noise, looked out of the window and saw her husband hanging to the branches of the tree. She hastened to the spot, and with the help of Pudney, succeeded in disengaging him from the tree in safety. The circumstance afforded great amusement to the bystanders; his vrow at the same time advising him to go in his shop, and let the boys do the work of ploughing. Clump instantly obeyed.

The following is an extract from a newspaper published at the time to which it refers, July 12th, 1765: "We hear from the Fishkills that for a week or two past a tiger or panther has been seen in the woods in that neighborhood, not far from Mr. Depeyster's house. It has killed several dogs, torn a cow so that she died the same day, and carried off the calf. It likewise carried off a colt of about a week old. Eight men with their guns went in search of it, and started it at a distance. It fled with great swiftness, and has been seen since at the Fishkills."

The first Baptist church in the original town of Fishkill was at Gayhead. The precise time when it was built is not known. It existed as late as the revolution, and then they abandoned the ground and built a church in Middlebush, which they sold to the Methodists in 1826. They then built a church at Fishkill Plains. The Baptists now have four churches in the two Fishkills.

The first Methodist church in the original town was built at Fishkill Landing in 1824. The building is now known as Swift's Hall. They have now eight churches in the two towns.

The first Presbyterian church in the original town was built at Brinckerhoffville, in 1750. They have now three churches, all in the original town.

The first Reformed Dutch church in the original town was built at Fishkill Village in the year 1731. They have now five churches in the two towns.

The first Episcopal church in the original town was built at Fishkill Village about 1770. They have now five churches in the two towns.

The reader may probably see some errors in perusing this history, but it was the best the writer could do under existing circumstances. Many of the old records have been mislaid or lost, and the writer has had in some instances to follow tradition, which is imperfect at best. He has labored hard, walking on foot, exposed to heat and cold, to obtain what information he could get from the old inhabitants, but it is almost too late to get a perfect early history, for many generations have passed away since this town was first settled. The writer has tried to rescue from oblivion, history that in a few years more would be irrecoverably lost.

HISTORICAL SKETCH OF FISHKILL

VILLAGE.

Fishkill Village, in the time of the Revolution, was one of the largest villages in Dutchess county. It could boast of an academy, two churches, one school house, a hotel, and a printing press, and it was the theatre of many thrilling incidents, although no battle was fought in the vicinity. General Washington, with his army, quartered there in 1777, for several months. The headquarters of the officers was at the dwelling now occupied by Sidney E. Van Wyck, generally known by the name of the Wharton House, a fictitious name given by Cooper, the novelist. The barracks commenced about thirty rods north of this dwelling, and extended near the line of the road to the base of the mountain, where the old road turned east from the main road leading to Fishkill Village.

We will commence at the west end of the village, and try to give information as to the names of residences at that time. The first house still exists, and is now owned by the Southard family, whose grandfather, Zebulon, then resided there, and who purchased his farm of Madam Brett in 1760. This farm is the first after crossing the creek at the west end of the village.

The next house east of the creek was the residence of John Bailey, great grandfather of the writer, who was born about 1704, in the town of Westchester, Westchester county, N. Y. He was a builder in early life, and took contracts for building mills in New Jersey, and came to Fishkill in 1730 or '31. He purchased a farm of Madam Brett, containing 214 acres of land, and then made farming his occupation. The farm is now owned by Charles C. Rogers and William M. Baxter. He married Mary, daughter of Johannes Terbush, who then lived in Fishkill. Mr. Bailey had six children, four sons and two daughters: John, born December 4th, 1732; Esther, born February 5th, 1735; Nathan, born June 22d, 1738; James, born June 7th, 1741; Elizabeth, born July 20th, 1743; Henry, born November 16th, 1745. When my great grandfather purchased this farm, the country was new, and tribes of Indians yet remained in Fishkill. Wild animals abounded in the mountains, wolves howled around his dwelling nights, and the beavers had built a dam across the small stream that runs through the farm at its mouth, where it empties in the large creek. In the revolution his children had all married and left home, except Nathan, grandfather of the writer, who married Abigail, daughter of John Pine, and remained with his father. Nathan had two children, John N., father of the writer, born November 11th, 1767; Mary, my aunt, born December 31st, 1772. In the revolution, the family consisted of John Bailey, my great grandfather, then about 72 years old; Nathan, his son, 36 years old; John N., grandson and father of the writer, aged 9 years; Mary, a grand daughter, aged 3 years; and a number of negro slaves. The house they owned and occupied, stood near where William M. Baxter now resides, and was built by the great grandfather of the writer, soon after he purchased the farm. It fronted the south, which was the custom of the early pioneers, and the highway was in the rear. This house was roofed and sided with cedar shingles, except the west end, which was built of stone. It never was painted, and some fifteen years ago it was taken down, and the present edifice, now owned by William M. Baxter, was built. Three years after the battle of Lexington was fought, in 1778, my ancestors sold this farm and removed to Poughkeepsie, and purchased a farm near the village, and the father of the writer was sent to school in the village. The schoolhouse was located in Main street, near the present City Bank, his parents living near enough for him to attend school in Poughkeepsie on foot. None of the family has lived in Fishkill Village since.

When the British took possession of New York, in the Revolution, many families left the city and sought residences elsewhere, for places of safety. Among the number that found a home in Fishkill, was Samuel Loudon, a printer, who established a printing press at now the residence of Mrs. John C. Van Wyck; and John Bailey, a cutler by trade, who set up his work shop not far from the residence of Charles C. Rogers. The old shop existed as late as 1820. He made or repaired the sword of General Washington, and stamped his name on it: "J. Bailey, Fishkill." This Bailey was nowise connected with our family. After the

British evacuated New York, in 1783, he and Loudon returned to their homes in the city.

The next house was on the north side of the street, near where the Bryson House now stands. It was occupied by a Dutchman, whose name was Tryer. He was a tanner by trade, and carried on the business there.

The next house east, was the residence of Johannes Terbush, which now is owned by Lewis H. White. The old Terbush house was taken down by his father, Dr. Bartow White, who built the present one about the year 1808.

The next house is the one William Van Wyck owns and which is now occupied by a man named Redman. Allard Anthony came in possession of this house soon after the Revolution.

The next house was on the north side of the street, where John P. Green now resides. Johannes Swart lived there, and he had one of the finest residences in the village. His house in height was two stories. It is said that he kept a store there before the Revolution, and a tavern was kept there for some years after. This house has been rebuilt several times. Swart had several sons and daughters, and owned a farm where he lived.

The next house east, on the north side of the street, was the residence of Stephen Purdy. He married Esther Bailey, a daughter of John Bailey, great grandfather of the writer, who had five children, four sons and one daughter: Elizabeth, born September 3d, 1758; Francis and James, twins, born January 14th, 1760; John, born August 14th, 1765; Stephen, born October 10th, 1767. The house was located opposite the Bank of Fishkill. It was built of wood, roofed and sided with cedar shingles, and was never painted. The roof was very steep; the length of the rafters reached two-thirds the width of the building, what carpenters used to call a square roof. There was no stoop, the front door opening from the yard. This house existed until 1835, when it was taken down by Nelson Burroughs, who then owned the premises, and erected the present building, now owned by Oliver W. Barnes.

The next house was the Union Hotel. Part of the hotel then existed, and was kept by James Cooper. This hotel was destroyed by fire in December, 1873.

On the south side of the street from the hotel, formerly lived a Rosacranze, who owned a farm which joined Terbush's, who was one of the first settlers in Fishkill, but whether he was there in the Revolution is uncertain.

East of the Union Hotel, on the north side of the street, there was only one small house before you reached the Dutch church, and was occupied by Abraham Smith. It is owned by James E. Dean, and has been recently taken down.

Beyond the Dutch church there was but one house on that side of the street, until you arrived at the residence of Mrs. John Van Wyck. Robert Brett, son of Madam Brett, lived there, and owned a large farm, containing 650 acres of land. His farm extended east to the residence of Henry D. B. Sherwood, and west to what is now known as Osborn Hill. The house was built of stone, and was demolished by Obadiah Bowne, in 1819, who then owned the premises, and built the present beautiful structure. Robert Brett was a man of eminence, occupying a high position in society, and holding offices of trust in the county. The first constitutional convention held a session in his house, in the autumn of 1776. He gave shelter to the printer, Samuel Loudon, and General Washington was afterwards a guest in his house. Robert Brett had two sons, whose names were Matthew and Robert. Matthew died in the morning of life, aged 28 years. Robert was the father of James Brett, who resides in Fishkill Hook; he died in 1831, at the advanced age of 80 years. The highway then was very close so Robert Brett's house, and wound around the brow of the hill, crossing the creek near Isaac Cotheal's house. Capt. Richard Southard lived there then, and owned a large farm, extending up the creek, including the farm owned by the heirs of Cornelius Burroughs. The old house was taken down by Richard Rapalje, who came in possession of the farm soon after the Revolution, and erected the present house in 1800. Southard had six children, four sons and two daughters.

The next house was the old Van Wyck homestead, now owned by Sidney E. Van Wyck, a descendant of the family, and was erected by Cornelius Van Wyck in 1737. This house was the headquarters of our officers while in Fishkill, and it remains much the same, although it has been built more than a century and a quarter.

On the opposite side of the street from the Dutch church was a school house, and west of the school house, on the same side of the street, was a small house occupied by Edward Griffin, and then there were no more houses until you reached the Rosacranse place.

The Episcopal church was built in 1770, which was six years before the Declaration of our Independence. The architect who had the supervision of the building got so befogged that he and his workmen left before they finished framing. It was said that they were more or less intemperate. The building committee then went to New York, and procured another set of mechanics. They had to commence anew and reframe

EPISCOPAL CHURCH, FISHKILL VILLAGE.

the building, and it is said the two framings can be seen in the upper part of the structure. This church was formerly surmounted with a towering steeple, running up in four sections, and its height was only three feet less than the spire on the present Reformed Dutch Church. This steeple was very heavily timbered, and a sad accident occurred when it was raised. One of the workmen fell from a height of nearly sixty feet, striking on a stick of timber, and was instantly killed.

The steeple, with the exception of the lower section, was taken off in 1810. A complaint was brought against the congregation, saying that the steeple was not safe; that it might fall and endanger the life of some person. The last section was taken off some thirteen years since, otherwise the church remains the same. The exterior has never been remodelled, although the church has stood more than a century. The convention of the representatives of the State of New York, held a session in this church in the Revolution. It was used as a hospital when the army encamped on the flats south of the village, near the Highlands. The small pox breaking out in the army, the sick were taken to this church. The father of the writer was then a lad, ten years old, and he caught the small pox when going to see the soldiers in their encampment. The board of health waited on his father and informed him that he must be taken to the hospital. His father prevailed on them to let his son remain at home, on account of his being so young. The board then informed him that if he would keep his son where the disease would not be likely to spread, they would consent for him to remain with his parents. This his father promised to do, for the small pox then was a terrible scourge, and it was a terror to civilized as well as savage nations. It was not until 1798 that vaccination was discovered by Dr. Jenner. Mr. Bailey placed his son in a bedroom, and with the assistance of a negro slave whose name was Cæsar, who had had the small pox, took care of him, and grandfather Bailey altered the road that ran close to the house, through a woods on the north side, which was some distance off, for it was said that the disease could be taken from the smoke of a chimney, nearly fifty rods. The boy's mother never had had the small pox, and she could not see him, and it was thought that he could not live. She became almost frantic with grief, when grandfather and Cæsar made an opening in the bed-room door, and placing a window light in the opening, then making it perfectly tight, which afforded the mother great consolation to look through the window and see her son, who, after a very severe sickness, recovered. The following spring, in 1778, our family, as I have stated above, left Fishkill, and moved to Poughkeepsie.

While the army was encamped at Fishkill, the soldiers would pass the sentinels at night, and commit many depredations. They robbed hen roosts for miles from their barracks, and every fence rail along the highway from Fishkill to Brinckerhoffville they took for fuel. They stripped the siding off the old Presbyterian church, as high as they could reach, to boil their camp kettles. Abram Brinckerhoff kept a store and owned a mill. The soldiers would come to his store to get something to eat and drink. One night his mill caught fire, and mill and contents were all consumed. How the fire originated was not known; it was supposed it was accidentally fired by the soldiers. General Washington ordered his officers to send what men Mr. Brinckerhoff needed, gratuitously, to help him rebuild his mill. A large gang of soldiers were sent, and immediately set to work; some hauling timber, others in hewing and framing, and the mill now occupied by Alexander Dudley was then built.

The Reformed Dutch Church in Fishkill, in the revolution, was built of stone in 1731. In shape it was quadrangular, and the roof came up from all sides to the center. From the apex of the roof ascended the cupola; in that the bell was suspended, and surmounting the cupola was the bird which veered with the

REFORMED DUTCH CHURCH, FISHKILL VILLAGE.

wind and told from what quarter of the compass it came. The window lights were very small, set in iron sash frames, with port holes in the upper story for a place of defence against Indian incursions, which the settlers were exposed to. In front of the church was a large oak tree, whose giant arms extended across the street. One large limb came in close proximity to a window in the upper story. This church was used as a prison in the revolution, and the celebrated spy, Enoch Crosby, who figured in Cooper's writings as Harvey Birch, was confined there, and tradition says that he made his escape on one dark stormy night by leaping from an upper window to a limb of this tree. The tree was taken down when the present edifice was erected. The father of the writer recollected attending church there with his parents before they left Fishkill. He informed the writer that the pulpit was on the east side of the church, and a gallery extended all around. It is not definitely known what year the present edifice was commenced, for the records of that period of the church's history is lost, but from information derived from aged residents of the town, it must have been only a few years after the revolution.

An old and highly respectable inhabitant, who was born in 1774, and whose death occurred some years since, informed me that after peace was proclaimed, a great Fourth of July celebration took place in Fishkill, and he went with his father to the village on that day to witness the celebration. The old church then existed. He went into the gallery to hear the oration. The church was densely crowded, when the galleries began to give way, and a general rush was made for the doors. He being small, succeeded in getting out very soon; but no serious accident happened. As near as he can recollect, he was then some ten years of age. When this church was rebuilt, it was enlarged and extended further west on Main street, covering Madam Brett's family burying plot, where she and some of her children and grandchildren repose—underneath the present church. One grave was not disturbed, and was where a grandson of hers was buried, 98 years ago, and who was a son of Robert Brett. This grave lay at the furtherest east end of the plot, and some twelve feet from the present edifice, which was far enough so as not to interfere with the building when erected. A tower and steeple were added to the church; the height of the spire is 120 feet. When the present church was built, the congregation was poor, they having just passed through a seven year's war, which had impoverished them, and with little or no money, they undertook to erect a church, which took some ten years to complete.

They had only a few years before separated from the church at Poughkeepsie, the latter having abandoned their old ground in what is now known as Market street, where their first church was built about 1718, and commenced building a new church on the opposite side of the street, near the Poughkeepsie Hotel, in 1782, where the old burying ground is still to be seen. In 1822 they abandoned that site, and built a new church on the old Glebe property, which belonged to the two congregations before they separated. This church was destroyed by fire in 1857, when the present edifice was erected on the same site. It is one of the finest churches in the county. There was a great deal of spirit manifested between the two congregations, which should have the finest church. Poughkeepsie had got the start of Fishkill, and commenced building in 1782. Their church was nearly finished before Fishkill had commenced. Their structure was much like the present one at Fishkill, only when Fishkill had completed theirs, it was thought to excel Poughkeepsie. The church at Fishkill went up slowly; the walls are three feet thick and thirty feet in height, and the timbers placed upon the walls that support the roof and tower, are of oak, and of such enormous size that it must have been attended with a great deal of labor to have placed them there, and the building appears as durable now as when first finished. The architect's name was Barnes, and the boss mason was Manney. Every stick of timber, load of stone, lime and sand, was hauled and carted on the ground by the congregation, gratuitously. Not one cent was paid for carting any of the material that was used in the building.

There was then no church in the town below the village; all came to church at Fishkill Village, if they went anywhere. Much of the wealth of the town was there, in this and the Episcopal church. The inhabitants would come from below Fishkill Landing, south as far as Pollipel's Island, to Fishkill, on the Sabbath, to attend the Dutch and Episcopal churches. General Swartwout, Abram Brinckerhoff, Christian Dubois, and Cornelius C. Van Wyck, were among the number that composed the building committee, and whenever any timber, stone, lime, sand, or brick, was wanting, they promptly responded to the call. General Swartwout bestowed most of his time in assisting while the church was building, and it was a common saying in the neighborhood where he lived, that General Swartwout and all of his hands, have gone again to work at the church. It was said that he neglected his farm for the interest of the church, and he furnished one hand at his own expense all the while the church was building. He gave the shingles for the roof. The timber was mostly obtained from the Highlands, which was then of little value, for the country abounded with heavy forest. Large trees were taken down, whose diameter at their base was three and four feet. The congregation turned out in full force, with horses, oxen, carts, wagons, negro slaves, and hauled the timber to the spot. But their funds gave out before the main structure was finished, and it would not do to stop building then, and to obtain a loan was almost impossible, for there was but little money in the country, so impoverished was the country after the war. Long Island then was an old country, and they concluded to try to raise some money there. The building committee sent Abram Brinckerhoff there to try to borrow a sum sufficient to finish the church, in which he succeeded, giving the building committee for security. This money completed the church, with the exception of the spire, which for the want of funds stood nearly three years without covering, and it was not entirely completed until 1795, when the spindle, ball and bird were placed upon it. There has been no alteration of the exterior, except a recess in the rear of the church. The interior has been remodelled several times, but with little or no improvement. Originally the galleries were supported from the ceilings, with iron rods fastened to the timbers above the arch. Then there were no columns in the church to distract the view, and the pulpit and side pews were elevated six inches above the floor. The first alteration was made in 1806, when the iron rods were taken down, the pulpit and side pews lowered, and columns placed underneath the galleries. The second alteration was made in 1820, when the entrance on Main street was closed, and the pews all taken up, and new aisles made, pews lowered, and one entrance only, and that in the tower. The third and last alteration was in 1854, when the interior was entirely remodelled, with new and modern pews and pulpit; the galleries narrowed and lowered, and a number of pews added to the audience room, and a furnace placed underneath. This church has stood more than three quarters of a century, and is as durable now as when first completed, and shows no sign of decay, and with all the churches which have been erected since in the two Fishkills, there have been but few if any that has eclipsed it, and it is now an ornament to the village.

Soon after the Revolution, and before the present Reformed Dutch Church was erected, four dwellings were built in Fishkill and vicinity. The old Cornelius C. Van Wyck mansion, still owned and occupied by his descendants; the house on the opposite side of the street from the Episcopal church, which has a gambrel roof, owned by Isaac Cotheal, and first occupied as a store, kept by Abram Rapalje; the house known as the Baxter house, now owned by John Beecher, part of which existed before the Revolution, and when the present Reformed Dutch church was building, was occupied as a tavern by William Ward; the house now the residence of Leonard B. Horton, built by Doctor Hunting, which had a gambrel roof, and was remodelled by Andrew Wight, some twenty-five years ago, who then owned the premises.

Methodism was introduced in Fishkill about 1794; the first sermon was preached in the street, under a poplar tree near the Baxter house. The preacher, whose name was Croft, attracted a large crowd, many coming merely out of curiosity; and the first society formed was in Fishkill Hook in 1800. Then costly and pewed churches and extravagance in dress, was forbidden in their discipline. The ministers wore coats with straight collars, and broad-brimmed hats; the women straight bonnets. Their quarterly meetings were conducted with closed doors and no one was admitted in their love feasts more than two or three times, unless they became members.

Soon after the Revolution, several prominent men made Fishkill their permanent residence. Among the number was Joseph I. Jackson, a member of the bar, and since Judge of Dutchess county; Dr. Bartow White, who came from Westchester county in 1800, while a young man, and became eminent in his profession; James Given, who came to Fishkill in 1798, and engaged in the mercantile business. He first tried to locate near the Episcopal church, which then was the most attractive place for business in the village, but could not purchase any ground there. He was obliged to select a place where the store of Hayt and Benjamin is now located. There he built a store in 1810, and commenced business, and in 1812 he erected his dwelling, which is now occupied by his descendants. The year previous he set out those beautiful elm trees in Main street, which now are such an ornament to the village. Allard Anthony, who in early life was a manufacturer of leather, and afterwards engaged in agriculture. As a citizen and a man, his character for truth and integrity was proverbial. Being once called on in court to testify, the court did not administer the oath to him, being perfectly satisfied with his stating what he knew. John Bedford, who was a silversmith, and was diligent in business, accumulated a large estate. Greenleaf Street, who filled offices of trust in the town for many years. He was one of the vestrymen in the Episcopal church in 1796. In the Revolution farms within a radius of five miles of Fishkill could be bought for £5 per acre.

The Fourth of July, 1826, which was the fiftieth anniversary of our independence, a banner was strung across the street from the top of the poplar tree where the first Methodist minister preached in Fishkill, to the spire of the Reformed Dutch church, and the whole surrounding country assembled to celebrate that day. A procession was formed at the lower end of the village, headed by a body of cavalry dressed in blue and scarlet uniform, and followed by the citizens with flags and banners. Arriving near the church, the cavalry dismounting, the procession marched into the Dutch Church, between a large company of boys, from ten to twenty years of age, who lined the street on either side for several rods. The writer was one of the number, and before the procession got in, the church was filled to repletion, the cavalry filling the main body. A band of music occupied the whole front of the gallery, playing "Hail to the Chief." Rev. Doctor Dewitt delivered the oration; Rev. Doctor Westbrook was marshal of the day; General Swartwout and other Revolutionary worthies, participated in the celebration. A splendid dinner was served at the two hotels, the Mansion House, which was only built one year previous, and was then kept by Major Hatch, and the Union Hotel, kept by a Mr. Vail; the cavalry dining at the Union Hotel, and the citizens at the Mansion House.

In 1789, there were but seven post offices in the State. Fishkill Village was one of the number. After the Revolution, Fishkill progressed very slowly in population, and as late as 1810 the village contained only two churches and a small collection of houses, while Poughkeepsie contained 422 inhabited dwellings, 49 stores and shops, five churches, an Academy, Court House and Jail, two weekly papers, and a population of 2,981.

Fishkill Village, at the present time, contains about one thousand inhabitants, four churches, a select and free school, National and Savings Bank, and a weekly newspaper. The New York, Boston and Montreal Railway passes through the village.

EARLY SETTLERS NEAR FISHKILL

LANDING.

The first settlers at Fishkill Landing, after Peche Dewall, who was a squatter, were Roger Brett, the Duboises, Pines and Van Voorhises. Roger Brett built the first house, known at the present day as the Teller mansion, at Matteawan, in 1710. This house has had an extension roof and a wing added to it, otherwise it remains the same. The Duboises settled on the south side of the Fishkill creek, near its mouth, on the great Highland Patent granted to Adolph Phillips in 1697. This patent included all of Putnam county. The division line of Phillips and Rombout was at the mouth of the Fishkill creek, where it empties into the river. The Pines located east of Matteawan, on the Fishkill road. One house is still standing, known at the present day as the Birdsell house. The other the Pine family sold to Mr. John Boice some sixteen years ago, who demolished it and erected the present stately mansion. The Pine that owned the Birdsell house sold the farm in 1790, and removed to Delaware county. The Verplanck and Newlin mansions were also among the first houses erected, and are still standing and in good preservation. The Van Voorhises located on the Stony Kill road, one mile north of the village of Fishkill Landing. The old dwelling yet stands, and is located a few rods north of the residence of Mr. Wm. Henry Van Voorhis. It is only one story, with an open garret and a cellar kitchen beneath. The roof is very steep, and the roof was covered with red cedar shingles. John Van Voorhis,

VERPLANCK HOUSE, FISHKILL LANDING.

father of William Henry, was one of the lineal descendants, and lived there many years. Before it was vacated by him, the writer and his mother were invited to pay it a visit, as they had a peculiar interest in its history, for grandmother was born in this house, April 13th, 1744. Mother and soon visited the old house for the last time, on the 1st of February, 1842. We spent the day examining the ancient landmark. My mother pointed out to me the places where she used to play when she was a little girl, when she came to visit her grandmother. On the mantel piece in the parlor were scripture pieces, representing some of the miracles our Saviour performed while here on earth. Grandfather Peter Dubois married his wife in the old house, November 17th, 1768. He was born on what is now known as the old Dubois place, near Swartwoutville, June 13th, 1746. His father, whose name was Christian, was born in Kingston, Ulster county, Nov. 15th, 1702, and grandfather Dubois purchased the farm of the Beekmans, about the year 1710. The farm, when he came on it, was all woods, for the country was then a wilderness. He struck the first blow with his axe on his farm to fell the trees where the house now stands. The house was built of stone, and like all of the ancient Dutch houses, had very steep roofs and low walls. In 1812 another story, of wood, was added to it. This farm remained in the Dubois family until 1839, when Coert Dubois, who then owned it, sold it to Alfred Storm. It is now owned by a Mrs. Sparks. Peter Dubois died the 16th of June, 1737. He was buried in the Reformed Dutch Churchyard, in Fishkill Village. It was not known where his remains laid until recently, when James E. Dean, of Fishkill Village, reset and scoured some of the old tombstones so that they could be deciphered. A tombstone near Main street, all covered with moss, was scraped, and this proved to be that of Peter Dubois.

The inscription is in the Dutch language, and is as follows:

"Hier lyde her lighaam,
Van Pierer D Bois
Overleeden Den 22' van
Januarie Anno, 1737–8.
Oudi Zynde 63, Jaar."

[TRANSLATION.]

"Here lies the body of Peter Du Bois, who departed this life the 22d day of January, in the year 1737–8, aged 63 years."

A slave, a colored woman, who was born in the old Van Voorhis house at Fishkill Landing, long before the writer's mother, was purchased by my father when he married in the Dubois family in 1805. My father gave forty pounds for her, when he first commenced keeping house. She expressed a great desire to live with my mother. The writer well remembers the old slave, whose name in Dutch was Nanna, taking him on her lap and relating to him incidents which took place when she lived in the old Van Voorhis house. She told the writer that she had often carried his mother, when an infant, in her arms, and when grandmother was married to grandfather Dubois, what a wedding they had—how they danced. She informed me that when the British fleet came up the river, the family, all except her master and herself, left home and sought a place of safety in the Great Nine Partners, at Filkins', who was one of the original purchasers. Her master declared that he would not leave his house; he would lose his life first, for he was a staunch Whig; and she said that she would not leave her master, so they two remained at home. When the British fleet arrived in Newburgh bay, they commenced firing their cannon. Their house was secluded from the river, but several balls came over the house and struck near by; one came very near striking the house. Her master told her to go into the cellar kitchen, as they might get hurt. They remained there until the fleet passed by.

She said when our army arrived at Fishkill, her master was glad to think that they now had protection. General Putnam came to Fishkill Landing on horseback. Her master took her to Fishkill Village. She said that she saw Generals Washington, Lafayette, and Staff, and our army encamped on the flats just north of the Highlands, near the residence of Sidney E. Van Wyck, and on one occasion she assisted in making some arrangements at the house of Robert R. Brett, now the residence of Mrs. John C. Van Wyck, for Washington and his staff, who was then staying there. She helped light the candles for them to transact business.

Here it may not be amiss to relate an incident that occurred when the writer was a mere lad. Nanna was going to Fishkill Landing to visit her son Thomas, and she got mother's consent for me to go with her. A colored man, whose name was Jack, drove for us. We stopped near where James Rogers' harness shop is now. The writer thinks that is the identical spot, and the store-room the same place they visited Thomas. He recollects looking out on the opposite side of the street, and seeing but two or three small houses from where Snook's saloon is to where the First National Bank is now located. The writer recollects Jack taking him by the hand and walking through the street towards the river, on the side of the street where he made his visit, to the Stony Kill road. He recollects seeing but two houses. We walked beyond to where Baxter & Martin's store is now. He recollects of seeing no bustle, no passing or repassing of sleighs, for it was in winter time. Along that street there was a small cluster of wooden buildings. He recollects seeing people crossing the river on the ice. Then there was no road to Matteawan, except the old Fishkill road.

Nanna could speak the Dutch and English languages, and she often told the writer that she regretted leaving Fishkill Landing, and at last when freedom was proclaimed throughout the State, in 1828, she made up her mind to live with her children the remainder of her life. Her son Thomas and daughter Rose came to our house to take her home with them. My parents tried to persuade her to remain with them what little time was allotted to her on earth, but the boon of freedom was too great for her. When she left the house, we all wept, and could it be wondered at when she was born and reared in the family, and now she was probably beyond three score and ten years, for she did not know her age. But Nanna found freedom far different than she expected. The colored people were poor, and there was no fuel in the country but wood, and that even at that day commanded a high price at Fishkill Landing, and she found that the fire of freedom did not suffice. She did not find wood and provisions as plenty there as she had in the days of slavery, and she wished herself back again in the old kitchen, a slave under her old master. She went out doing house work, but being old she soon gave out and returned to her daughter's, sick. The writer's mother sent him to her daughter's to enquire after her and fetch her back, bag and baggage, but she was not well enough. Finally pinching want began to stare her in the face. A colored man was dispatched to inform us of Nanna's destitution, but he was unable to find our place of residence, and the next news we heard was that Nanna was dead. She died in a little house near where the Dutchess Hat Works are now located, in 1830.

A VISIT TO FORT HILL.

Fort Hill is located in Fishkill Hook, on the farm recently owned by Joseph Beecher. It derived its name from a tribe of Indians that formerly owned the county, known as the Ninham tribe. Their village was located in a valley north of the hill where their fort was located. This was once a powerful tribe, for as late as the year 1700 they numbered more than a thousand warriors, and it is but a few years since this powerful tribe became extinct.

They erected a fort on that hill for their defence and safety when engaged in war with other tribes, and when compelled to retreat they would flee to the fort and barricade themselves, and keep the enemy at bay. Curiosity induced me to pay a visit to the spot where the fort was once located. Accordingly, Mr. Beecher and myself set out one day in the year 1861 for that purpose. The morning was pleasant, and the clouds that appeared in the horizon partially screened us from the scorching rays of the July sun, and at ten o'clock we had ascended the hill, and stood on the ground where the fort was supposed to have been located. It was a well chosen spot for defence. On all sides, with but one exception, the ascent was very precipitous, and that would afford a safe retreat to the mountains. The

Sachem erected his fort on the first elevation of the hill, where the ascent was most difficult and dangerous, and here he erected a parapet, and surrounded it with palisades for the safe retreat of his tribe. I could discover no traces of the ruins, for the plough had for so many years been used by the hand of civilized man, in turning up the earth, that every vestige of the ruins was obliterated. I looked around and surveyed the country. It was a beautiful day, and being elevated above the valley of the Hook, the western breezes swept rapidly by, and tempered the atmosphere, which caused the heat to be less oppressive. The sun had arrived at the zenith, and from the spot where I stood the view was of surpassing beauty and loveliness. The harvest was ripe and ready for the sickle, and the farmers had commenced gathering their sheaves in their garners. As far as the eye could reach was presented fields of grain and grazing pastures, spotted with sheep and cattle. Far ahead in the distance I could see the Catskill Mountains, whose blue tops rise one above another, and stretching beyond the vision's utmost limit. Casting my eye back again across the valley, it presented one of the most beautiful farming districts in the county, inhabited by an intelligent class of farmers. The stately farmhouses that were scattered over the valley, the village of Johnsville, with its hundred chimneys, the snow white church, the heaven pointing spire, the stately schoolhouse, surmounted with a cupola, added a zest to the enjoyment, and heightened the beauty of the surrounding scenery.

The mansion of H. D. Sherwood was then located a short distance from Fort Hill, and his grounds were laid out with great taste. His artificial ponds, with jets of water spouting upward, and filled with gold fish, his beautiful lawns interspersed with evergreens and fenced with hedges of living green, his fields of grain waving their yellow ridges before the wanton breeze, and chasing each other like successive generations. But what a contrast does the appearance of the country present now to that of a century and three quarters ago. The great Sachem and his tribe then occupied the valleys, and the primitive forests stood in all their grandeur, and from Fort Hill then might have been witnessed the Indian sporting in the valley, hunting in the forest, and fishing in the Wiccapee; the great Sachem at the head of his tribe, teaching them the art of war and the amusement of the chase. The howl of the wolf and the scream of the panther might then have saluted the ear.

I call up before my imagination the secret windings of the scout, the bursts of the war whoop, the fury of an Indian onset, the triumphant display of scalps, and the horrors of the war dance before the tortured and expiring captives. But now the scene has changed. Civilization has taken the place of savage life. The forests have been leveled, and the valleys have been converted into meadows and wheat fields. Instead of beasts of prey we see grazing herds; instead of the kindling of fagots we witness the worship of God, and instead of the appalling war whoop we listen to the Songs of David. In the beautiful words of inspiration, "The wilderness has been made to blossom as the rose, and the valley is now vocal with the praises of God."

But the time admonished us to leave, for we had lingered on the spot longer than we had anticipated, for the history and scenery it afforded us was doubly interesting. We descended the hill, and was soon at the residence of Mr. Beecher, and I was highly entertained by himself and lady with a sumptuous repast, and then made my way home, greatly pleased with what I had seen, and shall ever remember my visit to Fort Hill.

THE BRICK MEETING-HOUSE.

I have been for several weeks this year, (1874,) snugly ensconsed in an isolated farm-house in the town of Washington, Dutchess county, N. Y., one mile from the village of Millbrook, on the Dutchess and Columbia railroad. This village has been built since the completion of the road. Adjoining this village are the villages of Mechanic, Hartsville and Four Corners. They lie contiguous to each other, as Fishkill-on-the-Hudson and Matteawan, and sooner or later will be included in one village. The Reformed Church, in the village of Four Corners, is a magnificent structure, of Gothic architecture, built of wood, with stained glass windows. Over the north entrance the tower commences, and surmounting the tower is a spire which shoots up to the height of one hundred and thirty feet from the earth. A fine-toned bell and clock is placed in the upper section of the tower, and the sound of the bell and the striking of the clock is distinctly heard from my boarding house, distant two miles. As you enter the church from the north, an aisle crosses to the entrance on the opposite side. Intersecting this, two aisles lead the way to the preacher's desk. Behind this is the choir's seat, which faces the congregation. The interior of this church appears at first to the stranger, too low and narrow for its length. The pews, which are of black walnut, are elegant, and the church will seat comfortably three hundred people, and I am informed that they have a large Sabbath school and lecture room.

Millbrook has two churches, Episcopal and Catholic; Mechanic has two Friends' meeting-houses, Orthodox and Hicksite. The town of Washington is on the great Nine Partners' patent, purchased in the year 1697. This is a beautiful farming country and some portions of this town will vie with any in old Dutchess, which is saying much. From Millbrook to Washington Hollow, a distance of three miles, is a beautiful rolling ridge of land where the mansions of Messrs. Brown and Thorne are situated, and the mansion of Mr. George H. Brown is not excelled in the State, outside of our large cities.

Among the early settlers was the Society of Friends, who came from Long Island about the middle of the last century, and located on the great Nine Partners' tract and Beekman's patent. One of their first churches in this town was erected at Mechanic, known at the present day as the Brick Meeting House. Curiosity induced me to attend their meeting, as I had but twice in my life entered a Friends' Meeting House. Accordingly, on one pleasant Sabbath morning, myself and chum, a mere youth of sixteen years, who was a member of the family where I boarded, wended our way on foot to that venerable edifice. Deviating from the main road, we took a by-path which led us to the graveyard, which had been the burial place of the Society of Friends for more than a century. We entered the city of the dead, and surveyed the place where death had so long scattered the discarded relics of his ruthless pastime. The silence of the death sleep was there. Plans, purposes, toils, and cares were ended. I talked to my chum on the brevity of life, how that I had recently been shocked on reading in the death column of THE FISHKILL STANDARD of two young men who had died since I left Fishkill, only twenty-one years of age. One was of a robust constitution and his prospect of living to the age of three score and ten was as bright as his, and as we stood near the burial plot of his ancestors he might in a few months or years be lying there beside them. He seemed to drink in every word that I said, as I reminded him of his pious mother; how often she had urged and entreated him to seek the Saviour. As I uttered these words he clung to me with greater tenacity, as I held up to him a crucified Saviour. We then left this consecrated spot, and came to the rear of the Brick Meeting-House. We clambered over the fence in the yard, and our attention was arrested at the long rows of sheds which sheltered their horses and vehicles during the time of worship, but are now in a dilapidated state. From appearance a horse had not been tied under some of them for a score of years. Large forest trees, whose age appeared to reach far beyond the period when the first white man ever saw the great Nine Partners' tract, with staples drove in them, rings where horses had been tied, but the earth at their base, which had been so often trodden beneath the horse's hoofs, was now overgrown with grass; long rows of tie-posts, too, stood along the high board fence, presenting to my mind the large congregation that assembled within those walls a half century ago. Two large horse blocks stood in front of the Brick Meeting-House. Time had rendered one unserviceable; the other was used, and on it was a sun-dial placed there by Jacob Willet sixty years ago.

Presently a stranger entered the yard and gave us a cordial greeting, and we informed him of our object in coming here. He seemed pleased to meet us and then he offered to conduct us through the building, which offer we kindly accepted. We were struck with its appearance; the walls were of brick, two feet or more thick; large windows with heavy sash frames set in deep embrasures; yellow pine floors, fastened to the timbers with large wrought nails; box stoves, with brick flooring beneath, which had stood there longer than our guide could remember; the same pews and unpainted columns which support the galleries have not been altered or remodeled since the meeting-house was built. A winding stairs led us to the gallery, which had not been used for many years, even the window shutters in the upper story had not been opened for years. He opened one of the window shutters to give us an opportunity to view the upper part of this sanctuary. How gloomy and melancholy was the scene presented to us. Here those long rows of empty benches which once were thronged with worshippers, were now silent as the chamber of death. My mind reverted to the time when that yard, on every Sabbath morn, contained more than a hundred vehicles, and that venerable and ancient edifice was filled to overflowing. We asked our guide when this meeting-house was built. He led us to the rear wall and pointed out to us a brick bearing date 1780, almost a centuary ago when those walls went up. Time as yet had made little or no impression on this building. The same windows and shutters, sills and frames, all of cypress wood, are in good preservation, and the walls appear as durable as when the last brick was laid.

The congregation is so small that they have abandoned one-half of the first story, and what few worshippers now assemble, sit on the women's side. Myself and chum guessed the number that would assemble there that morning, which we thought would amount to thirty all told. Presently the congregation commenced to gather, and our guide conducted us to a seat, and when we were all seated we had only nineteen. The services then commenced, and the stillness of death pervaded the whole house. One of our number was a little boy, apparently about eight years old, and he seemed to know and feel the solemnity of the occasion. How still he sat as he watched the solemn worshippers, with their broad-brimmed hats on. Some twenty minutes or more had passed, when a mother in Israel arose and doffed her straight bonnet and commenced speaking. The theme that she presented to us was the narrative of the Saviour with the woman of Samaria at Jacob's well; when He was wearied with His journey and sat on the well, when she came to draw water, and He said to her: "Whosoever drinketh of this water shall thirst again, but whosoever drinketh of the water that I shall give him shall never thirst, but the water that I shall give him shall be in him a well of water springing up into everlasting life."

How she went to the city and said, "Come and see a man which told me all things that ever I did; is not this the Christ?" So it is with us; the Saviour knows the hearts of all present, and like the woman of Samaria He tells us all, and knows the wants of all, and he is ready and willing to give to the uttermost, and if we seek we shall surely find Him. We listened with intense interest to her pathetic appeals as they fell from her lips, until she finished her narrative. The same stillness again pervaded our little assembly, and the writer thought that this was none other than the house of God, the very gate of Heaven. The same stillness again pervaded the meeting, when about 12 o'clock one of the grave members commenced the shaking of hands, which was the signal that the services were ended. We then left this hallowed spot and returned to our home.

Attached to this meeting-house was one hundred acres of land, which was purchased by the Friends before the house was built. In 1794 they erected the Nine Partner's boarding school, which was once noted for distinguished teachers. Willet, Tabor, and others, are fresh in the memory of the historians. After standing three quarters of a century, the Friends sold ninety acres of land, including the Nine Partner's boarding school. The purchaser demolished the building, and now nothing remains of it but its past history. The Friends have now about ten acres of land, including the burying ground, and the two meeting houses. The Orthodox house is a plain wooden structure, built when the Society was torn asunder by dissensions about forty-five years ago, which it is needless for me to relate here. The Orthodox has a flourishing congregation and Sabbath School. As I have said, the Brick Meeting House was built in 1780, when our country was struggling for her Independence. In the darkest hours of her adversity, the devoted followers of George Fox erected this time-honored meeting house. The brick and lime were burnt in kilns near-by, and the timber was obtained from the forests near where the house stands. The past history of the Friends, or Quakers, as they are sometimes called, is written in tears of blood. They have suffered persecution, imprisonment, exile, and death. They were foremost in modifying our laws, reforming our prisons, breaking the shackles from off the slaves, and forming treaties with the untutored savages without the effusion of blood. Peace and Love have always been inscribed upon her banners, which she has carried for more than two centuries. May she renew her strength, marshaling her hosts with her banners streaming, marching onward until our swords shall be beaten into plow-shares, our spears into pruning hooks, and that banner, emblazoned with letters of living light, Peace and Love, encircles the whole earth.

On Sabbath morning, August 9th, I made a second visit to the Brick Meeting House, it having been announced by posters put up in conspicuous places through the village, that a distinguished speaker was to hold forth there at 4 o'clock on the afternoon of that day. It stormed all the morning, and as the day progressed the storm increased, and at noon the rain fell in torrents, but suddenly, as if He had said, "So far shalt thy proud waves come, and no farther," the rain ceased, the murky clouds that hung as a pall over the heavens began to disperse, and by two o'clock the sun was shining brightly, and at three o'clock the writer was on his way to the Brick Meeting House. When I arrived there, the people were assembling; vehicles, carriages and splendid equipages were thronging the yard. The two entrances in the Meeting House were thrown open, the inner doors were hoisted, and the two sexes were assigned to their separate floors. The writer took his seat as directed, and sat anxiously waiting for the distinguished speaker to arrive. Presently it was announced that he had come, and soon he made his appearance. Passing through the aisle, he took a higher seat, where he had a commanding view of the two separate floors. His appearance commanded respect; his dress, his venerable look and snowy locks, with covered head, reminded me of the patriarchs. He sat for some minutes in silence, when taking off his hat, he arose, and casting his eye over the congregation, stood motionless. The scene was impressive. Some were dressed in the Friend's costume; others again were most elegantly attired. The sun shone through the large windows, throwing his rays athwart the massive brick walls, when every eye was riveted on the speaker. He commenced first by alluding to this venerable Meeting House; the changes that had taken place there since his remembrance; the fathers and mothers in Israel that had fallen, and then, pointing to the graveyard where their ashes lie, he said that he had witnessed the death bed scene of many lying there. What bright evidences they had given of their faith in God; how calm; no doubts, no fears; they were joyful, even in the immediate prospect of death. What a vacuum, he said, death had made here. "Who is to fill the places of the fathers and mothers that have fallen?" he asked, as he looked around upon the assembly. The speaker at last came squarely on his own platform. He held up to us his own colors. He said he loved every Christian, of whatever name or sect; he could clasp them all in his arms, but the Christian that draws his sword to spill his brother's blood he held no fellowship with. That was the spirit of Anti-Christ; that no man can be a Christian and at the same time have malice and envy rankling in the heart. The Saviour used no sword; the doctrine he taught while here on earth was love, boundless love, and he exhorted all to imitate his example, to love our neighbor as ourselves and to love our enemies; that, he said, was the spirit of Christ; this the temper of Heaven. The speaker occupied the floor three-quarters of an hour, and then resuming his seat, a stillness pervaded the house for some minutes, when the shaking of hands commenced and the services were ended.

PINE PLAINS.

Pine Plains was formed from the town of Northeast, March 26th, 1823. It lies on the northeastern extremity of the county of Dutchess, on the Little or Upper Nine Partners patent, purchased by Sampson Boughton and others, April 10th, 1706. The ancient name of Pine Plains was Shekomeko, derived from a tribe of Indians who inhabited that part of the county when first settled by the Europeans. Its present name was taken from a dense forest of pines, which originally covered the plains where the village is now located. The first settlers were Moravians, who established a mission among the Indians, in September, 1740. Ebenezer Dibble, C. W. Rauty, James Graham, John Tice, Smith and Snider, were also early settlers. In the year 1800, the village of Pine Plains contained only a hotel and four or five isolated dwellings. Two are still standing, in a dilapidated state. One was occupied in the revolution by one Lewis, who committed suicide. It was said that he was linked in with several others, who had formed a conspiracy against Congress. A tract of land containing about fourteen hundred acres near the village, is still owned by the heirs of the original proprietors, and are leased to the occupants. In 1808, some enterprising men commenced improving the village. A large and commodious dwelling of brick, a store and hotel, were erected by a Mr. Dibble, who carried on the mercantile business for many years, doing a large trade in barter, buying all the grain the surrounding country produced. The store is still standing, and is now occupied by Messrs. Chase and Dibble, who have recently added twenty feet to its length, and otherwise improved the interior and exterior.

The first church, Presbyterian, was built in 1816, as a union church, all denominations worshipping in it until 1830, when the Presbyterians purchased the rights of the other denominations, and they have since had sole possession. The church in height is two stories, surmounted with a steeple running up in two sections; over the upper section is a vane placed on a spindle. A fine toned bell is suspended in the upper section, and as often as the blessed Sabbath returns, its sound is heard reverberating over the Plains, summoning the worshippers to the house of God. The exterior of the church remains the same as when first erected, except the windows, which recently have had blinds put on them, which adds very much to the appearance of the church. The interior has been remodeled, with modern pews and pulpit, and the aisles carpeted. A gallery extends all around the church, and is supported by heavy columns. Above the gallery are also columns, which support the roof. An organ has been placed in the front gallery. The pastor, Rev. William Sayres, was installed in this church in 1833, and for thirty-seven consecutive years has preached to this congregation, and the same ardor and zeal which characterized him for more than a third of a century, still distinguishes him, and age as yet appears to have made no impression. May he be spared yet for many years to labor for Christ and his church, and be instrumental in bringing many more to the Saviour.

Stissing Mountain lies about two miles west of the village, and its highest summit is some 700 feet above the valley. At its base are several ponds, well stocked with fish, and the tourist and men of leisure often spend several days here in sailing and catching pickerel and fish of different varieties, and I apprehend that the time is not far distant when this place will be a fashionable retreat for citizens of the great metropolis to spend their summer months, for the scenery is not surpassed. All that is now wanting, is the accommodations to make it a fashionable summer resort. It was the fortune of the writer to spend a few months there in 1870, and he was well repaid, for the rural beauty, the village and the surrounding country, the mountains, ponds, rivulets, and landscapes, all added a zest to the every day scenery. Stissing Mountain is a fashionable resort for pic nics and pleasure seekers, and the writer concluded to pay a visit to its highest summit before leaving Pine Plains. So on one pleasant morning, in the latter part of September, having procured a conveyance, and accompanied by three lads selected from the village, he set out to spend the day on Mount Stissing. Having provided ourselves with refreshments, we left the village about eight o'clock. Our guide drove us around to the opposite side of the mountain, saying that the ascent was less steep and precipitous. An hour's drive brought us to the foot of the mountain, when the road became so rough and uneven that we had to leave our conveyance, and perform the rest of the journey on foot. Having obtained the best information from our guide how to gain the summit, and appointing an hour when he should meet us at the same place, he returned to the village. My companions and myself then commenced the ascent, and each one carrying a portion of the luggage, we proceeded up the rough and rugged road. It required considerable effort for us to overcome the steep acclivities, and we were obliged to rest before reaching the summit of the mountain. Finally we arrived at the top. The mountain appears like a huge boulder transported there by some convulsion of nature, for it is situated in a beautiful valley; from the top we had a commanding view of either side. It was difficult for us to decide which view was the most picturesque. Westward lay a valley extending to the noble Hudson, a distance of some eighteen miles. The glories of a September sun painted its dark blue waters with a blue still darker. Beyond lie the Catskill mountains, whose blue tops rise one above another, stretching beyond the vision's utmost limit. The far famed Mountain House could be distinctly seen, it being nearly three thousand feet above the river. Eastward the view extended to the Taghkanic mountain. The village of Pine Plains, and the adjacent valleys, afforded a charming prospect. The church spires were glittering in the rays of an Autumnal sun. The western slope of Taghkanic was one of gorgeous splendor, reaching to the fartherest limits of the landscape. Farm houses dotted the plains, and small streams wound their way through the valleys like threads of silver. So absorbed was the writer in gazing at the scene before him, that his companions had retreated unperceived by him to the shades of the forest. He set out to regain them, and found them lying under a huge pine tree that overshadowed them. Our appetites now reminded us that it was necessary to supply the inner man, and spreading out the contents of our baskets, we were all soon enjoying ourselves in partaking of the dainties which had been provided for the occasion. After finishing our repast, we spent the remainder of our time in various amusements, till the hour arrived for us to leave Mount Stissing, and bidding adieu to the place where we had spent a few hours so happily, we commenced descending the mountain, which was easily accomplished, and we reached the foot before our conveyance had arrived. But a little time elapsed before the rattling of a vehicle warned us our time was up. Soon it came in sight, and seizing our luggage, we were ready as soon as it arrived. Seating ourselves, our driver was soon wending his way to Pine Plains. Taking a circuitous route, and passing over an undulating country, we arrived home at last, and were warmly greeted by the villagers.

In 1853 the village of Pine Plains contained twenty-four houses, several stores and shops, a post office, etc., and the growth was rapid for several years after, when it came to a stand still, and then for many years there was little or no improvement, and as late as 1860 the village contained only 382 inhabitants. The completion of the Dutchess and Columbia Railroad added a fresh impetus to the growth of Pine Plains; a number of dwelling houses were in process of erection at the time of my visit in 1870. Two buildings by Messrs. Eno and Chase are on a magnificent scale, and add much to the beauty of the village. Real estate is greatly enhancing in value, and new streets are opening. The village now contains four churches, a union free school, two hotels, and about 800 inhabitants. Pine Plains is only four hours from New York, via the Dutchess and Columbia Railroad, which connects with the Hudson River Railroad at Fishkill Landing. Trains arrive at Pine Plains several times a day from the latter place. In the next score of years Pine Plains may double, if not quadruple, her population.

ISAAC VAN AMBURGH.

Isaac Van Amburgh was born at Fishkill Landing, May 26th, 1808. His mother's second husband was Benjamin Hutchings, who owned and occupied the farm now owned and occupied by Isaac M. Knapp, situated one mile east of Johnsville, East Fishkill. Van Amburgh was but a small lad at the time of the marriage, and he then went and resided with his stepfather, who was then a large landholder in Fishkill; under the supervision of his mother and stepfather, he was sent to the district school in Johnsville. The old school house then stood on the opposite side of the street. It was an ancient structure, built in 1794. School houses then were built the same as churches are at the present day, by voluntary subscription. It was not till 1813 that our people passed a law taxing the people to support schools, and dividing the State into districts. This school house was small, the height of the ceiling scarcely admitting a tall man. In the west end was a huge stone fire place and chimney, and the building was roofed with cedar shingles. The floor was laid with oak plank fastened to the sleepers with wooden pins, as nails commanded a high price, for it was before the invention of cut nails. The cross seats were slabs, taken from the saw mill, which made them very heavy. In 1810 the old stone chimney and fire place were taken out, and an addition made to the west end, and a Franklin stove superseded the fire place. This was the school house in which Van Amburgh, in company with the writer, received the rudiments of education. This old school house was demolished in 1847, and the present noble structure was erected on the opposite side of the street.

Van Amburgh was a self-made man. This school house was the only one in which he and the writer were taught the useful branches of learning. There they spent many happy years together. The winter of 1827 was very severe, and the snow had fallen very deep, and a cold snap was followed by a January thaw. The scholars erected a snow fort, and when finished, put a flag on it. The school was very large, numbering more than fifty scholars, and they divided for a battle. The larger scholars were commanded by Van Amburgh, and the smaller ones by Rowland. Rowland's army numbered about five to one of Van Amburgh's, and, as the writer was small, he was enlisted under Rowland. Rowland's army occupied the fort, and Van Amburgh was to take it. The teacher, Mr. Graves, had certain rules drawn up, to prevent any scholar being hurt. Snow balls were to be thrown, and wrestling allowed, and when a scholar was thrown, they could wash his face with snow before he was permitted to get up. Further violence was prohibited. Both parties were eager to commence the fight. The day was appointed, and the teacher, Mr. Graves, and several other spectators stood on an eminence where they could overlook the battle. Rowland ordered his men to make a large supply of snow balls for the occasion. Van Amburgh's men were large and strong, and also well drilled, but Rowland depended on numbers. Van Amburgh commenced the attack, when Rowland's men threw such a volley of snow balls that it was impossible for Van Amburgh's men to discern from whence they came, for they were completely blinded. Van Amburgh, seeing it was useless to contend with such superior numbers, in throwing snow balls, ordered his men to make a charge on the fort, Van Amburgh himself leading the way. As he was very tall, his height even then being nearly six feet, and his strength in proportion, he opened his way to the fort, followed by his men, scattering Rowland's small troops in every direction. Rowland then retreated a little way from the fort, and made a stand, and ordered some snow balls soaked in muddy water, and then attempted to drive Van Amburgh from the fort. This proved a failure, as Van Amburgh's men were partially shielded inside the fort. Rowland's men were the smaller scholars, but numbering five to one of Van Amburgh's. He divided them into small bands of five each, and gave the name of one of Van Amburgh's men to each of his bands to attack. This rule was to be strictly adhered to. Rowland then ordered an attack on the fort. In the meantime Van Amburgh had torn down the flag, and had commenced destroying the fort. This stimulated Rowland's men, and the five attacked one of Van Amburgh's, and it had a good effect. Van Amburgh, seeing his men thrown, and as fast as he succeeded in getting one on his feet, another was down and calling for help, and the snow continually pouring in their faces, ordered a retreat on the hill near the school house, when the teacher ordered a cessation of hostilities. The scholars were then all called together, and Van Amburgh made a speech to his men, saying how nobly they had taken the fort, torn down the flag and scaled its walls, and he was loudly cheered by both parties.

Van Amburgh was very fond of such sports, and after school hours, instead of going directly home, he often would linger around the school house, wrestling with some of his school mates, and from his superior strength, he was always a match for his competitor. He was of a mild disposition, seldom if ever was angry, and he won the affection of both teacher and scholars. Sometimes it was necessary for him to remain at home a few days to assist his parents.

Van Amburgh even then manifested a fondness for natural history, and he had asked the writer of this for books that treated on that subject. He afterward became familiar with the works of Buffon and Goldsmith, and the perusal of those essays created in him a desire for the study of this science. After leaving school Van Amburgh went to reside at Fishkill Landing, the place of his nativity, and undertook to learn the tailor's trade. But his eyes failing him he abandoned it. We next find him in the city of New York, engaged in the mercantile business, on the corner of Broadway and Bleecker street, with a partner whose name was William Hutchings. This copartnership was of short duration. He then set up business for himself in South street, near the old screw dock. But the genius and taste of Van Amburgh was not suited to mercantile life, and he soon gave up the business. He then made a tour through the Southern States. How long he remained there is not definitely known. There now appears to be a vacuum in his life, of which we cannot gather any information. It is supposed that he applied himself to his favorite study of Natural History, until he engaged his services to Raymond & Co., who then owned the largest menagerie that, up to that time, had ever been collected in Europe or America. Van Amburgh soon astonished Raymond and all connected with the menagerie, with his bold and fearless attempt to subdue and tame those wild and ferocious animals, the lions and tigers.

After performing feats which no man heretofore had attempted with wild animals, it was announced through the press that Van Amburgh would enter the den of lions like Daniel of old. A thrill of mingled amazement and horror ran through the city, and strong appeals were made to the manager from the pulpit and the press, imploring him to desist from such an undertaking, fraught with such foolhardiness and danger. It was idle to convince the masses that he could enter a den of wild beasts and leave it unscathed; but they were soon convinced to the contrary, for in the fall of 1833, at the Richmond Hill theatre, Van Amburgh performed a feat with the lions and tigers that, with the exception of the prophet Daniel, had baffled the skill and sagacity of man in all former ages. Goldsmith says that Mark Antony rode through the streets of Rome in a chariot drawn by lions. Van Amburgh would have performed a greater feat than this, for he volunteered to drive through Broadway and the principal streets in the city in a chariot drawn by lions and tigers, but the authorities interfered.

His next appearance was in the Bowery theatre in a play entitled the Lion Lord of the first Monarch, in which he introduced a royal Bengal tiger, apparently loose on the stage.

Van Amburgh's fame had now spread throughout the United States, and many of his old schoolmates went to New York to see him enter the den of lions and tigers. Among the number was the writer of this biography, and he will never forget the impression that it produced on his mind in witnessing so sublime and fearful a spectacle. Van Amburgh was attired in a dress which his own good taste and judgment had designed for the occasion. As he approached the door of the den of lions a thrill of horror involuntarily escaped the audience, but with a firm step and unaverted eye he opened the door, and went through with the programme without manifesting any fear, to the astonishment and entire satisfaction of the large audience.

From 1833 to 1838, Van Amburgh performed every winter in the old Zoological Institute in the Bowery, where there was an extensive menagerie. He now contemplated visiting Europe, and accordingly, in the summer of 1838, he sailed for England. His fame had already preceded him, and his arrival in England had produced a great sensation. His first appearance in public was at Astley's, where his success was of an unprecedented character. In London he was courted by the nobility and gentry, and her royal majesty, Victoria, of England, extended to him repeated marks of royal patronage and approbation. On one occasion the Queen, apprehending that there was something talismanic in the whip with which Mr. Van Amburgh forced the inmates of the den into obedience, requested him to lay it before her, when to her utter astonishment she discovered that it was nothing but a common cowhide.

Afterwards, in partnership with a company of Americans with a menagerie, Van Amburgh traveled through England, Ireland, Scotland and Wales. He then visited France, and throughout the length and breadth of his travels, Mr. Van Amburgh was the favorite pet of the royalty and aristocracy, but he always manifested a strong attachment for the free institutions of his own country. Nothing could wean him from the love that he cherished for his native land, especially the place of his birth.

Returning to the United States in 1845, crowned with European applause, Mr. Van Amburgh once more presented himself to his countrymen. Uniting himself with his former friend, Mr. James A. Raymond, they collected the largest menagerie ever exhibited and commenced a campaign throughout the Union, and wherever they exhibited their large collection of animals, the masses collected to witness his entrance into the dens of the lions and tigers.

Van Amburgh now had accumulated a fortune. At the age of nineteen, when he left home, he was penniless, and was sent adrift on the world to get his living. A kind mother gave him her parting blessing when he left the maternal roof, and many prayers had she offered up for the welfare of her son. A kind Providence watched over him, and that mother lived to see her son reach the top of the ladder of fame.

Van Amburgh afterward made several temporary visits in Europe, and traveled more or less in his own country. The last time the writer had an interview with him was in 1848, when he traveled through Fishkill with his menagerie. Nearly the whole two Fishkills were present to see him, for it was said that it would be his last visit to his native place, except as a private citizen. The writer saw him enter the cages of the lions and tigers for the last time, and with what thrilling interest did the large audience witness the wonderful control he had over those ferocious beasts of the forests. In conversation with him my mind reverted to the scenes of our childhood, when we went to school together. All those ties that united us together in by-gone days came up before me in vivid recollections. I saw at a glance that he had not deviated from the path of virtue, and had shunned the intoxicating bowl. His appearance was noble; his height rather more than six feet. Age had made no impression on that powerful frame. I felt myself in the presence of more than an ordinary man.

Van Amburgh has no brothers living. An only sister survives him, living at Gayhead, East Fishkill. He died November 29th, 1865, at Philadelphia, aged 57 years, six months and three days. He had selected Newburgh for his last resting place, and there his remains were interred.

Essays.

Essays.

CIVILIZED AND SAVAGE LIFE

CONTRASTED.

When the Almighty created man, he said, "Let us make man in our own image, after our likeness," and he created him thus, and placed him in the garden of Eden, and there he was sinless and happy until he ate of the forbidden fruit. The Lord then drove him from the garden and commanded him to earn his bread by the sweat of his brow. But he did not curse him with savage life, for he knew that it would afford him no happiness. After this man became very wicked, and it repented the Lord that he had made man on the earth. And the Lord said, "I will destroy man whom I have created, from the face of the earth," except Noah and his family, whom he preserved in a certain ark or vessel, with such kind of living creatures as he took with him. The ark was built of gopher wood, probably what we call the cypress, a strong and durable wood, not easily subject to rottenness. And this naturally leads us to think that it was built in Chaldea, where vast quantities of cypress wood was found as late as the time of Alexander the Great. The earth was made sixteen hundred and fifty-six years before the flood, and some historians assert that it was as densely populated then as at the present day. This to me appears reasonable, for man then lived centuries, and sixteen hundred and fifty-six years now would carry us back almost to the commencement of the Christian era, a sufficient time to elapse to populate the earth. Large cities probably then existed, mighty empires flourished, all since sunk to oblivion.

The ark was 547 feet in length, 131 feet shorter than the Great Eastern, but its tonnage was much greater, being 81,000 tons, while that of the Great Eastern is 22,500. The height of the ceiling of the ark was eighteen feet; that of the Great Eastern thirteen feet eight inches. The ark consisted of three stories, and the extreme height was about 55 feet, sufficiently large for Noah and his family, and the animals and winged fowls and their provisions for a year. The ark rested on Ararat. It is the finger mountain near the northeast of Armenia, and it is visible nearly two hundred miles distant. The height is so great, and the snow which covers it so deep, that its top is inaccessible. Infidels object to the general deluge by saying that if Noah was buoyed up on the water over the tops of the highest mountains he must inevitably have perished, for the cold would be intense. I suppose that the water tempered the atmosphere and made the climate more genial. Some philosophers assert that when the earth was created, it was tropical from pole to pole; that flowers bloomed perennial in what geographers now call the frigid zone; that as late as the Christian era the elephant existed as far north as our latitude. Some again assert that the flood was limited to a certain part of Asia, that the Western Hemisphere, or that portion of the globe, was saved. The Western Hemisphere probably in ancient times was covered with water, and those immense steppes or prairies now existing in the Western States were covered with water, and the Atlantic and Pacific oceans were united, and the bridge of islands that now exist in the Pacific ocean extended to the Atlantic, which now are the tops of the highest mountains extending throughout our continent.

When Noah came forth from the ark, he settled in Mesopotamia, and before his death he divided the world among his three sons, giving to Shem Asia, to Ham Africa, and to Japheth Europe. The descendants of Shem settled from Media westward to the sea coast of Aram or Syria. His sons were Elam, Ashur, Arphaxad, Lud and Aram. Elam possessed the country now called Persia. From him it had the name of Elymae and Elymais. Ashur settled on the west or northwest of Elam in Assyria, called likewise after him Ashur, at present Curdistan. Arphaxad peopled Chaldea. Lud is supposed to have wandered as far as Lydia. Aram and his descendants inhabited Armenia, Mesopotamia, and Syria. From his son Uz, a tract about Damascus, the stony and desert Arabia, was called the land of Uz. Ham, the second son of Noah, removed into Egypt, which in Scripture is often called the land of Ham. The sons of Ham were Cush, Mizraim, Canaan and Phut. Cush, his eldest son, possessed Arabia. Mizraim and his descendants inhabited Ethiopia, Lybia, Egypt and the neighboring countries. Canaan and his posterity settled in Phœnecia, and the land of Canaan, lying on the east and southeast of the Mediterranean sea. This was the land afterwards promised to Abraham, which he and his posterity accordingly enjoyed, and was then the land of Israel and Judah Phut, the youngest son of Ham, planted himself in the western parts of Africa, on the Mediterranean, in the country of Mauritania, whence this country was called the region of Phut, in St. Jerome's time. The Scriptures leave us very much in the dark as to the country where Japheth, the eldest son of Noah, settled. All we can collect respecting him is, that he retired with his descendants to the north of the countries planted by the children of Ham. His sons were Gomar, Magog, Modi, Javan, Tubal, Meshech and Tivas. Gomar, the eldest son of Japheth, was the father of the Gomorites, called by the Greeks Gallatins, who were the Gauls of Asia Minor, inhabiting part of Phrygia. The families of Gomar soon grew very numerous, and sent colonies into several parts of Europe. They first settled at the lake Boestris, and so gave the name of Bosphorus Cimmerius to the strait between it and the Euxine sea. These, in time, spreading by new colonies along the Danube, settled in Germany, whose ancient inhabitants were the Cimbri, so called of the Cymmerians. From Germany they afterward spread themselves into Gaul, where they were originally called

Gomerites, then by the Greeks Galutæ, and at last Gauls. From the colonies of Gaul, or Germany, came the first inhabitants of Great Britain.

From the information we gather from Biblical history, Great Britain was first peopled by Gomer, the son of Japheth, grandson of Noah, probably about two thousand years before the Christian era. Rome then was the place where man had made the greatest progress in civilization and learning. She had her orators, statesmen, heroes, poets and sages, and she was then the mistress of the world, occupying all of the important parts of Europe, Asia, and Africa. Her imperial city contained four millions of inhabitants. Her victorious armies had overrun Gallia, and Julius Cæsar, willing still further to extend his fame, determined upon the conquest of Britain. When the troops destined for the expedition were embarked, he set sail about midnight, and the next morning he arrived on the coast near Dover, where he saw the rocks and cliffs covered with armed men to oppose his landing. After several hard fought battles, the Romans were victorious, but what was the condition of the Britons when they were first known to the civilized world! What description does Cæsar give of the inhabitants. He says that they were in a savage state, and living in cottages thatched with straw, with their cattle. They lived mostly on milk or flesh procured by the chase. What clothes they wore to cover any part of their bodies were usually the skins of beasts, but much of their bodies, as the arms, legs, and thighs, were left naked, and those parts were usually painted blue. Their hair, which was long, flowed down upon their backs and shoulders, while their beards were kept close shaven, except upon the upper lip, where it was suffered to grow. The dress of savage nations is everywhere pretty much the same, being calculated rather to inspire terror than to excite love or respect. Their religious superstitions were terrible. Besides the severe penalties which they were permitted to inflict in this world, they inculcated the eternal transmigration of souls, and thus extended their authority as far as the fears of their votaries. They sacrificed human victims, which they burned in large wicker idols made so capacious as to contain a multitude of persons at once, who were thus consumed together. To these sights, tending to impress ignorance with awe, they added the austerity of their manners and the simplicity of their lives. They lived in woods, caves, and hollow trees. Their food was acorns and berries, and their drink water. This was the condition of the Briton at the time the island was invaded by the Romans. They introduced civilization there, and from that time savage life gradually declined, and as early as the invasion of the Danes, Britain could boast of learned men. Her learned Alfred, who flourished at that time, cultivated both learning and the Muses, when barbarism and ignorance overspread the rest of Europe.

Learning and civilization had progressed so far as early as the reign of Henry II, that the use of glass in windows, and stone arches for building, were introduced, and in the reign of King John the famous Magna Charta was framed, the very bulwark of English liberty. Nor must we omit to mention Roger Bacon, who flourished in the dark ages, and was the forerunner in science to the great Bacon, Lord Verulan, as the latter was to Sir Isaac Newton. Among the other curious works written by this illustrious man, we find a treatise upon grammar, mathematics, physics, the flux and reflux of the British sea, optics, geography, astronomy, chemistry, logic, metaphysics, ethics, medicine, theology, philosophy, and upon the impediments of knowledge. He lived under Henry III, and died at Oxford about the year 1294. The industrious Leland, who was himself a moving library, was the first who published a short collection of the lives and characters of those learned persons who preceded the reign of Henry VIII. Edward IV, during his short life, did a great deal for the encouragement of learning, and encouragement was given to learned foreigners to settle in England. The Liturgy of the Episcopal church was composed in this reign, and with the exception of two articles, is the same the church uses at the present day. Learning as well as liberty suffered an almost total eclipse in England during the bigoted bloody reign of Queen Mary, but it revived again in the reign of Elizabeth. Although she was so dictated to by her ministers, as to suffer the poet to languish to death in obscurity, she was no stranger to Spencer's Muse. She tasted the beauties of the divine Shakespeare, and raised genius from obscurity. During her long and peaceful reign knowledge shone with effulgent brightness. Sir Walter Raleigh, Sir Francis Drake, and the Earl of Essex, the politest scholar of his age, flourished in her reign. Her successor, James I, son of Mary, Queen of Scots, gave encouragement for learned foreigners to reside in

England. He was himself no great author, but his example had a considerable effect upon his subjects, for in his reign were found those great masters of polemic divinity whose works are almost inexhaustible mines of knowledge. He was likewise the patron of Camden and other historians, as well as antiquaries, whose works are to this day standards in those studies. What was most noted in his reign was the translation of the Bible from the original tongue by the learned men, and is the same used at the present day. His son, Charles I, had great taste for the polite arts, especially sculpture, painting, and architecture. He was the patron of Reubens, Vandyck, Jones, and other eminent artists, so that had it not been for the civil wars, he would probably have converted his capital into a second Athens. The Earl of Arundel was, however, the great Maecenas of the age, and by the immense acquisitions he made of antiquities, especially his famous marble inscriptions, he may stand upon a footing as to the encouragement and utility of literature with the greatest of Medicean princes. The distinguished Milton, and poet laureate, also flourished in his reign. The public encouragement of learning and the arts suffered indeed an eclipse during the times of the civil wars, and the succeeding interregnum. Many very learned men, however, found their situation under Cromwell, though he was a stranger to their political sentiments, so easy that they followed their studies to the vast benefit of every branch of learning, and many works of vast literary merit appeared even in those times of distraction. Usher, Walton, Wallis, Harrington, Wilkins, and a number of other great names were unmolested, and even favored by that usurper. The reign of Charles II was chiefly distinguished by the great proficiency to which he carried natural knowledge, especially by the institution of the Royal Society. The king was a good judge of those studies, and though irreligious himself, England never abounded more with learned and able divines than in his reign. His reign, notwithstanding the bad taste of his court in several of the polite arts, by some is reckoned the Augustan age in England, and is distinguished with the names of Boyle, Halley, Hooke, Sydenham, Harvey, Temple, Tillotson, Barrow, Butler, Cowley, Waller, Dryden, Wyckerly and Otway. Classic literature recovered many of its native graces, and though England under him could not boast of a James and a Vandyck, yet Christopher Wren introduced a more general regularity than had ever been known before in architecture. St. Paul's cathedral was built by him, which was thirty-seven consecutive years in building. He lived to see it finished after himself had laid the corner stone. The reign of James I, though he likewise had a taste for the fine arts, is chiefly distinguished in the province of literature by the compositions that were published by the English divines against popery, and which for strength of reasoning and depth of erudition never were equalled in any age or country. The names of Newton and Locke adorn the reign of William III, and he had a particular esteem for the latter. Learning, says the historian, flourished in his reign merely by the excellency of the soil in which it was planted. The improvement which learning and all of the polite arts received under the auspices of Queen Anne, put his court at least on a footing with that of Louis XIV, in its glorious and palmy days. Many of the great men who had figured in the reigns of the Stuarts and William, were still alive and in full service of their faculties, while a new race sprung up in the republic of learning and the arts. Addison, Prior, Pope, Lord Bolingbrook, Lord Shaftsbury, Arbuthnot, Congreve, Steele, Rowe, and many excellent writers, both in verse and prose, need but to be mentioned to be admired, and the English were as triumphant in literature as in war. The learned ministers of George I, were patrons of erudition, and some of them were no mean proficients themselves. Although George II was himself no Maecenas, yet his reign yielded to none of the preceding in the numbers of learned and ingenious men that it produced. In the reign of George III the great Earl of Chatham made the United Kingdom ring with his eloquence. In the reigns of William IV and Queen Victoria, there are Sir Robert Peel, Sir Walter Scott, Lord Palmerston, Lord John Russell, Chalmers, and Whiteside.

From what we have collected from history, we learn that it was civilization that roused England from her lethargy and barbarism, where she had been slumbering for the long lapse of ages. It was civilization that enabled her to arise upon the wings of destiny, and throw her future glories and splendors around her. It was civilization that enabled her to spread her commerce over the fairest portions of the globe, from the east to the west, from the Arctic ocean of the north to the great southern ocean. She has sent her couriers over the bounding seas, and every gale of the ocean has laughed through the cordage of her laden ships. England for the last several centuries has spread her conquests over all North America, conquered part of the Eastern world, and given birth to some of the greatest men that have existed in modern days. There was a Fox, a Pit, a Sheridan, and others whose fame and glory shone through Europe, like a meteor that bursts and sheds its blaze throughout the heavens. As far back as the commencement of the reign of the Tudors she has not been wanting for a succession of learned men to gild the pages of her history. Even down to this day her lustre is undiminished, and she still remains the guiding star for history to emblazon. But contrast her happiness now to her misery eighteen hundred years ago. Then her inhabitants were immersed in all the horrors of savage life, living in huts with their cattle, clothed with the skins of beasts, and sacrificing human victims to their gods. Their religious superstitions alone were enough to blacken the pages of history, and make the heart of the philanthropist bleed.

Thus I have reviewed English history, and traced that nation from savage to civilized life. And I have done this to show that savage life does not afford any happiness, but on the contrary it adds infinitely to the weight of man's calamities. It has filled ancient Britain with tears, and clothed barbarous nations in mourning; it has brought upon the savage race the wrath and curse of Heaven. It may be asked is there no remedy for this degradation of savage life. Is there no way in which truth, reason and mercy can rear a superstructure that will suppress it. I answer yes. That superstructure is civilization and religion. Let the gospel of Jesus be preached throughout the world, and let the waste places in Zion be built up, let the missionary of the cross of Christ proclaim the glad tidings of salvation to a guilty dying world, then savage life will become totally annihilated, and civilization wave her white banner throughout the earth.

BOOKS THE GREAT SOURCE OF

INFORMATION.

It is through the information of books that we can learn what has happened in all ages of the world. It is through books that we learn what a great Empire the Assyrian was, founded by Nimrod, that mighty hunter, which increased in splendor for the long period of fifteen centuries, spreading itself over the fairest portions of the globe, and at length overturned and subdued by the immortal Cyrus. And there was the Persian Empire, shining like a meteor for nearly two centuries, swayed by the scepter of Cyrus, conquering the surrounding nations, and adding strength to its greatness, and at length totally subjugated under Darius their last king, in the memorable battle on the Granicus at Issus, on the plains of Arbela, by the all-conquering arm of Alexander. View next the Grecian Empire, brilliant but brief, existing but a few years in a blaze of glory, and terminating with its hero in an ignoble death, and dividing itself into several kingdoms, stretching their petty scepters over the disjointed parts of the continent. View next the Roman

Eagle, wheeling its victorious flight over the fertile plains of Asia, the burning sands of Africa, and the genial soil of Europe, conquering Carthage and Britain, and giving laws to the then known world. It existed under a republican government for nearly five centuries, and gave birth to some of the greatest writers, poets, statesmen, heroes and sages, that have existed at any period of the world. View the imperial city, spreading itself over seven hills, and at the birth of Christ containing over four millions of inhabitants. But view its decline. Headed at last by an ambitious set of demagogues, such as Cato, Cataline, Nero and others, it falls. The imperial city is sacked and pillaged, and overturned by successive hordes of fierce barbarians, and in the fourth and fifth centuries after Christ, the semi-savages from the north, the Saracenes from the east, the Goths and Vandals from the west, complete its destruction. To this deplorable state succeeded the dark ages of the world. It is through the information of books, that blessed book the Bible, that we learn of the dispensation of a cloud of ignorance, through the herald of the cross sent over that dark benighted land.

After England was converted to christianity, she arose as upon the wings of destiny, and became one of the greatest nations on the globe, and since the Reformation she has spread her conquests over all North America, conquered a major part of the eastern world, and given birth to some of the greatest men that have existed in modern days.

Again, it is book information that has raised individuals to the very pinnacle of greatness. It was book information that enabled Wesley to be the founder of a sect which has since spread itself over the civilized globe. It was book information that enabled the Earl of Chatham to be England's greatest statesman and orator, and Goldsmith to be one of the ablest historians that ever existed. Book information then is power. It is the scepter that gives us dominion over nature. It is the key which unlocks the storehouse of creation, and opens to us the treasures of the universe.

Take for example the man that has no book information. Can he gain any information on a tour through the old world? No. Let him travel through those oriental countries, let him wander if you please over the hills of Greece, and everything that presents itself to his eye is of a dreary aspect, bounded on one side by sterile hills, and on the other lashed by the eternal waves of the Ægean sea. Let him look over Egypt and he will see nothing but the ruins of ancient cities and temples. He can get no information of the ancient beauty, grandeur and magnificence of those countries. The information he will impart on his return, will be cold and uninteresting. It is only the man of book information that can learn the rise and fall of those nations and cities, that can rake up their mouldering ashes, that can collect and gather together their scattered fragments as they rot, and hand them down through books from generation to generation.

SLEEP.

How refreshing is sleep to one who has been toiling through the day, and burdened with its cares. To such a one sleep is a happy period, when the business of the day can be dismissed from the mind and forgotten, when we are conscious of having done nothing the world refuses to overlook or forget, to such a one sleep is one of the most happy periods of his life. Sleep is something with which we cannot dispense, for everything that exists, all animal creation, must sleep; and man, the noblest being that God has created, has been obliged to sleep when he knew that danger was threatening him. Alexander slept on the plains of Arbela just before the decisive battle was fought. Hannibal slept while his destiny was shaping, while disputing with the armies of the "mistress of the world;" and Bonaparte slept on the battle field of Austerlitz. Charles I. slept on the night before his execution, when the noise of the workmen engaged in erecting his scaffold was ringing through his cell, and Marie Antoinette, when under sentence of death, was aroused from her slumbers and led to the guillotine. Sentinels have slept at their posts, and soldiers on forced marches, and so essential is sleep to man, that under the most trying circumstances he cannot long exist without it. The mother that manifests the tenderest affection for her child in sickness, when she sits beside the dying couch witnessing the intense suffering it must endure, must sleep, perhaps, when her darling is in the agonies of death; for her powers of mind and body are exhausted, and she sits unconscious until aroused to witness the departure of her child.

Our beneficent Father has so beautifully arranged the time for sleep, separating the light from the darkness, giving man all necessary time for sleep to restore exhausted nature, so as to enable him to bear the heat and burden of the day through the short pilgrimage of his earthly existence. But alas! how many there are at the present day, especially among the young, whose time for sleep is so limited that life to them gets to be a burden. Sauntering night after night in those dens of iniquity that infest our cities and villages, spending their time and money, immersed in dissipation till their wretched existence is terminated with a horrible death. Happy they who have retired to rest when exhausted nature demanded, and have had sufficient sleep in order that they may transact the business of life with the strictest exactness, when called to give an account of their stewardship here below, they can say with the Apostle Paul, "For if ye believe that Jesus died and rose again, even so them also which sleep in Jesus will God bring with him."

ADVERSITY.

Adversity overtakes almost every man at some period of his life. It often comes at a time when he is most prosperous, when everything he had undertaken has added to his wealth. It then thwarts his plans, and strips him of his property, which has cost him years of anxiety and toil. The Christian also has experienced the severe trials of adversity. Often has his cup of sorrow been full to overflowing, and he has been compelled to drink from the very bottom of that cup, the bitter dregs of trouble. This was strikingly illustrated in the case of Job; when his children and property were taken from him he murmured not, but cheerfully submitted to the will of Providence, and submissively said, "Naked came I out of my mother's womb, and naked shall I return thither. The Lord gave, and the Lord hath taken away; blessed be the name of the Lord." The worldling that has been prosperous for years, that never as yet tasted of the bitter disappointments of adversity, how forgetful is he of the maxims that have been taught him; and when adverse winds begin to howl around him, when his earthly props are knocked from under him, how unwilling is he to submit to the will of Providence. How apt is he to find fault with that great and good being that has watched over him from his earliest years to the present time. Misfortunes may have overtaken him, friends may have deserted him, and his heart is now bleeding with anguish, yet there is a sovereign balm that can heal those wounds which adversity has thus inflicted. If he would but flee to the Saviour for refuge, the shafts of adversity would point in vain against him. This was the case with the Psalmist, who when afflicted, said, "It is good for me that I have been afflicted. Before I was afflicted I went astray, but now have I kept thy word." The Christian that believes that an unseen hand rules his destiny, is patient in adversity, thankful in prosperity, and in all things which may befall him, will place his trust in his faithful God and Father, and when times look dark and threatening, when the enemy rushes in like a flood, what comfort would he have if he did not believe that God rules, sustains, and governs all things. It calms the perturbation of his mind and enables him with a peaceful resignation to say, "Not my will, but thine, O Lord, be done." Through all of the vicissitudes of this life, his faith remains firm and unshaken as the ponderous rock. The warm zephyrs of prosperity breath meltingly upon him, the rough storms of adversity descend, the heaving billows of affliction dash, but nothing can move him. His eye is fixed on God, and his hope is in that glory that fadeth not away. These comfort and support him.

FASHION.

How prevalent is the force of fashion, and to what excesses of extravagance has it led, as may be witnessed at the present day. It pervades all ranks of society, the poor as well as the rich, and the influence it exerts over the masses is truly appalling. It causes those in affluence to live beyond their means, while those in poverty are made to suffer the effects of still more abject penury in order to make an outward display. Intemperance is justly styled a mighty evil, and the philanthropist has long sought means for the recovery of the poor inebriate, while the orator has portrayed in vivid colors his career from the first glass to the lowest depths of miserable degredation. Half a century ago, when intemperance was at its height, it was not tolerated in the church of Christ, and if a member of any Christian church became intoxicated he was expelled and disreputed; but not so with fashion at the present day. The clergy, even, and the members that compose the church, rather lead the van, and it is to church that we may go to see the fashions of the day. There we may witness the fine equipage, the full display of dress and the proud show of gewgaws. Every religious society, except perhaps the Quakers, is contaminated with the lust of fashion, which they allow to pollute their sanctuaries. How melancholy it is to see a society like theirs on the decline, merely because they will not yield to its corrupting influences. Fashion at the present day is a greater evil than was slavery at the South, and it travels over the country with more than railroad speed, while to the rising generation it is as destructive as death itself. It begets habits of indolence and extravagance in youth, and what property they may have inherited is soon wasted, when having no habits of industry, they soon become poor dependents and here their career of infamy begins. How often have the fashionable youths of wealthy parents been drawn into the vortex of vice until they have been plunged into utter ruin. This truly is a prominent cause of all the failures that occur, and the fashionable family that is living up to if not beyond their means, invariably find that their expenses, instead of lessening, will constantly increase, until they are borne along with the current, their property spent, and a failure ensues; and if this evil increases at the same ratio for half a century to come, as it has done for that now past, we may read the doom of our country as did King Belshazzar that of the ill-fated city of Babylon, written with the finger of inspiration on its walls.

APRIL DAYS.

How beautiful and pleasant are the sunny days of April. The long dreary winter has passed and the balmy days of Spring have come. The rippling brooks have broken their ice bound fetters, and the snow has vanished from hill and valley. The trees and fields are beginning to clothe themselves with verdure, and the works of nature display beauty. The husbandman has dragged his plough from its resting place and commenced turning up the earth and burying the seed in its bosom. As the months advance the warmth increases and the days appear more lovely and the hazy mists that rises in the atmosphere (as the sun gradually approaches the west) and slumber in the valleys, appears like the smoke of so many bonfires. The voice of the robin and blackbird is heard, and the soft showers fall like mists upon the earth. All nature is awake, her slumbers are broken. The cattle, released from their long confinement, roam joyously over the fields, and the bleating of sheep proclaims that the icy bars of winter are burst asunder. How visibly we see the spring advance as the days glide along, and late in the month that welcome guest and forerunner of summer, the swallow, returns; at first here and there only one appears glancing by, as if scarcely able to endure the cold. But in a few days their number is greatly increased, and they sport with much seeming pleasure in the warm sunshine. Lovely month, what happiness it affords us as the genial sun darts its rays upon the earth each succeeding day from the first of April onward.

www.ingramcontent.com/pod-product-compliance
Lightning Source LLC
Chambersburg PA
CBHW051736300426
44115CB00007B/590